D1601299

THE ROLE OF

RELIGION

IN HISTORY

THE ROLE OF

RELIGION

IN HISTORY

GEORGE
WALSH

BL
85
.W34
1998
WEST

TRANSACTION PUBLISHERS
NEW BRUNSWICK (U.S.A.) AND LONDON (U.K.)

Copyright © 1998 by Transaction Publishers, New Brunswick, New Jersey.

All rights reserved under International and Pan-American Copyright Conventions. No part of this book may be reproduced or transmitted in any form or by any means, electronic or mechanical, including photocopy, recording, or any information storage and retrieval system, without prior permission in writing from the publisher. All inquiries should be addressed to Transaction Publishers, Rutgers—The State University, 35 Berrue Circle, Piscataway, New Jersey 08854–8042.

This book is printed on acid-free paper that meets the American National Standard for Permanence of Paper for Printed Library Materials.

Library of Congress Catalog Number: 98-23864
ISBN: 1–56000–368–5
Printed in the United States of America

Library of Congress Cataloging-in-Publication Data

Walsh, George, 1923–
 The role of religion in history / George Walsh.
        p.   cm.
 Includes bibliographical references and index.
 ISBN 1-56000-368-5 (alk. paper)
 1. Religions. 2. History. 3. History (Theology) I. Title.
BL85.W34 1998
200'.9—dc21   98-23864
                                                              CIP

Contents

Preface

The present work originally appeared in the form of lectures to a popular audience. Since then it has been revised, mainly by the addition of new material. The outlook governing the work is naturalistic and seeks to interpret religious phenomena in the light of Objectivism. Chronological accounts come first and they are then supplemented by interpretations and hypotheses. The book is divided into two main parts entitled respectively, *Rise of the Two Major Forms of Religion* and *Ethos of the Judeo-Christian Tradition*. The first chapter of the first part serves as an introduction covering my view of the nature of religion in general, then moves on to an account of primitive religion. This account serves as a backdrop for the role that religion plays once society has become historical. Two basic forms of historical religion are described in terms of their chronological development. This description is laid out in the three remaining chapters of part 1. These chapters deal with Indian and Middle Eastern forms of religion respectively. We then move on to part 2 which is concerned entirely with the Judeo-Christian tradition. The analysis here is mainly in terms of *the basic philosophical principles*. The world outlooks of the Jewish and Christian traditions are compared, contrasted, and then exhibited in their solutions of everyday problems, ethical, political, and sexual.

I would like to express my appreciation to the following people: to David Kelley, who conceived the project and guided it to completion; to my son Michael Walsh, who challenged and encouraged me, to my wife Cathy Walsh, who contributed that scarce coin—sabbatical time—both to discussion of old topics and to practical arrangements; to Murray Franck, my continual Socratic interlocutor of shared interests especially in the subject of the present work, to D. Andrews Reese, the very helpful member of the staff of the library of Salisbury State University; and praise must go to Jaime Dorrian of the Institute for Objectivist Studies staff for her highly competent transcription of the original oral audio-tape form of the work. Finally, high praise must go to Mary Ann (Molly) Hays who was present at the original delivery of the lectures upon which the present work is based, who read the work in its entirety, and who all along made many comments and suggestions for its improvement. Her help has been invaluable. Without her encouragement and assistance it would not have been completed.

George Walsh
Professor Emeritus, Salisbury State University
Salisbury, MD, 1997

Part I

Rise of the Two
Major Forms of Religion

1

Introduction:
The Nature of Religion and Primitive Religions

I will begin by submitting a definition of religion. A religion is a system of beliefs and practices resting on the assumption that events within the world are subject to some supernatural power or powers such that human needs, either physical or psychological, can be satisfied by men's entering into relations with such powers. The supernatural powers in question are called supernatural in virtue of the fact that they can allegedly be known, related to or influenced primarily by means other than those of reason and sense experience. The fundamental belief characteristic of all religions is, thus, belief in a higher supernatural power which can control everyday events, and the fundamental practice characteristic of all religions is the attempt to influence this power. The power, however, is conceived of in two basic ways which differ sharply from one another. One way sees the power as an impersonal energy, a kind of supernatural electricity, which can be manipulated and controlled. Obviously that manipulation is what we have always called magic, which is the art of compelling a supernatural power to do one's will. The root concept of magic is the belief in a supernatural energy which can be concentrated or dispersed and which is subject to invariable laws. These laws are somehow learned by the magician and then applied by him according to certain formulas as he chants his incantations or performs his rituals. If these incantations and rituals are correctly performed, the desired results are inevitably achieved. If the desired results are not achieved, the conclusion is that something went wrong with the ritual. Francis Bacon said that to command nature you must obey her. The magician believes that to command supernature you must obey her, obey her by learning her laws and applying them. Magic shares with science the characteristic of seeking invariable laws, but it departs from science with respect to the object of these laws—the supernatural rather than the natural. The means of learning these laws are dreams and visions rather than observation, experiment, and reason.

We have said that there were two basic ways of conceiving supernatural power. We have been talking about the first way, the impersonal. The second basic way is the personal, the I-Thou relation. Supernatural power is conceived here in terms of disembodied persons— gods, spirits, angels, demons. Man's relation to them is, in intention, an interpersonal one. You enter into interpersonal relations with the gods, in prayer. Man begs them, cajoles them, loves them, hates them, is faithful to them or is unfaithful to them. His attitude is that of a suppliant, whereas the magician's attitude toward the supernatural is that of an engineer. These disembodied persons relate to man in a personal way. The gods love him, they hate him, they choose him, they reward him, punish him, and so on. Any number of models of interpersonal relationships may operate in this kind of religion. The gods may be regarded as friends or enemies, for instance. Or a political model may be used; God is a king and men his subjects. Or a family model may be used, God is the heavenly father and men his children. Sometimes holy mothers are brought in, then holy infants. Under this scheme, all men are conceived as brothers and they are said to be each others' keepers.

The best examples of these strongly personal religions are Judaism, Christianity, and Islam. The God of these religions is conceived as personal. I am using the term *personal god* to mean a god who is thought of as a person, or three persons as in the case of Christianity. God thinks, wills, watches, evaluates; gives out commandments, rewards, punishments; has mercy, seeks for his lost sheep; and so on. The impersonal and the personal concepts of religion can be thought of as two ends of a spectrum. At one end you have nothing but magic, the impersonal force being collected, stored, routed, rerouted, and dispersed by magicians. At this end of the spectrum, the supernatural power is completely impersonal, the magician is in control, he is an engineer of the supernatural. The witch doctor curing somebody or putting a curse on him is an example. At the other end of the spectrum, you have a personal, absolutely omnipotent God who decrees all things from moment to moment. Islam is the perfect example. The word *Islam* means surrender; the basic idea is total prostration before God's will. In between, toward the magic end of the spectrum, you have Greek polytheism, where, although the gods are persons, they are in constant conflict with one another, and their action is limited by the amount of divine power they can work up for the occasion. The gods had, so to speak, to do push-ups in the Greek polytheistic system. Further over toward the personal is Catholicism, where God is omnipotent but who confers upon his priests the power to perform rites which work more or less automatically; *ex opere operato*, that is, efficacious when correctly and seriously performed. Think of the traditionalist Archbishop Lefevre and his ordinations disapproved by the pope. The pope was very upset, but he had to admit these were *valid* ordinations, even though "irregular" and therefore disapproved of by God.

If you recall the movie, *The Exorcist*, there was a scene in which the bed containing the little girl was suspended in the air, and the priest, sweat rolling down his face, with a crucifix in his hand, kept repeating, "by the power of Christ I compel you, by the power of Christ I compel you!", until finally the bed returned slowly to the floor? This is an example of the mixture within religion of the personal and the impersonal, of God-controlled power and man-controlled power.

Our next step is to trace the origin and fortunes of religion in human society. We should note first that religion, as we have defined it, is universal; not in the sense that all men are religious, but in the sense that religion has been present and has exerted a very perceptible force in almost every known society in history. Furthermore, almost every nation and every ethnic group has either a prevalent religion or has some background which is religious in character. We will look first at religion in its early forms in the hope of shedding some light on its origins. We will look at prehistoric societies to see what religious institutions were present there. Prehistoric societies were, obviously, primitive. By primitive societies, I mean "small-scale societies with a simple material culture and lacking literature." I have adopted this definition from *Theories of Primitive Religion* by E.E. Evans-Pritchard.[1]

There are, of course, two classes of primitive societies; those which are prehistoric and those still surviving today and open to direct study by contemporary cultural anthropologists. The prehistoric societies, those which didn't survive, can only be studied by archeological remains—stone instruments, pottery, cave paintings, and the like. These archeological data have to be interpreted, and for their interpretation we have to turn to the living practices and beliefs of surviving primitive tribes.

In this volume, I will analyze a number of religious institutions existing among today's primitive tribes and ask what are the essential characteristics of those institutions. Then I will look at the archeological data of prehistoric societies to see if there is any evidence of such institutions in these prehistoric societies. Now, however, I will begin by examining the specific beliefs and practices of primitive religion. I shall refer to these beliefs and practices as religious institutions.

First, we have the belief in a powerful supernatural energy that pervades nature, but apparently at different densities, for it becomes concentrated in persons and things and is transmissible from one person to another. For instance, it may be concentrated in a grove of trees and then this sacred grove is regarded with awe and treated with respect. It is frequently regarded as the force behind chance or luck. For instance, if you can summon enough of the energy concentrated in the head of your spear you can become invincible. The concept is therefore that of a special force which is responsible for whatever cannot be explained by everyday forces like fire and wind. Therefore, whenever it is encountered, it causes awe and anxiety. Nevertheless it is assumed that it is subject to some kind of regular laws which are partly known by man, and the application of these laws is magic, a subject I will discuss later.

Another institution is *animism*. Primitive man recognizes the fact of consciousness. (At least he *does* recognize it. The modern radical behaviorist is pre-primitive). Primitive man recognizes that his consciousness is not identical with his body and not identical with the external objects of which he is aware. But how clearly he draws these distinctions is uncertain. For instance, he explains his dreams as due to his consciousness leaving his body and traveling to distant places. This leads him to the concept of a disembodied spirit. He then notices the similarity of sleep to death and he concludes that, if he can be temporarily out of his body in sleep, he can be permanently out of his body in death. So out of this primitive distinction between consciousness and body is born belief in immortality. So there are disembodied spirits around, and maybe spirits who have never been embodied at all, and maybe there are spirits in trees and stones and brooks; all these spirits are selves, egos, centers of consciousness just like you and me, with their own perceptions, memories, ideas, emotions. Note the difference between spirits and supernatural energy. Spirits are personal. By calling them personal I mean that each of them is a person. If I believe in a tree spirit, I mean that there is a center of consciousness up there peering through the leaves at me. My relations with these spirits will be personal—I will address them, I will pray to them, I will conjure them up, and so on.

So we come to worship and veneration. *To worship* means to give homage or honor to, as to one's superior. This homage and honor is directed to the spirits, and they are worshipped as more powerful and sometimes, but not always, as more worthy than we are. Sometimes they are worshipped with fear and loathing—worshipped in order to persuade them to go away, as in the case of demons. *Veneration* is recognition of and reverential regard for the presence of a sacred personal power; thus stones and meteorites may be venerated by kissing, or objects worn as amulets may be kissed before being worn. Plants and trees may be venerated, especially those which are used for crops or lumber. Animal veneration is widespread among primitive peoples. They will venerate a lion in the hope that by drawing close to him they may share in his strength, or a snake in the hope that they may share in his cunning, or the phallic power which he symbolizes.

Let us now look at *taboo*. A taboo is a prohibition against contact with a person or a thing. The contact may be direct bodily contact or it may be prohibition against conversation with a certain person, or it may be prohibition against approaching a person or object, or a prohibition against entering a house or a room, or against eating a certain animal or plant, or eating with certain classes of persons. The prohibition may be very strong. For instance, in certain societies you must not allow your mother-in-law's shadow to pass over you. In others, women are regarded as taboo during menstrual periods and for a time after childbirth.

It is important to see that a taboo is not the same as a moral prohibition. A moral prohibition is a warning not to endanger a value. To illustrate the difference between a moral prohibition and a taboo, let me cite an example from the Hebrew Bible, or Old Testament. At a certain point, King David decided to move the ark of the covenant from a house in another city to Jerusalem. This is related in 2 Samuel, chapter six. "And they carried the ark of God upon a new cart and brought it out of the house of Abin'adab which was on the hill; and Uzzah and Ahi'o the sons of Abin'abad were driving the new cart with the ark of God and Ahi'o went before the ark. And when they came to the threshing floor of Nacon, Uzzah put out his hand to the ark of God and took hold of it, for the oxen stumbled. And the anger of the Lord was kindled against Uzzah; and God smote him there because he put forth his hand to the ark; and he died there beside the ark of God."[2] Now this is one of the many vestiges of primitive religion in Judaism, a religion which is especially full of taboos. Had a *moral* prohibition been involved, it would have gone something like this: the ark is a symbol of God, it must not be allowed to fall to the ground. This fall is what poor Uzzah was trying to prevent. Had a moral principle been involved and had the religion at that stage been built on moral principles, Uzzah would have been made a saint. That is the difference between a taboo and a moral prohibition.

Many taboos are based on fear of the supernatural energy. It is obvious that the fear is either of suffering harm oneself or of damaging someone else. There's something obsessive about taboo, and this is obvious in some of its parallels in civilized society, for instance, if you step on a crack in the sidewalk, you'll break your mother's back. Many different things are tabooed: objects, places, names. Thus it may be forbidden to utter the sacred name of God. Sharp weapons, hair, fingernail cuttings should be avoided according to the Pythagoreans. The rule is that if anyone accidentally eats a certain food, the person will die. Frequently he does die of fright after having swallowed the food. Notice how powerful these religious taboos are. As for the person who has transgressed a taboo, he must be avoided, too. Warriors must be avoided before battle because they are in a dangerous state of excitement. Women, especially, must not approach the warriors lest they drain some of the excitement away. Warriors, immediately after battle, must be avoided because they've been polluted by bloodshed. Blood pollutes.

This brings us logically to the next institution, *purification rites*. A person who has broken a taboo must be ostracized lest he infect the whole community. But the ostracism can be avoided by putting him through a purification rite; common methods are ritual baths, fasting, shaving the hair, covering the body with ashes or white paint, or passing through fire or cutting the body or scourging it. Purification ceremonies are also used after childbirth and after menstruation. Purification ceremonies are also performed in preparation for some ritual, when one fasts, abstains from sex, and so on, and for ridding the body of unclean spirits.

And now we come to a great institution, *sacrifice*. Sacrifice is the giving up, by forfeiture or destruction, of some valued object, in order to cause it to pass from human possession to the possession of a supernatural power. (In terms of religious sacrifice.) Sacrifices may be very simple—as in the pouring of a cup of wine on the ground. But they also may be more radical. Animals may be sacrificed, ranging from single chickens to whole herds of horses. Humans may be sacrificed starting with criminals, then prisoners of war, then fellow tribesmen chosen by lot, and finally one's own children. The motive of sacrifice may be propitiatory: for instance, a virgin may be thrown into a volcano to keep it from erupting. The propitiation may be by way of atonement, to blot out sins; the sacrifice may be sacramental, to tap a source of power for oneself; or it may be to insure that the crops will grow. Enter the concept of dying and rising. Death of a human being may be balanced by the raising of a good crop, or sacrifices may be performed in order to ensure that spring arrives.

Another institution is *the cult of the dead*. There is a whole complex of beliefs, attitudes, and practices relating to death. All primitive people, without exception, show evidence of the belief that some part of the personality survives death. How did they arrive at this belief? We have already seen how easily they may have arrived at the belief in disembodied spirits. So why shouldn't they conclude that death was simply permanent disembodiment? Furthermore, certain experiences may corroborate the belief that a dead man remains after physical death. The survivors can't help thinking of him or dreaming of him; memories linger. Sometimes the memories are so vivid that they give rise to auditory and visual hallucinations. Man alone among the animals conceptualizes death and knows that he is going to die. Since survival is a basic wish, this knowledge must strike the primitive, at least, with disappointment. He wishes he would not die, and the wish is father to the thought that he will become a disembodied spirit. Once the theory of survival after death is accepted as fact, some unpleasant corollaries are manifest to those who believe it. They may wish, for instance, that certain of their enemies would not survive, for their spirits may come back to haunt them and seek revenge.

Thus out of a great variety of mixed wishes, beliefs, and fears may arise a whole complex of burial practices. Primitives may pile a heap of stones over the dead body to keep it from rising again. This may be the origin of gravestones. They may tie the body with cords or drive a stake through its heart, and food offerings may be left at the burial place to satisfy the hunger of the dead. The corpses may be carried out feet first in order to "point him away from the house." The pall bearers may even carry the dead body in a zigzag line. Why ? To confuse the dead man so he won't know his way back! The body may be taken out of the house by a special door, never used for any other purpose—the "funeral door." I saw this custom observed in a house I frequently visited as a child, although I never found out if it was being deliberately followed as a tradition or whether it was believed that some practical reason justified it. These customs do not necessarily imply fear or hostility toward the dead. They can just as well be interpreted as rites of passage designed to encourage the dead not to linger but to continue on to the next phase of existence. Leaving food at the grave can be interpreted as a gesture of partial support, while the dead are getting used to their state of being independent, pushing them out of the nest so to speak. It is a very widespread custom to bury with the dead man clothing, weapons, furniture, ornaments, and so on. Sometimes his favorite dog is killed and buried with him, sometimes his favorite wife is sent along to accompany him by being killed on the grave, buried alive, or even burned alive, as widows are in remote parts of India still today.

As for beliefs about life after death, there seem to be three basic forms: (1) the spirit goes to a realm where earthly joys or woes continue as before; (2) the spirit is reborn on earth in another body, usually a human body; and (3) what survives death is something less than a full human personality, but a sort of shadow or weak image which wanders forlornly in the regions of the dead. None of these theories contain any reference to reward or punishment for the moral quality of one's life on earth. Sometimes there is, in primitive society, after-death punishment for having broken a taboo, but never for being a good or bad individual. In the first theory that I mentioned, the *heaven theory*, all warriors go to heaven whether they've been good or bad. In the second, or *rebirth theory*, a person's new life tends to depend on his former status in society. A barber is born again as a barber, in the same social status under the same totem sign. In the *wandering shade* theory, everybody's shade has to go to the place of aimless wandering regardless of his or her personal merits or faults.

I just mentioned totem, so we will deal next with *totemism*. Totemism is a system of beliefs and practices based on the assumption that there is a special relationship between groups of humans and certain species of animals, plants, (or even occasionally inanimate objects) which are called totems. The recognition of this special relationship results in social groupings or clans which find their identity in their association with the totem. In most cases, the sense of special relationship with the totem results in the myth that all members of the group are descended from the totem. Totemism is accompanied by something called *exogamy*, the rule that members of the totem group must "marry out," and any sexual relations within the group constitute incest. Also the eating of the totem by the group is taboo except on periodic occasions when the whole clan can make a kind of sacramental meal of the totem, giving them a sense of unity in identification with it—"all one body we" as the Christian hymn goes.

The next institution is *magic*. Magic is the attempt through the utterance of prescribed words or the performance of prescribed acts to control the supernatural powers for ends desired by man. Magic is the system of incantations and rituals designed to bring about the kind of impersonal control we mentioned previously. It is usually connected with belief in supernatural forces and it is always based on the assumption that there are certain laws governing the supernatural forces. Magic is the practical application of these laws. The magician, as I mentioned before, is a supernatural engineer who has graduated from engineering school—instruction by another magician. The founders of the study of primitive religion made many contributions to our understanding of magic. Among them was E.D. Tylor in his great work *Primitive Culture* (1871). He regarded magic as a pseudo-science in which the primitive postulates a cause-and-effect relationship between the magical act and the desired outcome, whereas in reality the link is one of *association of ideas only*. Tylor's characterization is, I think, correct. It is important to note that it has two aspects. One, the believer in magic really does think there is some kind of objective order, some system of laws to which he is conforming and which he is setting in operation by his rituals. He thinks it is like striking a match, and he keeps the precaution of not letting his children play with the magic paraphernalia. In intention, therefore, magic is a kind of science. Its laws are conceived as part of objective reality. Objective reality as a whole, therefore, exists, the magician thinks. It is composed of what we would call the natural plus the supernatural, although the believer in magic does not have a clear conceptual grasp of the difference between the two. So magic is conceived as a kind of dealing with an alleged two-story objective reality.

The second part of Tylor's theory—that magic does not really deal with authentic objective reality—would lead us to agree with him. Of course it doesn't; it's a pseudo-science. But what kind of pseudo-science is it? Look at its alleged laws. They are based on the association of ideas; for instance, if I steal a pair of gloves from somebody and put a curse on them he will die. The magician tries to induce rain by beating drums. What do these drums sound like? Thunder. The basis of the whole theory is the association of ideas, and ideas are *freely* associated *in consciousness*, so consciousness takes over. Now what principle is this, that consciousness takes over? *Primacy of consciousness*, as Ayn Rand called it. Magic assumes this primacy. It is a pseudo-science based on the primacy of consciousness. Considered as an *applied pseudo-science*, it seeks control over reality, but a control based on consciousness alone, specifically, on the *stream* of consciousness. Control is the assertion of the supremacy of some wish or whim.

Let's now pass to the contributions of another great student of primitive religions, Sir James Frazer's *The Golden Bough* (1890). According to Frazer, magic is based on two principles of thought, the *law of similarity*, which says, like produces like; and the *law of contact*, which states that things which had once been in contact with each other continue to act on each other at a distance, even after the contact has been severed. From the law of similarity, the magician infers that he can produce any effect he desires merely by imitating it. From the law of contact, he infers that whatever he does to a material object will affect the person with whom the object has once been in contact. That is, he could cast a spell on you, as I said before, by stealing a glove and putting a curse on it. Magic based on the law of similarity Frazer called *imitative* magic. Magic based on the law of contact may be called *contagious* magic. The law of similarity and the law of contact both fall under the *law of sympathy*, which assumes things act on each other at a distance through a kind of secret sympathy, perhaps a kind of ether, if you can imagine such a thing. All magic in accord with the law of sympathy is called *sympathetic magic*.

How does the law of similarity work in imitative magic? Suppose your totem is corn, and it is the job of your totem group to "get the corn up" in the spring. Well, you just go out into the fields, utter certain words like "up corn," and start jumping as high as you can. Now, suppose your totem is kangaroo. You are the consultant on kangaroo multiplication. You gather all the men and women of your consulting group and organize a jumping orgy. You go out into the fields and leap while coupled until you fall down in total exhaustion. But meanwhile the kangaroos have gotten the idea at last, and the meat supply of the tribe has been secured for the year. Another form of imitative magic is to make an imitation of your enemy and to stick pins in it until he dies. This is black magic, and of course it is an important part of the cult of voodoo. The practices of imitative and contagious magic may be applied in various ways, as in *fetishism*, in which some inanimate object is supposed to be full of magical power, either occurring naturally as in a strangely shaped stone or put there by an incantation such as the blessing of a medal. The fetish may be venerated or it may be whipped in case it doesn't work. Very often the fetish is thought to be the dwelling place of a spirit. The spirit of one's fetish may be rendered powerless by one's enemy's fetish, in which case one dismisses one's magician and takes the fetish somewhere else to be supercharged.

Another method of dealing with spirit power is *shamanism*. A special class of men called shamans or witch doctors are able to work themselves up into a frenzy perhaps by whirling, perhaps by taking drugs, and in that trance the shaman establishes control over certain spirits, especially those of disease and death, so as to be able to drive them out of people.

Yet another is *popular* magic. For instance, a whole community may try to rid itself of some evil by rendering the spirit which produced it a scapegoat and then driving the scapegoat out of the locality.

Then there is *divination*, an important epistemological activity. Divination is the method by which supernatural laws and facts may be learned. Divination is divine research. It may be by reading the stars or tea leaves or entrails or palms; this is visual divination. Or it may the hearing of divine utterances and being inspired to speak what one has heard in prophecy; this is auditory divination. Students of the history of philosophy should note that Frazer and Tylor are dependent on Hume. Hume says there are three types of association; resemblance, contiguity, and causation. Here the magician is using resemblance and contiguity or contact and confusing it with necessary connection. The magician jumps to an inference of necessary connection by observing resemblance and contiguity.

Ritual is yet another institution. We have seen that the impersonal means of dealing with the supernatural is magic. The *personal* means is prayer and devotion. The practical application of both is found in ritual. Ritual is the whole system of selected programmed words, bodily actions, and gestures in terms of which religion is enacted. Many rituals are called *expectant* in character. They are conducted in such a way as to bring about what is imminent anyway; like trying to make spring arrive, or to make the kangaroos multiply, or to make the monsoons come. As a result people become anxious or upset if the ritual is omitted or if there is some slip-up during the ritual. And the chief witch doctor tells the assistant witch doctors to start the whole thing all over again and so they have to go back one week and start chanting again. Now these expectant rituals turn into great celebrations and in early times motivated an interest in the calendar and in astronomy. Priests became astronomers and bureaucrats in control of irrigation systems. Another important use of ritual occurred during rites of passage; rites making birth, initiation, marriage, and death possible. One was socially lost unless one underwent one of these rites—like the brith or barmitzvah—or saw to it that members of one's family did. The initiation rite, in practice, transformed one into a full man or woman. In the course of the initiation rite, one was deliberately terrified, had one's genital organs mutilated to a greater or lesser extent, and was finally told the secrets or mysteries of the tribe. In these initiations one had the sense of being born into one's new status or role. One was regarded as born again and given a new name, as in confirmation, for instance, or baptism. Rites of initiation seem to be an essential part of all tribal life. When the tribal form of social organization dissolves and is replaced by urban society, a hunger for a return to tribal forms seems to linger endlessly and to be passed on from generation to generation. This hunger is expressed in the rites of passage of organized religions such as circumcision, bar mitzvah, baptism, confirmation, and so on, the omission of which causes a sense of lack of identity and of rootlessness. Also there are remarkable survivals of tribalism and totemism in fraternities with their hazing and initiation rites, and in such secret societies as the Masons, even the Lions and the Elks.

Now we pass to *myth*. Myth is universal among primitive men. One function of myth is to answer the questions naturally raised as to the importance and the origin of the ritual such as the question asked by the youngest child on Passover night; the four questions adding up to the overall question of why this night is different from all other nights. This is what the youngest child asks, and so he is told a story. The story explains and justifies the ritual. *To explain and to justify without special regard to truth is the essence of myth.* Occasionally, of course, the myth may be true, but its function is to give an explanation in reply to a question. The word myth means story, a story used to explain either the origin of a custom or the origin of the whole universe. The word myth came to mean a fiction, only after men discovered that myths were, as a rule, fictitious. A myth is a story explaining the origin of a custom, the origin of our tribe, the origin of the universe. Or they may be stories of heroic deeds such as that of Prometheus. Out of myths have grown great oral traditions, out of the oral traditions scriptures, out of the attempt to systematize these and give them a semblance of rationality, theology.

We now come to an important question. Why do people do these things? Don't they grasp the distinction between consciousness and existence? Well, Ayn Rand said in *The Metaphysical versus the Man-Made* that "very few men ever choose to grasp it and fully to accept it." And that is even more so of infants and savages who, "as far as can be observed do not grasp it at all, although they may perhaps have some rudimentary glimmer of it,"[3] according to Rand. We have further seen how religious practices are a function of the primacy of consciousness. But anyone who operated wholly on the primacy-of-consciousness level could not survive. Now primitive men did survive, as you and I know, otherwise we wouldn't be here. And primitive man could not have survived if he used magic all the time, so he must have used ordinary methods of knowledge a good deal of the time. If he switched to magic from time to time, or even often, he must have known *when* to switch. There must have been some *signal* in his life that told him it's time to switch. Primitive man has very keen senses. In many ways he's a better observer of nature than civilized man; *he* can tell what animals have just been through the woods here, when *we* don't have a clue. So there's nothing wrong with his powers of sensory observation. Furthermore, he can think abstractly. He can make elaborate calendars and calculators—Stonehenge is evidence of that.

His systems of totem relations are so elaborate as to baffle cultural anthropologists. So there is nothing wrong with his conceptual ability. Out of observation and thinking he has developed amazing arts and crafts making it possible for him to survive under adverse conditions. Think of the enormous skill involved in setting out from the coast of southeast Asia in canoes and settling all of the Melanesian and Polynesian and Malayan islands all the way from Easter Island to Madagascar! Those people must have been reality-oriented to a large extent, not merely dreamers.

Primitive man has built up an enormous number of arts and skills and crafts based on everyday observation and rational thinking. On the basis of these, he has survived. When and why then does he turn to the supernatural? No one truly tackled this question until about 1925 when the great anthropologist Bronislaw Malinowski wrote, "In a maritime community depending on the products of the sea, there is never magic connected with the collecting of shellfish or with fishing so long as these are completely reliable. On the other hand, any dangerous, hazardous and uncertain type of fishing is surrounded by ritual. In hunting, the simple and reliable ways of trapping and killing are controlled by knowledge and skill alone, but let there be any danger or uncertainty connected with an important supply of game and magic immediately appears." So they know the difference, after all. "Coastal sailing as long as it's perfectly safe and easy commands no magic. Overseas expeditions are invariably bound up with ceremonies and ritual." In the face of sudden changes of wind and current, the savage must "admit that neither his knowledge nor his most painstaking efforts are a guarantee of success. Something unaccountable usually enters and baffles his anticipations. But although unaccountable, it still appears to have a deep meaning, to act and behave like a purpose. The sequence of events seems to contain some inner logical consistency. Man feels that he can do something to help and abet his luck."[4] So he turns to magic to deal with the otherwise uncontrollable. This element of chance or fortune fills him with what another anthropologist, George C. Homans, called *primary anxiety*, the sense that things are out of control. You turn to a ritual. But then suppose you fear that the ritual has not been performed correctly, you get *secondary anxiety*, and so you develop a tremendous, gigantic obsessional neurosis in your whole culture.[5] You have a whole Talmud full of directions and exceptions and opinions of this and that authority on what to do. I think this helps to explain man's turn to the supernatural. The *signal* to do so is anxiety over lack of control. His wish for assurance is so great that his ability to see the difference between consciousness and existence is reduced to the glimmer that Ayn Rand was talking about. He returns to an infantile state. "Except ye be converted, and become as little children, ye shall not enter the kingdom of heaven," a famous authority once said.[6] The same authority said, "take no thought, saying What shall we eat? or What shall we drink? . . . for your heavenly Father knoweth that ye have need of all these things. But seek ye first the kingdom of God, and his righteousness; and all these things shall be added unto you."[7]

Primitive man is neither lacking in sense observation nor in reason, but in philosophical development. He projects a primitive philosophy, which is religion, and he relegates to a separate order, the kingdom of heaven, precisely the element of chance which he cannot control. He calls this "providence." Later on in his career man gets more and more control over nature and his own life. He learns that all of nature is one uniform system and that chance is not a metaphysical but an epistemological category (at least some men learn that). As his control and confidence advance, religion retreats, but tends to come back again whenever certainty and confidence retreat. In addition to this there are certain things which escape our control: death is one of these. And we remain finite in our knowledge of many of our powers. The most advanced physicist, the most sophisticated statistician or seismologist, cannot predict the moment when an earthquake may wipe out his institute and reduce him to a paraplegic. The facing of these unavoidable slings and arrows is the supreme philosophical test for the individual.

Let us now look at religion among prehistoric men, the genus *homo*, species *sapiens,* and Neanderthal man. Man is a member of the genus *homo*, which is characterized by erect posture and the ability to make tools. This genus has been on earth for about two-and-a-half million years. One species of that genus is *homo sapiens*, distinguishable by his reason. The broadest definition of *homo sapiens* would include Neanderthal man, who appeared about 100,000 years ago. If we adopt this classification, *homo sapiens* have been around only 4 percent of the total time that a manlike creature has been around. There was no sign of religion before the appearance of *homo sapiens*, in other words, *no sign of religion before the appearance of reason.* Neanderthal man buried his dead in a crouching position. Accompanying the corpse were tools and food offerings. There are also signs of a bear cult; the skulls of bears are deposited in niches in caves.

Then came Cro-Magnon man. Cro-Magnon man is now generally placed together with modern man in a subspecies called *homo sapiens sapiens*—especially rational. Cro-Magnon man, besides having a more elaborate culture had a more elaborate religion. Like Neanderthal man he buried his dead, but he put the body under a stone for safe-keeping. He put in the grave not only tools, but weapons and ornaments. He painted the body with red ochre (iron oxide), to simulate blood. We know from the customs of later people that painting with red ochre is a magical procedure to encourage blood flow. Cro-Magnon man painted colorful and elaborate pictures of animals in the remote interior of caves, areas that sometimes can be reached only by swimming. These paintings seem to have a magical purpose; they include painted spears thrust into the animals. There is a picture of a shaman, a man wearing a costume of reindeer antlers, owl's eyes, patched animal skins, bear's paws, a horse's tail, a man's beard. It is believed that what happened in the caves was a pre-hunting ceremony like a war dance, and that the job of the shaman was to rev up the hunters for the kill. The dance was also meant to bring success to the hunt. The shaman probably ritually painted the spears into the animals as the ritual progressed. Another phenomenon was the presence of sculptured figures of the human female, two to four feet high with greatly exaggerated sexual characteristics. There is also a picture of nine women surrounding a naked male, apparently the idea of a perfect initiation ceremony.

When we go from Cro-Magnon man to related peoples of the upper Paleolithic, we see definite signs of sacrifice from about 15,000 years ago. We find the corpses of young does filled with rocks and sunk in lakes. With the coming of the Middle Stone Age, about 10,000 years ago, we get to the first signs of agriculture. This period is associated with symbols of the sun and the moon, the worship of the ax and spear, and apparently a mother goddess. The New Stone Age lasted from 7,000 to 3,000; it was characterized by active agriculture, the domestication of animals, permanent housing, wheeled carts, and the first surgery. The cult of the mother goddess expanded. Burial rites became more complicated. The corpses of the wealthy began to be interred in enormous underground stone chambers accompanied by human sacrifices. During this time the great megalithic monuments of western Europe were built, and fertility rites were held that in some way connected the death of humans with the return of vegetation.

The next stage in the development of religion is the religion of civilized societies. I am here using the term *civilized societies* in a technical, not in a moral, sense. Civilized society includes those societies marked by a written language, the amenities and comforts of urban life, and considerable advances in the arts. In the remaining chapters of the book I will deal with the religion of civilized societies. Although there have been many such societies such as those of Mesopotamia, Egypt, Greece, Rome, and China, I will not be analyzing these. Instead I will confine my attention to certain religions that had widespread, indeed enormous effects beyond the boundaries of societies in which they originated. They are the religions of the Indian and Near Eastern traditions. Our next chapter, will be concerned with religions of the Indian tradition.

Notes

1. E.E. Evans-Pritchard, Theories of Primitive Religion, Oxford University Press, 1996, p. 18.
2. 2 Samuel 6:3–7 Revised Standard Version
3. Ayn Rand, "The Metaphysical Versus the Man-Made," in *Philosophy: Who Needs It?* Indianapolis and New York, The Bobs Merrill Co., Inc., 1982. The whole essay is instructive on this point.
4. Bronislaw Malinowski, "Culture" in *Encyclopedia of the Social Sciences,* edited by Seligman and Johnson, vol. 9, New York, MacMillan Publishing Co., 1931, pp. 632–634.
5. George C. Homans, "Anxiety and Ritual: The Theories of Malinowski and Radcliffe-Brown," *American Anthropologist,* vol. 43, 1941.
6. Matthew 18:3 King James Version
7. Matthew 6:31–33 KJV

2

Religions of the Indian Tradition

In our first chapter, we dealt with primitive religions. We now turn our attention to the religions of civilized societies. As I said at the end of the first chapter, I use the term civilized societies in a technical sense, to mean those societies marked by a written language, the amenities and comforts of urban life, and considerable advances in the arts. We cannot, I said, deal with all the religions of civilized societies. We are concerned only with those which achieved global significance. Among these we can distinguish two major families, those in the Indian tradition and those in the Near Eastern tradition.

In the present chapter, we shall be dealing with the three main religions in the Indian tradition: Hinduism, Jainism, and Buddhism. Since Jainism and Buddhism are offshoots of Hinduism, we shall take up Hinduism first.

Hinduism has half a billion adherents, 90 percent of them in India. They make up about 85 percent of the population of India. The association of Hinduism with the unique type of society indigenous to India is therefore something essential to the religion. Hinduism means *Indian*, and is the religion that undergirds, pervades, and crowns Indian civilization. It can only be understood in conjunction with this civilization, and it can only be understood in its historical development.

Hinduism had no founder. It developed along with Indian civilization over a period of about 2500 years, from about 1500 B.C. to about A.D.1000. After this date it was more or less fixed in its essential characteristics.

Indian civilization had a precursor civilization, which existed from about 2500 to about 1500 B.C., about a thousand years, but which existed in mature form about half that time, from about 2200 to about 1700. This civilization, the Indus River civilization, which was in the area of present-day Pakistan, consisted of about seventy good-sized towns strung over 1,000 miles. There were two metropolises, the agricultural base was wheat and cotton. In the metropolises, there were storehouses and processing factories for these products. A brisk trade was carried on with Sumeria. The streets in the cities were laid out with great regularity. There were storied apartment houses, elaborate indoor plumbing, and trash disposal systems. Everything was standardized. All the bricks were of the same regulation size, there were exact weights and measures and thousands of inscribed seals. All the evidence seems to indicate a highly regimented centralized society ruled over by a priestly bureaucracy. The way in which the streets are divided into major blocks and the ruins strongly suggest the separation of different occupational or kinship groups from each other. The cities are surrounded by vast walls forty-feet high from their base and citadels raised fifty feet. The walls seemed to have been built against both flood and invasion. Outside the walls lived a mass of very poor inhabitants. Inside the cities were ritual purification baths. The lower classes apparently did the manufacturing work, and did it on an assembly-line basis. Everything suggests a caste system ruled over, as I have indicated, by a priestly bureaucracy that was immensely preoccupied with orderliness and cleanliness. Technologically, once a certain level was reached, about 2200 B.C., everything was standardized and there was no growth from then on. No change occurred for the next 500 years until the destruction of the civilization. The parallel to the society described in Ayn Rand's *Anthem* is startling.

The religion of the society is revealed by its artifacts. It was a fertility religion. There are figurines of females with enlarged sexual organs; and there are stone images of female sexual organs called *yonis*. And there are rather ambitious representations of male sexual organs, two feet high, called *lingams*. There is a male figure with horns wearing an animal skin, seated in a yoga position with an erect penis. He resembles the later Hindu god Shiva, the god of fertility, orgiastic rites and destruction. There also appears to have been a cult of sacred bulls. The Indus River people buried their dead, sometimes a man and a woman together, foreshadowing the later Hindu practice of widow-burning. Skeletons reveal the physical type of the people to have been Mediterranean so far as the upper classes are concerned, and so far as the lower classes are concerned probably Australoid, a flat-nosed people related to the Australian aborigines. There is no agreement concerning the language inscribed on the soapstone seals, but many scholars believe that it is Dravidian, a family of languages widespread today in the south of India.

This society contributed many elements to later Indian civilization: the caste system, the overwhelming tendency toward bureaucracy, the concern for purificatory bathing, the fertility cult, the worship of animals, especially the sacred cow, and probably the practice of yoga. An obsessive concern with regulation and control seems to have been a pervading note of the whole society. This civilization began to disintegrate about 1700 B.C. There is much disagreement about the causes, but there seems to have been some kind of disaster involving the river system followed by the attacks of invading people.

The invading people, the Indo-Aryans, came into India from the northwest. They were a semi-pastoral people who settled down wherever the grazing was good and raised crops. The cow and the horse predominated among their animals. They had tamed the horse in their probable homeland in the south of Russia, a feat requiring great ingenuity and courage. They traveled in covered wagons and they fought in two-wheeled chariots. Their social structure was intensely patriarchal, centering in the nuclear family and spreading out to the clan, the tribe, and the people. The individual was involved in a complex network of allegiances based on mutual trust, support and confidence. There was a class system in which the warrior caste the Ksatriyas, seemed to have been, at first, on top, the priest magicians or Brahmins second, and the farmers or vaisyas third. The society was ethnocentric and xenophobic, hospitable to insiders but closed to aliens. Within the group, apart from the normal cycle of exchange, many services were offered as pure favors without expecting anything in return. Beef was their chief diet. They took great pride in their war-like prowess. They also took great pride in how much they could drink. Their favorite drink was soma, a highly intoxicating beverage, possibly extracted from a species of mushroom.

The invading Aryans had closer cultural connections with Europeans than they did with the Indus River people, and this can be demonstrated by comparing their language with Dravidian. Let us compare the numbers one to ten in a modern Dravidian language and the numbers one to ten in a modern Aryan language. The Aryan is Hindi in the north, the Dravidian is Kannada in the south. Here is the Dravidian: *vondu, yardu, muru, naku, aydu, aru, yawu, yentu, ombatu,* and *hattu.* Here is the Hindi: *ech, do, teen, char, ponch, chech, sot, ot, now* or *non,* and *dos.* Now what do you see there? The latter are like English, Latin, French, or Greek, so you can immediately see that they had a closer cultural connection with the European people.

The religion of the Aryans was polytheistic. They worshipped the personified forces of nature. Their gods were anthropomorphic, often of the warrior type. A few were identical with those of Greece and Rome. For instance, the Indo-Aryan sky god was Dyaus Pitar; in Greece it was Zeus pater and in Rome, Jupiter. So, there is a definite connection here. To these gods they make sacrificial offerings of soma and horses, soma by turning their cups upside down. Our knowledge of the early Aryan religions comes from the sacrificial hymns or *Vedas.* These hymns were transmitted orally from generation to generation.

The Aryans apparently fell upon the decaying Indus River civilization, destroying its forts, its cities and probably its irrigation system. The following extract from a hymn to the war god Indra has been interpreted by some scholars as the celebration of the destruction of a great dam system on the southern tributaries of the Indus River. The dams are supposed to be here symbolized by a serpent called Vitra. Now here is the hymn:

I will proclaim the manly deeds of Indra . . . , impetuous like a bull he chose the soma, drank down three vessels of its juices. Indra slew Vitra, the mighty serpent. He slew the serpent then discharged the waters. The waters deep have hidden Vitra's body plunged in the midst of never ceasing torrents. He lies beneath the very feet of rivers which with his might he had before encompassed. The cows, o hero, thou didst win and soma, and free the seven streams to flow in torrents.

That is one interpretation of the hymn, not the only one, but the one I think most plausible.[1]

The Aryans conquered the remnants of the Indus River civilization and then they faced the problem of how they would deal with its inhabitants whom they referred to scornfully as *dasas,* dark-skinned, and *anasas,* people without noses. It is probable that the Aryans intermarried with the priestly bureaucracy among the conquered and consigned the rest to manual labor. It is also likely that the priestly bureaucracy joined forces with the priests among the conquerors and imparted to them some of their mentality.

At any rate, a new class system emerged in which there were four main castes, *varnyas*, or colors. The priests or Brahmins were now on top. The warriors or Ksatriyas were second; the small farmers and merchants or Vaisyas were third. These three castes were called "twice-born" because they had been invested with a sacred thread at puberty. They alone were allowed to learn the sacred hymns, the Vedas. The menial laborers were organized in a fourth class called *Shudras*. Those whose occupations made them ritually impure, such as cow slaughterers and leather workers, were classified as untouchables.

The natural question is how the priests got on top. This can only have been done by the consent of the warrior land-owning aristocracy. The priests must have appealed to some interest of the aristocracy. Fear of the unknown, fear of uncertainty, of not attaining victory, of not attaining wealth, health, children, land, perhaps. What did the priests do? They propagated an ideology, distinctive to India and different from that of the Judaic tradition. The ideology runs as follows: There is a universal causal order which they called *Rita*. This causal order not only includes everyday causal natural events such as the fact that water puts out fire; it also includes magic. You will remember how in the first chapter I defined magic when we were discussing primitive religion. Magic is the performance of certain actions, the making of certain gestures, the utterance of certain words, which literally compel reality to respond in certain ways. Information about these actions is not attained by reason, but is a matter of revelation. Now, said the Brahmins, if you try to perform these actions without the detailed knowledge of just how to perform them, you are not going to succeed. We are the professionals, we alone know how to perform the *soma* sacrifice, the horse sacrifice, and so on. This knowledge has been handed down from father to son, from teacher to student, in our own caste from the beginning of the world. Not only do we perform the ceremonies necessary to win victory and health, we perform the ceremonies necessary to bring on the monsoons, indeed even those ceremonies necessary to make the sun come up in the morning.

The warrior class, awed like Attila before Pope Leo the Great, bought this claim and all that it entailed and paid enormous fees to the most expert Brahmins for the correct performance of the sacrifices and rituals, which sometimes lasted for more than a year and in which hundreds of animals were slaughtered. According to the teaching, the universe itself had been produced by sacrifice, and constant sacrifices were required to maintain it, and this called for highly trained professionals to intone the hymns with the appropriate mantras or sacred phrases, and to perform the elaborate ceremonies with scrupulous accuracy. Let me give you a couple of such incantations. To get rid of jaundice: "unto the sun let your yellowness go up; with the color of the red bull do we envelope you. Into the parrots do we put your yellowness, into the yellow-green birds." Formula against serpents: "Let not the serpents slay us with our children and with our men, the closed jaw shall not snap open, the open jaw shall not close. Homage to the divine folk, [the serpents,] homage to the black serpent, homage to the one with stripes across its body, homage to the brown constrictor, homage to all the divine folk. I smite your teeth with tooth, I smite your jaws with jaw, I smite your tongue with tongue, I smite your mouth, O serpent, with mouth."[2] (Observe the principle of association.)

At this point it is about 900 B.C. and the religion is still very worldly. We have two bodies of scripture in place, the Vedas or hymns to the gods, and the Brāhmanas or manuals for the priests. The Brāhmanas are like rubric books, telling the priests how to apply the sacred hymns, how to perform the ritual. Every hymn praises a god and makes a petition. The priest accompanies the hymn with ceremonies. Now here is an excerpt from a hymn to Bitu, the god of food. If you think that Hinduism started out on an ascetic note, be disillusioned by this. The hymn to Bitu the God of food: "I glorify Bitu, savory Bitu, honeyed Bitu, we who eat you and drink your juices get fatter and our necks get longer. Since we enjoy plants and juices, O body may you grow fat, and since we enjoy Bitu's mixture of soma with boiled milk and barley, O body, may you grow fat." Worldly indeed! The purpose of all the ritual was to help us to enjoy what they called a hundred autumns on earth and at death to go to paradise where we would have more of the same, something like Valhalla.

Next we come to the age of *Brahmanism* from 1000 to 700 B.C., called that because during that time, the authority of the priestly caste was unquestioned. The religion continued to be a religion of worldly values: wealth, love, marriage, children, food and drink, victory over one's enemies, luck in gambling, the joys of the elephant hunt, and so on. A life of a hundred autumns. The only goals of life on earth were *artha*, power, and wealth and *kāma*, pleasure especially sexual pleasure. Their word for manual is *sūtra*; thus we have the Kāma Sūtra.

But what were the means by which these goals were to be assured? The performance of endless sacrifices. Sacrifices with increasingly elaborate rituals paid for by heavy fees to the Brahman priest. Good luck these people regarded as the result of good sacrifices. Some sacrifices seemed to be more effective than others. Sometimes the monsoon was delayed; and more skillful priests were called in. These more skillful priests soon began to receive fatter fees, and younger priests began to come to them for instruction. Naturally this encouraged the more skillful priests to elaborate the ceremonial ad infinitum, raising the tuition. The sacrifice now became more complex. Each gesture had to be carried out with precision, each word had to be pronounced correctly and to be expertly synchronized with the accompanying gesture. Since fire was essential to all sacrifices, the invocation of Agni, the fire god, was the necessary means of getting into contact with the other gods. He was the "control," like the "control" in a seance, and so Agni became more important than the other gods and soon began to absorb the other gods into himself. If a priest was sacrificing to Indra, he would say, "You, O Agni are Indra," now you see that's the denial of the law of identity as applied to a non-entity! "You, O Agni are Indra." But why was Agni more important? Agni was more important because he, Agni, was there on the altar under the control of the priest. So it is obvious that the priest's control was more important than Agni.

Now this ritual power, this supernatural energy, was called *Brahman*, from the root *brh*, meaning "to swell,"[3] because the Brahman belief was that, if the sacrifice was performed, the power just kept swelling in front of the priest. To expand, to be potent, is the meaning of this root. The name of the priestly class, *"Brahmin,"* was derived from the name of the power, "Brahman." Now in what did the power of Brahman consist? It consisted in the power of the mind to control reality by means of redefining things in a desired way. For instance, the priest pointing to the fire would say, "you O Agni are Indra, "then pointing to the square altar, "you O Ahavaniya are the altar of offering," then pointing to the semicircular altar, "you O Dakshina are the altar to appease the avenging spirits." Thus reality would be recreated and remolded by arbitrary definition. Such definitions by stipulation may recall the doctrines of those twentieth century philosophers who hold that all definitions are arbitrary, or those twentieth century economists who maintain that wealth may be created by decree. Cows would multiply, sons begotten, consciousness became primary, reality secondary. These definitions, these statements of identity, were called *mantras*. So you see, from these people way back 1000 B.C. down to the New Age people of today, it's the same idea. The *mantra* captured the holy power Brahman, which was the power binding a name to a thing. It was soon assumed that Brahman is the power which holds all things together; naming is causing to be, providing that the naming is done during a sacrifice with well-formed words in which the lips, the tongue and the palate moved exactly the right way. The word for well-formed speech was *samskrita*, from which we get the name of the language, Sanskrit.

The gods now began to lose their importance in comparison with the sacrifice. The priests taught that the gods had gained their positions in heaven by sacrificing! See how it comes down to the interest of a professional class. Obviously there was one thing that was now all-important, the Brahman, the sacred power in which all things live and move and have their being. This power was some kind of consciousness. It was controllable, and the way to control it was by sacrifice, for which one had to pay the priest. Some sacrifices lasted a whole year, accompanied by the slaughter of hundreds of animals and the performance of incredibly elaborate rituals, any deviation from which would invalidate the whole process, require it to be started all over again, require the offender to be purified in a series of baths in which you had to run the water just right and so on. Thus an enormous cultural obsessional neurosis was developing. These sacrifices were not only designed to ensure the patron of the good things of this world, they were designed to keep him in good health in heaven lest he become ill there (this is after he died). You performed sacrifices to keep the dead in good health, and thus avoid what was called "redeath." This is even more clever than the requiem mass system of the Western middle ages. Naturally the priest required directions, and the directions how to perform the ritual properly were in the scriptures called the *Brāhmanas*. To sum up, what we had in this period is a religion of this-worldly values which the people tried to gain by assuming the doctrine of the primacy of consciousness.

We now come to a turning point. Disillusionment with the system began to set in. As the smoke of thousands of slaughtered animals settled over the villages, people seemed to be no healthier, wealthier, or happier. The rain sometimes failed to come, and the Brahmins always departed with their payment in cows. Then disillusionment with the *means* began to spread to the *ends* of life. People began to get disillusioned with life itself. People began to argue, "if we can't achieve a better life through magic, maybe we can't ever achieve a better life at all." Anyway, death is inevitable no matter what you do, so is sickness, so are disasters of all kinds. Look at the pain; is it balanced by pleasure? Certainly not. We will get attached to the very things that give us pleasure and in time will lose those things, and so we will have sorrow. Life is full of sorrow. This might well be called the Great Disillusionment or Great Disgust, a kind of life-disgust that passed over Indian culture, and which eventually lcd to a new stage, the cosmic anorexia of Jainism and Buddhism.

About this time, a new doctrine emerged, the doctrine of rebirth or reincarnation. According to this doctrine, when an individual dies he is born again in another body. This doctrine was utterly unknown to the Aryan tradition. It probably came from the primitive tribes of northeast India, although this is not certain. However, as we saw in our first chapter, it is to be found in many primitive tribes in various parts of the world. However, as found among primitives, the doctrine of reincarnation is non-moral; if you're a barber you're reborn as a barber, or if a plumber you're reborn as a plumber, but it's not a reward or punishment for what you did in your previous life. Now, as adopted into the town society in northeast India in 600 B.C., the doctrine of reincarnation was *moralized*.[4] It now became this: if you live a good life you will merit greater good fortune in the next life as a reward, and if you commit moral offenses you will be punished in the next life. Everything we do has a lasting effect. This is called *karma*. It is the weight of sins and good deeds, vices and virtues that we carry with us from life to life. It goes on forever for most people. The whole wheel of rebirth with its circulating weights of *karma* is called *saṃsāra*.

Now, as we have already shown, life is not worth living, so we must do something about that. We must find some way of escape from the wheel. This is called release or *moksha*. This doctrine is going to be central from now on. People are looking for the cosmic ejector button. Now, this is actually the center and purpose of the religions which then began to develop. This development can be traced in the Indian scriptures. The earliest scriptures, as I said, are the *Vedic* hymns, then come the *Brāhmanas*. The next step is a group of scriptures called the *Aranyakas*. Now, these are hymns for hermits that go out into the forest to meditate. They begin to develop the doctrine that sacrifice can be performed mentally by meditation as well as physically, and that this mental performance is just as effective as the external performance. Now, since it had been taught in the Brāhmanas that the *physical* performance of the sacrifice could control the universe, this control was attributed by logical extension to the process of meditation; transferred to mental performance, to performing the image in your mind. In other words, consciousness can now control the existence and behavior of its objects. Now, the next step is to transfer the focus, from meditation to the self which is doing the meditation, for it is really the meditating self, rather than meditation, which is controlling the universe. By this time we reach the final chapters, which are called the *Upaniṣads*. "Upaniṣad" means "to sit down around [a teacher]," shad is "sit," "upan," is "near to." By this time we have an expanded doctrine of the self. The word for self at this time was *ātman*, which literally means, breath.

The two questions which most naturally arise are *one*, the nature of the self—what is the nature of ātman—and *two*, what is the relation between *ātman*, the self, and Brahman the magical power which holds together all things? Let us take the first question, what is the *ātman*, what is the self? Is it my body? No, I know that my body is constantly changing so that every few years I have a completely new body, yet I remain the same person. Is it my perceptions? No, they're always changing but the perceiving self remains the same. The self must be something independent of a particular body and of its sense organs. After all, the self, as we all know, can be reborn in another body with different sense organs. Well, then, perhaps the real self is the dreaming self. That is the self when it is free from the distractions of the senses. However, when a man is dreaming he is still affected by what he has experienced through his senses, for his dream images are derived from his sensations while awake. More than that, in his dreams he suffers the same anxieties he experiences when he is awake. For instance, he may dream that he is being trampled by an elephant, a great Hindu nightmare.

Well, then, where is the real self to be found? One of the Upaniṣads tells us that a man might get a taste of the true self in two experiences: when he's in a deep and dreamless sleep, and when he is "in the embrace of his dear wife." In either of these phases, he experiences a totally unified consciousness in which there is no awareness of the difference between himself and any object. That is the form in which his desire is fulfilled, says the Upaniṣad. That is the form in which the self is his desire, in which his consciousness is without any object. In other words, what is achieved in dreamless sleep or, in orgasm, is consciousness without an object. A consciousness, therefore, in which there are no distractions; a momentary, blissful release.

This highest bliss, the deepest stage of introspective withdrawal is called *ānanda*. But unfortunately it is only temporarily attained in every day life. The point is to remain in that state. This can be accomplished by *knowledge*. What do we need to know? We need to know three things: what the self is, what the Brahman is, and what the relation between them is. Now we've already found out what the self is; it is the pure ego after it has been stripped of all its perceptions, desires, and thoughts. It is a self in which there is no longer any duality. A self which has nothing to be conscious of. This is my real self, a consciousness without any object, *consciousness without existence*. I've achieved it by stripping off the outer layers of perception, memories, thoughts, and desires, all those things which Kant later calls the phenomenal self, and I've gotten to my pure ego. Now, after I have stripped off all these things, I have stripped off everything that is uniquely personal. What's the difference between myself and yourself after we've stripped off all the perceptions, desires, and memories that are unique to each of us? *I find that myself is identical with yourself.* Not a single difference between us can be found. By this philosophical argument the metaphysical basis of selfishness is destroyed. My self should be no more to me than yours should be to me, for they are one, one could be substituted for another or sacrificed to another. Now that we know what the real self is, let us note well its moral implications.

What is the *Brahman*? What is this power that underlies all things, that holds all things together? Is it physical? *Neti*; not that, for physical nature is one of the things it holds together. Is the Brahman a person? *Neti*, for it brings forth *all* persons. Is it a god? *Neti*, for it brings forth *all* gods. It cannot be defined, for to define it would be to identify it with something else, something other than itself; to identify it with one of the finite things which are its mere manifestations. *Neti, neti*, not this, not that. It's *beyond all distinctions*, it's the One beyond all duality. But we've already seen that the *real self* has been defined as a one beyond all duality. Now there cannot be two Ones, the *ātman* and the Brahman, for there is nothing to distinguish them from each other. Here, then, is the supreme doctrine of the Upaniṣad, *the Brahman is the ātman*, the magical power is the self and the ātman is you, *tat tvam asi*, that thou art.

Since the Brahman is you, and you are I, all we have to do is get together and know this. Not only intellectually but emotionally—then all our selfish desires will shrivel up and die, and we will be dead as separate persons, we will have obtained *moksha* or release. The Upaniṣads thus present a Gnostic scheme of salvation, or salvation by knowledge of some philosophical truth, not salvation by faith. And as a matter of fact the word they used for it, *jñāna*, derives from the same root *gno* in the hypothetical Indo-European mother tongue. It is also the root of "know." (jñāna is pronounced "gyana.") Now this Upaniṣadic teaching was later summed up by Sankara, who is regarded as the greatest Indian philosopher, often called the Kant of India. Sankara lived about A.D. 800 and lived to be only thirty-two years old. He taught that there is only one being which in a strict sense exists and that is Brahman, which is impersonal, absolute, pure consciousness and bliss. It is one and indivisible without a second being or division, without any internal differentiation. This Brahman is infinite energy which played (*lïla*) with itself and threw some of its energy out of itself, thereby creating the world. But this world is still an aspect of Brahman, and it has no existence apart from Brahman. When the world is considered apart from the Brahman, to the ignorant the result is *mäyä*, the veil of illusion. When seen through the veil, the Brahman seems to be a personal god; you look at him through the veil of mäyä and he then seems to be a personal god facing the world and looking out at the world. This creates the illusory distinction of God's world, versus God's person. But really there is only one being, that is Brahman, and that being is beyond all definition. Now, this is a *monistic* philosophy. Monism is the doctrine that there is only one being and within that being there are no differentiations whatsoever. In Greek thought we also encounter the doctrine that there is only an undifferentiated One, in Parmenides above all. The other Presocratics who were looking for the basic substance identified it as something distinguishable and inwardly differentiated, except possibly Anaximander.

The stage of Indian philosophy which we have now reached is called non-dual or Advaita, the final summing up of the doctrines of the *Veda*. (It is only fair to mention that other powerful schools of Indian philosophy are *dualistic*, rejecting the doctrine of the undifferentiated being.)

Now we come to the reforming religions, Jainism and Buddhism. About the year 500 B.C. we see the rise in the Ganges Basin of two new religions whose teachings are such as to exclude them from Hinduism. They both reject the whole body of Hindu scriptures. They reject the Vedic hymns, the Brāhmanas and the Upaniṣads; they reject the caste system and the animal sacrifices, but they retain the doctrine of reincarnation and release from the wheel of saṃsāra. They both teach a formula for release, but these formulas are different, and so are the metaphysical views on which they are based.

Let us look at *Jainism* first. Jainism was founded by a man called the Mahāvïra or great-souled one, a member of the warrior caste who left his family to become a wandering ascetic. He achieved what he called enlightenment after twelve years. He preached his new doctrine, and, at his death, left half a million followers. There are two million of his followers in India today. They hardly exist outside India but their doctrine is important because it embodies, in the purest form, certain principles which appear elsewhere only in a diluted or watered-down state. The whole intent of the founder was to present a concrete practical way of release from the wheel of rebirth. The way he proposed consisted of practical acts, not meditation, and this was because of the metaphysical system which he embraced: radical mind-body dualism. According to this doctrine, there are two kinds of stuff in the universe, mind and matter. Mind is conscious and occurs in the form of little centers of consciousness called *jïvas* or life monads. These monads are eternal and indestructible. There are quintillions of them in the universe. Matter, on the other hand, exists in the form of extended, shaped atoms. These atoms have mass.

Now some *jïva* is to be found in all matter, but the highest types of *jïva* can be found in living matter, plants, animals and men. All these can feel pain, and pain is the supreme evil. Now, the universe is arranged in such a way that the *jïva* of the being who inflicts pain on any other being, is invaded by *karma*, and *karma* is a kind of sticky stuff which weighs down the soul and postpones its release. So every time you give pain to any other living being you get a dose of sticky *karma*. Now, the soul without any *karma* is perfectly transparent (what David Kelley calls the diaphanous model is obviously at work here[5]).The *karma* is colored and soils the soul with stains of color. Black *karma*, for instance, is characteristic of mean, cruel, nasty, sadistic, merciless people; dark blue *karma* of sensual greedy people;

dove gray *karma* of angry people; these *karmas* all come from bad deeds. But there is some *karma* that comes from good deeds, this is because whenever you do a good deed you will hurt or annoy someone who didn't want the good deed to be done! The results are red *karma* which is characteristic of honest benevolent people; yellow *karma* which is characteristic of compassionate unselfish people; and at the highest stage, a kind of milky white *karma* which is characteristic of dispassionate, disinterested, absolutely impartial people.[6]

Now, if you accumulate *karma* by doing evil deeds, good deeds, or neutral deeds, how do you think you can avoid *karma*? By not doing anything at all. This is the Jain ideal. The trick is to attain a state of absolute passivity by not picking up any new *karma*, good or bad, and by purging oneself of all accumulated *karma*, good and bad. But, you exclaim, one cannot live like this! You'd be surprised. The Jain intends to do this in some life or other. In life after life he intends to purge himself gradually of all *karma* and then in some life to become a wanderer, a homeless one. Some Jains have already arrived at this state; you can see them in India today. They have renounced all their possessions including every last article of clothing. They walk around the streets of India stark naked carrying, at most, a staff. They do no work, they will not even pluck an apple off a tree. When they arrive at a Jain home—that is a home of people who haven't reached this state, in other words the laity, these co-religionists simply pour food into their open hands and the Jain ascetics will just eat out of their hands while standing. Eventually these wondering ascetics will reach the stage of complete detachment, at which point they will deliberately starve themselves to death and enter into complete release (*moksha*).

Now what kind of life does the Jain layman lead? The man who is not anywhere near the top? Well he tries to lead a life of *ahimsa*, which means nonviolence. Note the effect on Western civilization; we're beginning to experience it now. He is the total animal rights person. He will not engage in warfare, he is a complete vegetarian, he watches carefully as he walks, lest he step on the smallest insect. He often wears a gauze mask over his mouth lest he accidentally inhale a passing gnat. He shows the greatest reverence for the holy homeless ones and he supports them. For a Jain, *moksha* or release is defined as a state of complete isolation or *kaivalya*. He is now ridding himself of the last attachments, attachments to clothing and food. He is ready to go. His *jīva*, his soul, has become completely translucent. Then, after he starves himself to death, his soul goes to the top of the universe. Now what is the top of the universe? It is a great umbrella and on the inside surface of this umbrella the life monads stick, the *jīva*, completely impassive. He neither perceives nor thinks but knows everything directly and immediately *without any means of knowledge.* He is a pure spectator forever and ever and he is completely isolated from every other life monad. You see, at least these people are not social metaphysicians, holding that their own reality is founded in the consciousness of others.

Now what economic status do you think the Jains would have attained in India? Poverty? Well, more than half the manufacturing companies in India are controlled by Jains. The business card of one of my students reads: Jain Plastics, Fifth Avenue, New York. This small sect dedicated to poverty is the wealthiest group in India. What is the explanation? Well, the Jains are excluded from agriculture out of fear of killing worms and insects. They congregate in the trades and in banking. They are taught that industry and hard work are good things. They industriously accumulate as much good *karma* as possible, contributing lavishly to charities and supporting the homeless ones. So these people who contribute to charities, these rich people, you might call them the "limousine Jains," are supporting the homeless ones and sacrificing some of what they have. They hope in some life, preferably a million lives from now, to starve themselves to death, but not right now! The role of religion in their lives is to allow them to enjoy life in this world without guilt while holding on to a standard of radical altruism.

I now offer you a brief list of the ideas you can see embodied in extreme form in Jainism:

- mind-body dualism;
- the concept of involvement in life as a kind of stain or defilement;
- the concept of total detachment;
- the concept of animal rights;
- the concept of the *ahimsa* or nonviolence. It was from the Jains that Gandhi learned this doctrine of nonviolence;
- the concept of life as a kind of annoyance of which we must eventually rid ourselves, so that we can become pure contemplators and have no more worries about gnats, but will be completely isolated;
- the concept of a universe that is eternal with no supreme being.

Well now let us pass to *Buddhism*. Buddhism, like Jainism, is not a natural growth; it did not evolve from the customs of society. It is a system of thought and practice carefully worked out by a teacher who gathered around himself disciples and who founded an institution for the propagation of his view. This man has been known throughout history as the Buddha or the enlightened one. There are some people, of course, who question his very existence, but I'm going to assume there really was a historical Buddha. He flourished around 500 B.C. in the northeast of India. He was the son of a Rajah, the Indian title equivalent to the Latin "rex" or king, the ruler of a small kingdom on the border of Nepal. He came from the warrior caste. His name was Siddhārtha Gautama. His family was rich and powerful and they saw to it that he led a sheltered life of luxury. He had a beautiful young wife and a son. The family expected him to succeed his father as the Rajah. The turning point came when he saw "the four signs." One was a decrepit old man who tottered as he walked; the young Siddhārtha asked his charioteer why the man was in such a condition. The charioteer explained that eventually all men would become like him. Then the prince saw a very sick man sitting in his own excrement. The charioteer explained that all men are subject to sickness. Then the prince saw a corpse, and the charioteer explained that all men must die. Then the prince saw a shaven-haired ascetic walking along the street. The prince was impressed by the look of serenity on the face of the ascetic. He decided to leave his home, his beautiful wife, and his child; to go out in the world to find the solution to the problem of suffering. He tried the Brahman way, he achieved nothing. He tried the radical asceticism of the Jains. He got thinner and thinner but he achieved nothing. He abused his body without mercy, he reduced his diet to a few grains of rice a day, until as he said, "when I placed my hand on my stomach I had my backbone in my hand." Then he took food, and he meditated until he found what he regarded as enlightenment. Because of this he came to be called by his followers, the Buddha, the enlightened or awakened one. He imparted the desire for this enlightenment to a whole group of followers and shaped them into an order of monks. He taught for forty-five years before he died. His order gathered laymen around it and became a vast movement, eventually the dominant religious force in southeast Asia.

The following is a summary of the teaching of the Buddha as codified by a council of Buddhists of 250 B.C.[7] First there is a general metaphysical position: the universe is eternal; there is no God in the sense of creator or supreme ruler. So here is a religion without a God, or real supreme being. The universe is composed of events occurring in microseconds. There are no enduring physical entities even though there appear to be. (Here his position is the same as that attributed to a contemporary of his in ancient Greece. "There is nothing permanent," Heraclitus is reputed to have said.) The Buddha went on to say, "Neither are there enduring selves." What appear to be enduring selves are aggregates of physical forms, sensation, and habit; these are called the component bundles or *skandhas*, making up the self. The self is merely like the appearance of a continuous surface formed by the whirring blades of a fan; there is only an appearance of a solid surface. Causation is nothing but the regular succession of events. Here his teaching approaches that of Hume. There is no necessity involved. What then of the doctrines of *rebirth* and *karma*? Why should we care about being reborn if we have no real self anyway when we are alive? We are obviously not going to have a self after we die. So how can we be reborn? Buddha assured us that we *are* reborn and that what we do in this life will affect the quality of our next life. Well, how *can* we be reborn without a permanent self? He answered *that the strings of events which form the appearance of a self would carry over into the next life.* He said that there are strings of memory and perceptions and so on reaching back beyond our birth. Here, then is a radical Humean who believed in reincarnation!

Then the Buddha formulated the four noble truths, the bridge between his metaphysics and his ethics. The *first truth*: life is full of suffering. Remember the Great Disgust that I mentioned? Life is full of suffering. The word for suffering is *bukkha* in southern Buddhist thought. Life is full of pains, *bukkhas*. Pain includes longing and frustration and separation from the pleasant. This is the noble truth of suffering. *Second truth*: suffering is due to craving, clutching, wanting to hold onto passing pleasures as if they could be permanent. This is the noble truth of the origin of suffering, craving. *Third truth*: suffering ceases with the cessation of craving. This is the noble truth of the cessation of suffering. *Fourth truth*: There is an *eight-fold path* which leads to the cessation of craving. What that is we will see in a moment, but it is the practical application of the first three truths. Now, it is obvious that the misery of desire is caused by ignorance, the ignorance of him who thinks that the objects of desire are anything permanent.

The formula of that misery is the following: ignorance leads to will, which leads to action, which leads to consciousness, which leads to physical existence, which leads to the five senses, which lead to contact, which leads to feeling, which leads to craving, which leads to attachment or grasping, which leads to worldly existence, which leads to decay, death, grief, lamentation, physical dejection, and despair. This formula is called the *law of dependent origination*. Its opposite is the formula of *enlightenment* which means release from suffering, release from the wheel of rebirth. Enlightenment can come from following the noble, eight-fold path. *Right understanding*, first of all, the understanding that nothing is permanent. *Right attitude*: accept it and renounce all hope of changing. *Right speech*: abandon all frivolous talk and gossip. *Right morality*: do no injury to living things; do not steal, do not engage in sexual immorality, do not lie, do not drink intoxicating drinks. *Right occupation or livelihood*: do not be a butcher or slave dealer, a caravan trader, a publican or a poison-seller. *Right effort*: keep a guard over your mind, encourage good thoughts and suppress bad ones. *Right mindfulness*: avoid bad sense-perception, don't even see anything bad. *Right concentration*: achieve a feeling of purity and inner peace.

I'll give you just a little sample now of his words. "O priests, the learned and noble disciple conceives an aversion for the eye, conceives an aversion for forms, conceives an aversion for the impressions received in the eye. He conceives an aversion to the ear, conceives an aversion to sounds" This is an example of the style of the Buddha which is always didactic and utterly alien to the style of Middle Eastern or Western religious teachers.

Then we have, finally, the characteristic institution of Buddhism, the *religious order* of monks and nuns. The monks and nuns are closest to the Buddhists' ideal of release or *moksha*, which is called *Nirvāṇa*. It is the cessation of craving, when the flame of attachment is blown out, and this you can achieve in life, by knowing truth. For a time you remain as a living Buddha, you have achieved *Nirvāṇa*, yet you are still alive, but since you now lack all craving, your body begins to disintegrate and after a few years you die. This is called *paranirvana*, dying after having achieved *Nirvāṇa*. Everybody's goal should be *Nirvāṇa*, the blowing out of the flame. This *Nirvāṇa* can, under ordinary circumstances, be attained only by the monk or nun. This is because the later parts of the noble eight-fold path, right mindfulness and right concentration, can be practiced only in withdrawal from the world. The Buddhist world is therefore divided into the ordinary laity and the religious order, *sangha*. The layman simply obeys five commandments, prohibitions against taking life, drinking intoxicants, lying, stealing, and unchastity. He cultivates the virtues of kindness, affection, temperance, consideration for others, and pleasant speech. He supports the order and he hopes in some future life to be a monk or nun. This is basically the same pattern as that of the Jains. The monk and nun, meanwhile, are supported by the laymen, and they go around everyday begging their meals with a begging bowl. Thus, although Buddhism rejects the caste system, the caste system has re-emerged in the form of the difference between the laity and the clergy. The basic principle always affirmed by Indians is that he who devotes himself to a religious and intellectual life should not only be respected, but also supported by the rest of the world. That is the intellectual class following the love of higher truth. The very enterprise of loving higher truth and achieving it should be supported by the rest of the people. This class is to be separate, whether entered by birth or by decision. The holy man is honored not so much because *he* will render a return service, but to honor him is a good thing which sooner or later will bring reward to oneself.

Now I have been discussing the southern or orthodox form of Buddhism, which is called *Theravada*, the way of the elders, which is predominant in Southeast Asia. But there is also another form of Buddhism and this is *Mahāyāna* Buddhism, which means the Buddhism of the greater vehicle. Now the key concept in *Mahāyāna*, or greater vehicle, Buddhism is the concept of the *bodhisattva*. The bodhisattva is a man on his way to Nirvāṇa. He just gets to the edge of Nirvāṇa and he decides not to enter just yet. Not to enter? Why not? Because he wants to wait until all living beings can join him. He wants to say, "after you ...I will be unselfish, totally unselfish. I will not achieve the supreme good, which is release, until all of you have achieved it first, and meanwhile I'm going to work for all of you. I'm going to be reborn in life after life and be your guide, or in some *pre*-Nirvāṇa heaven, faraway I will be your intercessor, and you can pray to me by offering up the equivalent of masses and rosaries and things like that, and ultimately we will go together into Nirvāṇa. So that is the central doctrine of northern Buddhism, or Mahāyāna, which we have touched on here only so far as its essential principle is concerned.

Our task, in closing, is to determine what is the generic Indian pattern of religion. The Indian pattern of religion is based on revelation, like the Middle Eastern pattern which we will take up next. But it is a revelation which is a kind of intuitive insight into the nature of the universe, rather than a thundering out of heaven, "thou shalt—thou shalt not." In the Indian pattern, a seer, or a privileged, ecstatic visionary, ushers us into another realm. He sees something which is veiled to other men. He then expresses this knowledge in a song or poem. The word *Veda* means wisdom or knowledge. Indian religion is *wisdom religion*. The wisdom is transmitted from teacher, or guru, to student. It is like the tribal secrets which are transmitted at an initiation ceremony. The other word is *jñāna*, equivalent to the Greek *gnosis*, meaning knowledge. There is no hearing of a divine voice, no Mount Sinai, no threats to the unbeliever, very little, if any, appeal to faith. Secondly, there are hundreds of schools and subschools in Indian religion. All these schools contradict one another, yet the tendency is to ignore the contradiction and to claim that they all are, in a higher sense, one. The Indians thus blithely ignore the laws of identity, contradiction, and excluded middle, to such a degree as to give acrophobia to the most anti-Aristotelian Westerner.

Of course there are several patterns to be found in the development of Indian philosophy. But there is no pattern more prominent than that of the increasing stress on the primacy of consciousness. At the beginning there is ordinary magic: the *primacy of consciousness* shows up in the estimation of the *means* of life. I want good crops, therefore I sacrifice so many animals and the ritual will guarantee me the good crops. Then at the next stage I need perform the sacrifice only in meditation. Then the very *ends* of life became other-worldly and ascetical, and I cease to identify the gods as having a determinate reality. Then the indeterminate god that results is identified with myself. The Brahman is the Ātman. Then the very unity and existence of the self is placed in doubt: there is only a flow of impressions. The self has become a Humean flux and the remaining task is to extinguish the flux, to blow out the candle, as the Buddhists say. Indian philosophy, beginning with a hearty concern for the enjoyment of the things of this world advances through stages of increasing subjectivism to a complete detachment from the world and from all care even for one's inner impressions—in other words to complete nothingness.[8]

Notes

1. Rig-Veda 1.32, translated by A.A. Macdonell, in his *A History of Sanskrit Literature*, London, Wm. Heinemann, Ltd., 1928, p. 86.
2. Atharva Veda 1.22, quoted in *Sources of Indian Tradition*, vol. I, general ed. W.T. DeBary, New York, Columbia University Press, 1958, p. 18.
3. C.F. Heinrich Zimmer, *Philosophies of India*, Princeton, NJ, Princeton University Press, 1951, pp. 74-83.
4. See Gaananath Obeyesekere, "The Rebirth Eschatology and Its Transformations: A Contribution to the Sociology of Early Buddhism" essay 6 in *Karma and Rebirth in Classical Indian Traditions*, edited by Wendy Doniger O'Flaherty Berkeley and Los Angeles, University of California Press, 1980.
5. See Kelley, *The Evidence of the Senses*, Baton Rouge, Louisiana State University Press, 1986, et.passim, esp. 37-38 where he traces the origin of the concept in an explicit sense to G.E. Moore's "Refutation of Idealism."
6. Zimmer, *Philosophies of India*, edited by Joseph Campbell, Bollingen Series 26, Princeton, NJ, Princeton University Press, pp. 229-230.
7. The Council of Pätaliputra, called by King Ashoka, a convert, who ruled over two- thirds of India.
8. In addition to the works already cited, the following works contain further information on religions of the Indian tradition:
    Basham, A.L., *The Wonder That Was India*, New York, Grove Press Inc., 1954; Campbell, Joseph, *The Masks of God: Oriental Mythology*, New York, Viking Press, 1969; Conze, Edward, *Buddhism, Its Essence and Development*, New York, Harper and Row, 1951; Eliade, Mircea, *A History of Religious Ideas*, vol. 1, Chicago, University of Chicago Press, 1978; Macdonell, Arthur A., *A History of Sanskrit Literature*, London, Wm. Heinemann, Ltd., 1928; Organ, Troy Wilson, *Hinduism: Its Historical Development*, New York, Barron's Educational Series, 1974; *Sources of Indian Tradition*, vol. 1, general ed. W.T. DeBary, New York, Columbia University Press, 1958; Smart, Ninian, *Doctrine and Argument in Indian Philosophy*, London, George Allen and Unwin, Ltd., New York, Humanities Press, 1964. (This work is a good complement to Zimmer above. Whereas the former's emphasis is primarily psychological, the latter's is on the exact analysis of philosophical doctrines and the arguments actually advanced by each school. The result is a highly technical and exhaustive summary of over a dozen Indian schools, with charts both topical and historical.)

3

Judaism and Christianity

Now let us proceed to a very general and broad overview of Judaism and Christianity. The greater portion of this chapter is historical because historical context is a vital aid to the understanding of both religious and philosophical movements. So let us start immediately with the most remote origins of Judaism.

The only direct sources we have for the origin of the Hebrews are the mythical accounts in the biblical book of Genesis. These accounts center around the lives of the so-called patriarchs, Abraham, Isaac and Jacob. On the whole, the narratives present a true picture of life in the fertile crescent during the years 2000 B.C. to 1500 B.C. when Semitic speakers of the north central group of Semitic languages enter the stage of history.

According to biblical tradition, the original home base of the Hebrews was around a city called Harran, now in southeastern Turkey. I say home base because the very name "Hebrew" is a Babylonian word which means a wanderer or nomadic soldier of fortune who attaches himself to a host people as an ally and who then negotiates the acquisition of some grazing ground for his flocks.

The particular group descended from Abraham were attached to a warlike people called the Hurrians. We know this because the Hebrews adopted certain Hurrian customs such as the custom of selling one's birthright, or in the case of a woman, stealing her father's gods (idols) in order to make sure that her father's possessions came ultimately into the possession of her husband.

The Hebrews, in the beginning, spoke Aramaic, a Semitic language. Hebrew was the language they later acquired from the Canaanites, the previous inhabitants of Palestine or Canaan once they emigrated from farther east. After arriving in Canaan, they encamped in tents mostly near the Canaanite cities. They herded sheep, goats, and cattle and practiced seasonal agriculture. The Hebrews revered, as their ancestor, a man called Abraham. They were descended from him and his wife Sarah through their son Isaac who was (I think we're getting into pure mythology now) conceived when Abraham was 100 and Sara was 90. (You can always tell when the mythology starts.) Abraham had previously begotten another son, Ishmael, by Sarah's maid Hagar, from whom the Arabs are descended, according to both the Jews and the Arabs. That's one thing they are agreed on. Abraham worshipped a god called El, the strong one, the plural of which, Elohim, is used for God in certain component documents of the Bible.

The religion of Abraham was roughly the following: He and his descendants are the objects of the god's loving care. In return, the god asks for obedience, whose ordinary expression is prayer and animal sacrifices at outdoor altars, at stone pillars and sacred trees. Their god promises land and many descendants. Eventually there came a personal call by the god to Abraham, a promise of coming good fortune. Absent is the note of jealousy on the part of the god, or any note of tension with other gods or with people regarded as outsiders. It is important to note that the Canaanites also called the chief god El; from El, of course, comes the Arabic name "Allah."

Abraham made his first land purchase in Canaan in a place called Hebron, which is today venerated by both Jews and Muslims as his tomb. Now, there is no extra-biblical confirmation for the story of Abraham, but the logic of the myth and its general picture of conditions places him about 1750 B.C. as a contemporary of Hammurabi, the King of Babylon. The biblical tradition goes on to tell us that all the descendants of these people went down into Egypt, where eventually they were enslaved and then brought out in a sensational rescue mission led by a man named Moses acting under the direction of a God with a new name, Yahweh. So God now takes on a new name. Formerly El, sometimes in the plural Elohim, God is now Yahweh, who claimed to be identical to the original god El. That's what he said to Moses when he appeared to him in the burning bush. "I am the God of your father, the God of Abraham, the God of Isaac, and the God of Jacob."[1]

Moses is also said to have delivered to the people a law authored by

Yahweh. None of this has any support in contemporary Egyptian documents, not even the alleged drowning of the Egyptian Pharaoh as the sea closed back on his army after having parted to let the Hebrews through. Of course, the crucial question is what really happened at the time, but it is very difficult to reconstruct this. The key to the reconstruction is to be found, I think, in the idea that far out in the desert Moses forcefully initiated his followers into a new religion. New and yet old, for he forced them to return to a more primitive, more patriarchal form of Semitic tribalism than they had known for many generations. He forced them to turn away from their understandable desire to assimilate to the urban civilization of Egypt and to its customs. No one denies now that the name Moses is an Egyptian name. Moses was more assimilated than the other Israelites. He turned back violently from his course of assimilation when he realized that the path of assimilation was leading to slavery for many of the Jews. When he saw a labor boss beating an Israelite, Moses killed him and escaped out into the desert where he was welcomed by another, more primitive Semitic tribe, the Kenites of Midian, sometimes called Midianites, and from this tribe he got his wife. These Kenites were smiths.

There in the desert at Mount Sinai, he had the vision of God in the burning bush, the God who announced himself under a new name and who gave Moses the mission of leading the Israelites out of Egypt into a land of milk and honey, the old land of Canaan. But before he is to bring them into Canaan, he is to bring them to "this hill." Thus Mosesreceived his vocation in the desert as the primitive shamans did, as John the Baptist would, as Jesus did, as the monks of the desert would in time. Moses was to lead the Israelites out of Egypt and bring them to "this hill." He did just that. He initiated a whole people at once at Mount Sinai. Now some scholars believe that he actually did conduct a vast initiation ceremony here with all the theatrical effects which a primitive tribe has at an initiation ceremony. There is, for instance, a Dutch scholar named Eerdmans, who in his book, *The Covenant of Sinai*, hypothesized that the tribe of Kenites, the smiths, produced sound effects by beating loud drums and waving torches and so on, and this is the basis of the great awe which the Hebrews all experienced, but that is merely speculation.

There was, I think, an initiation ceremony in which Moses initiated the Israelites into a new way of life whose fundamental features were the following:

1. The worship of one God, or, henotheism, the worship of one God without any statement as to whether there does really exist any other god. This one people is to worship this one God;
2. The banning of female partners of the deity. This God goes it alone;
3. The banning of all magic and sorcery whatsoever. Remember that in the chapter on primitive religion I identified magic and sorcery as one form that religion can take. Moses is committing the Hebrew people totally to the *personal* form with all magic and sorcery excluded;
4. Images are out. Now why would images be banned? Remember the role of images in primitive religion? You have a control over the image, you can get it up in the morning, give it a shower, lead it in procession to its female partner at night the way the Hindus do; you can give it a present, you can start beating it if it doesn't do what you want. All such control over the deity is renounced in the banning of all images;
5. *All male* Israelites are initiated, not just some, as in a primitive adolescent, puberty initiation;
6. There is tribal equality, which you might call "democracy," rather than the highly structured hierarchical society of the Egyptians;
7. There is no emphasis on life after death.

All these were in conscious rejection of the Egyptian religion. In Egyptian religion you had polytheism, you had the cult of Osiris and his sister/wife Isis, you had magic, sorcery, and amulets. You had sculptured and painted images of deities, you had initiation mysteries in which individuals were initiated in special ceremonies, you had perhaps the most sensational degree of belief in immortality and care of the dead that you had in any religion, and you had a highly stratified class society.

Now Moses gave his followers, the tribes that he had brought together, a code, the earliest version of which is Exodus, chapters 19-24. This was promulgated about 1250 B.C. It follows the form of a Near Eastern treaty setting forth, at the beginning, the historical background, the purpose and nature of the undertaking, the benefits, the promises, and the curses. It's a treaty between God and a people. God is to be a truly arbitrary ruler whose mere wish is to govern every aspect of the people's lives.

The heart of the code is the Ten Commandments or Decalogue found in Exodus 20, 1– 17. All crimes are sins and all sins are crimes. *That is a crucial feature.* All breaches of the law offend God. Restitution to other people whom you may have hurt is not enough. God requires expiation, and this may involve drastic punishment. In other codes, a husband may forgive an adulterous wife and her lover; the

Mosaic code orders both of them to be put to death no matter what the husband may think. The Mosaic code was far stricter in matters of sex than other Near Eastern codes. All irregular forms of sex were banned. Incest was regarded as particularly horrible and was defined so as to include marriage with cousins. To quote a few provisions, "He that sacrificeth unto any god, save unto the Lord only, he shall be utterly destroyed." "Thou shalt not suffer a witch to live." "If thou lend money to any of my people that is poor by thee, thou shalt not be to him as an usurer, neither shalt thou lay upon him usury."[2] What is being prohibited was called the sin of "usury."

Now the Jews, in practice, forbade the taking of interest from fellow Jews but allowed it to be taken from people outside. In other words, the Jews were permitted to lend money at interest to non-Jews. But when Christianity and Islam *universalized* the basic Mosaic code, they forbade taking of interest, period. They took the basic Jewish idea, and they universalized what was originally a tribal prohibition. "If ever you take your neighbor's garment in pledge, you shall restore it to him before the sun goes down; for that is his only covering, it is mantle for his body; in what else shall he sleep?"[3]

"The first-born of your sons you shall give to me."[4] About this, the biblical commentaries say only that the commandment must have envisaged the redemption of the first born by substitute sacrifices, as in the case of Abraham and Isaac. This was a big thing in the Near East, the sacrifice of first born children. Sometimes children were thrown into fiery furnaces, the bellies of sculptured idols. And the great drama of the beginning of the children of Israel was a product of what happened when God demands that Abraham sacrifice Isaac, his son, and then says, in effect, I didn't mean it; here's an animal you can substitute for him. And ever since that time it has been a particularly horrible crime in Judaism to mistreat children, and always the opposite attitude has been maintained, at least in theory, that one treats one's children well.

Many of the provisions of the law are more humane than other codes. Actually, the statement "an eye for an eye and a tooth for a tooth" is a mitigation of the primitive idea of two for one. This is sometimes misunderstood, but the author of the law was trying, in my opinion, to humanize the practice. There is a great stress on the sanctity of human life, as you can see in the provision for capital punishment to be imposed for the violation of life. Offenses against property are generally played down. This is an expression of the tribal nomad's sense of communal possession and economic equality. But capital punishment is to be imposed for insults against God: rejection of his authority, the worshipping of any other god, the making of an image even of Yahweh himself, the sacred bull image. The unifying tenet is absolute authoritarianism so far as God's authority is concerned. But there is no earthly ruler allowed. God alone is king of Israel, and all men are equal before him. There is both political egalitarianism and economic egalitarianism. There is rough tribal justice tempered by mercy toward the weak, tribal responsibility, and collective guilt, "for I the Lord [Yahweh] your God am a jealous God, visiting the iniquity of the fathers upon the children to the third and the fourth generation of those who hate me, but showing steadfast love to thousands of those who love me and keep my commandments."[5]

Now upon such few simple commandments others were piled, in time, hundreds of dietary and Sabbath regulations amounting finally to 613, which the pious Jew is supposed to observe. Whatever the historical value of stories like the ten plagues, the crossing of the Red Sea, and the revelation on Mount Sinai, the account left a lasting psychological impression on the whole Hebrew people similar in function to a myth. The story of the Exodus became the symbol of Jewish history, religion, and nationhood. And the Ten Commandments, whose revelation at Sinai is the high point of the entire narrative, became the foundation of what we call the Judeo-Christian ethic as well as much of Islamic tradition.

The following material is what accompanied the Ten Commandments; what was "piled on top of it," so to speak. It has had much effect on these three religions but much moreso on Judaism. From this legal material we can make the following generalizations:

- The rules are formulated as expressions of God's will only. (I am the lord thy God who has brought thee out of the land of Egypt out of the house of bondage. Thou shalt have no strange gods before me. Thou shalt not make unto thyself a graven image the likeness of anything that is in the heavens above or in the earth below or in the waters that are under the earth.);
- They are promulgated to the people at large;
- The people at large are held responsible for their observance. Get him in there and make him do it if he says no;
- Obedience is somehow conceived as a *quid pro quo*. That is, there is not an absolute prostration before God such as you find in Islam. God

makes an agreement with you—the *quo* in this case was liberation from Egypt, liberation from slavery;
- The worship or service of other gods is forbidden;
- All recourse to magic is banned;
- The use of images is banned, probably because they suggest magical control of the deity; and finally,
- Sacrifice is interpreted as a tribute rather than as a giving to God what he needs. This is a new note.

Moses died without entering the promised land. He was the central figure of the epic. In a true sense, it may be said that he made the Jews *his* chosen people, for he devoted his whole life to an attempt to shape their mentality and their conduct forever. The Jewish community, as we now call it, was his project and to them he was a great liberator, leader, law-giver and the father of the prophets. Although no convincing extra-biblical evidence exists that there ever was such a man, the subsequent history of the Jews was profoundly effected by the belief that there was. After his death, the tradition continued.

His successor, Joshua, led the Hebrews across the Jordan, conquered Jericho, subdued most of Canaan west of the Jordan in the thirteenth century B.C. Now, actually, the conquest was by gradual incursion and Joshua may have had nothing to do with Moses or with any of the tribes that had been in and around Egypt. What seems to have happened is that one group of tribes in the south, saying that they had been led out of Egypt by Moses, persuaded the northern group of tribes to accept the whole Mosaic tradition and covenant as their own.

This new confederation of people was based on the idea of one God to be worshipped by us: "this is our God." This one God was regarded as the sole king of the whole confederation and his authority was exercised by charismatic military and political leaders called judges. The era of the judges was characterized by a continuing war to conquer the rest of Canaan and to abolish the Canaanite fertility cults to which the Hebrews were perpetually succumbing. The whole people now came to be called Israel after the alternate name of Jacob from which the tribes, the northern and southern tribes, were both descended. Israel, however, continued to be surrounded by hostile peoples. The confederation was too loose for safety, and what might be called a more perfect union was called for. This involved having a king "like other people."

Such a choice was a radical departure from the tradition of tribal life, when the God Yahweh was the only king. From now on there was a tremendous sense of tension between those who wanted to settle down and live as the Canaanites and those who wished to perpetuate the severe tribal tradition which meant, among other things, a more collectivistic and egalitarian economics and a puritanical sexual ethic. But finally the judges gave in to the idea of kingship and the last great judge, Samuel, anointed Saul as king. Later another Saul (St. Paul) was to try to undo the whole process, as we will see. Saul, in turn was succeeded by David about the year 1000 B.C. David defeated the Philistines, captured Jerusalem from the Canaanites and made it his capital. The Israelites then completed the process of settling down to an agricultural and town life. They began to experience in full the tension between that kind of life and life in nomadic circumstances. In Canaan every patch of fertile ground had its "baal" or fertility god. He died at the time of decay of vegetation and he came back to life again when the crops began to grow. There were high *baals* on the local hills. The dying and rising to life of all these *baals* and their female helpers were accompanied by orgiastic festivities. It was absolutely necessary to the science of agriculture that one engage in these rituals and it was great fun to go to the orgy. And so the Israelites were swept up in all of this, adding the worship of fertility gods and goddesses to the worship of Yahweh. The religion of the Israelites was well on the way toward syncretism, the merging of incompatible elements.

David, meanwhile, made peace with the Phoenicians, built an army, organized the kingdom, and moved the ark containing, supposedly the tables of the law, to Jerusalem. The ark he deposited in a tent. He brought a new ideology to Judaism, the idea that God had made a *parallel covenant* with the anointed king, channeling his benefits to Israel through the chosen dynasty of David. Henceforth the great leaders of Israel would be kings, sons of David. Here was the germ of the idea of Messiah, for whenever Israel was subjugated, the people looked for an anointed king of the house of David to arrive from nowhere and redeem the nation. David also introduced the idea of the inviolability of the king's person and a court rhetoric in which the king was styled "son of God." Solomon, David's son, succeeded him in 965. He concluded treaties with neighboring kings, made numerous diplomatic marriages, established trade relations with many countries, and was in many ways a master of international relations, as you can see in the famous episode with the Queen of Sheba. Internally he centralized the kingdom, imposed increasingly heavy taxes upon the people, and also forced labor. He built a great temple in Jerusalem to Yahweh in Phoenician style and also built on the Mount of Olives shrines for all the gods of his wives.

During his reign the native Canaanite population was largely absorbed, and the worship of their fertility gods flourished along with that of Yahweh. Following Solomon's death in 928 B.C., the dissatisfaction of the ten northern tribes, over the issues of heavy taxes, forced labor, and royal absolutism, led to the secession of a new kingdom which called itself Israel, leaving the kingdom in the south around Jerusalem to be called Judah. The kings of the north severed all religious ties with Jerusalem. They set up two northern sanctuaries to Yahweh and they put up the old totem image of the golden young bull or golden calf as the totem of Yahweh. For the next several generations, the process of syncretism continued in both kingdoms, and then the voices of reform were raised.

Now come the prophets. The prophets were very important in the history of the Israelites. Prophets had been around since before 1000. They were, essentially, dancing dervishes, who worked themselves up into a religious frenzy, which they called "being full of the spirit of God." Some of them were *baal* worshippers, others were Yahweh worshippers. They were essentially descendants of the primitive shamans. They gave out oracles, they praised and denounced, they made predictions about both private and public affairs. There were so many of them that there was even a union of prophets. Now, a considerable number of these prophets used to go out in the desert, fast, see a vision of Yahweh, and then come back and stand on the street corners of Jerusalem saying "repent, repent, the end is near," just as we see today.

From the standpoint of the writers of the Bible, there were two kinds of prophets, true prophets and false prophets. The true prophets were the prophets of Yahweh and the false prophets were the *baal* prophets, who were more like street corner gypsies reading your palm. They worshipped both the *baals* and Yahweh. On the other hand, the true prophet was often a kind of "back- to- the- simple- life- of- the- desert" type denouncing urban and civilized life. But we must be careful in evaluating them, for they mixed denunciation of riches with denunciation of plain decadence and dishonesty. They denounced seizure of property by the kings and so on.

So we have a kind of package-deal situation here. People were asked to choose between two value systems, one of which endorsed earthly pleasures and success, plus breaking contracts and robbery, plus the fertility gods, versus another which encouraged the life of the poor shepherd plus honest and decent living, plus the sole worship of Yahweh. To quote now the prophet Amos, "Woe to those who lie upon beds of ivory, and stretch themselves upon their couches, and eat lambs from the flock, and calves from the midst of the stall; who sing idle songs to the sound of the harp, and like David invent for themselves instruments of music; who drink wine in bowls, and anoint themselves with the finest oils, but are not grieved over the ruin of Joseph!"[6] "I hate, I despise your feasts, and I take no delight in your solemn assemblies." This is Yahweh speaking of course, through the prophet. "Even though you offer me your burnt offerings and cereal offerings, I will not accept them, and the peace offerings of your fatted beasts I will not look upon. Take away from me the noise of your songs; to the melody of your harps I will not listen. But let justice roll down like waters, and righteousness like an ever-flowing stream." [7] Thus spake Amos.

There were many prophets of this kind: Elijah, Amos, Josiah, Isaiah, Micah. They brought about a strong movement back to pure Yahwism for a time. But then, after the fall of the northern kingdom to the Assyrians in 722 B.C. and the exile of 25,000 of its inhabitants (the ten lost tribes) there came about a powerful reversion to *baalism* and syncretism in the south. The Yahweh prophets were suppressed by King Manasseh, shrines were erected to the Assyrian gods in the temple, and a kind of penthouse was erected on the top of the temple for the worship of the fertility god Adonis or Tammuz. A shrine also in honor of Ishtar, Queen of Heaven, was installed in the temple. King Manasseh burned his own son as a sacrifice.[8]

Suddenly the pendulum swung again and there came a tremendous reaction. With the accession to the throne of Josiah, Manasseh's grandson, the latter ordered the repair of the temple, and during the repair work that was going on, the high priest, Hilkiah, claimed that he had found, in a corner of the temple, the Book of the Law. This book he told the king is the original book of the law of Moses. The king consulted a prophetess who assured him that the book was genuine. The high priest then gave the king a second copy from which he told him he could rule the realm. He called the second copy "Deuteronomy," the second Law book. The king read the Law book, he cleared out all the idols and the sacred prostitutes from the temple, he took off the penthouse, he tore down the sacred pillars and poles, he raged through the whole kingdom demolishing the sacred places of the *baals*. He then centralized all worship in Jerusalem, bringing in all the local priests into the temple, and thus the income from the sacrifices were brought in, too, and centralized. The Jerusalem priesthood now had absolute control over the Mosaic tradition and a vested interest in it. This happened in about 622 B.C.

Judah lasted another thirty-six years until it was captured by Nebuchadnezzar, the king of Babylon, in 586, who destroyed the temple and deported about 5000 of the educated classes to Babylon, leaving the others behind. This ruling class in Babylon found comfortable homes for themselves. They did not disintegrate culturally or religiously. They constituted a distinct community in which religious observance increasingly took the place of the active secular life that they had lived in Judah. Their leaders evolved a new system of law and theology. A new concept of the people of Israel as a holy community, even in dispersion, or *diaspora*, came into being. The ideal activity of male Jews became no longer being a warrior, but studying and studying the law.

Suddenly, Babylon was conquered by Cyrus the Great, the king of Persia, in 538 B.C. Now, Cyrus was the adherent of another prophetic religion, Zoroastrianism. He was sympathetic to the Jews, and he allowed them to return to their homeland to rebuild the temple. Groups of zealous exiles began to return. Now, the people who had been left behind at the time of the exile were the less zealous Hebrews, and their whole attitude was: "Oh, here they come back from Babylon, here come the sticklers!" The temple was rebuilt. Nehemiah acted as the secular governor for the Iranian king, and Ezra was in charge of the religious aspect of things. A new religio-political establishment was in place by the year 444. Ezra ordered an assembly of all the Jews who had not gone to Babylon. He read the Law plus the riot act to them, forcing them to divorce their non-Jewish wives. He instituted a fanatical religious regime forcing on the people all the strict interpretations of the Law that the scribes had arrived at in Babylon. As you can guess, and as the Bible says, there was weeping and gnashing of teeth. As the commentator, W.K. Lowther Clarke says, "no more striking example is to be found in history of the power of a determined minority to influence the course of events than the fact that Judaism, as we now call Hebrew polity, was conceived in Babylonia and imposed on Judea."[9]

During the next hundred years, a large part of the Hebrew Bible was written or edited. This work of writing the Bible had probably started way back in David's time, around 1000.

Then the Persian empire was overthrown by Alexander the Great, in 333, and the Hellenization of the Near East begun. I want to quote again Clarke's biblical commentary. "Colonies of . . . Greeks were planted all over the vast area, but at best they must have formed a small minority of the population. The conquest was effective because it was a spiritual one, and the new civilization was accepted as definitely higher than anything previously known. For the first time Asiatics were introduced to political life; knowledge of Greek opened the door to drama, philosophy, and science; athletics and the cult of the body came in. A fuller and richer, if more secular, life could now be lived. Even among the stubborn Jews, many succumbed to the new influence.[10]

There was a profound antithesis between the Greek and Judaic spirits. At base were philosophical differences: reason versus authority; man-centered versus God-centered philosophy; the universal orientation; the Hellenistic world view of Alexander versus a particularistic orientation among the Jews of "our people." These differences came out in daily life. The Greeks were appalled at the Jewish dietary laws and the inability of their Jewish friends to dine with them. They were shocked at the Jewish practice of circumcision, which they regarded as a mutilation of the body. Many Jews, perhaps the majority, definitely wished to adopt Hellenistic civilization, to attend the schools and gymnasia. One of the signs of the times was that of enterprising Jewish merchants stationed outside the gymnasia selling artificial foreskins. Many of the Jewish priests, including the high priests, became half Hellenized or even fully Hellenized. The Jews tried to prevent this, and the Greeks having no more concept of rights than the Jews, tried to counterimpose their own civilization by force. The Greeks forbade Jewish observance, desecrated the Jewish temple, and many Jews became "martyrs," or witnesses, by death, to their beliefs. This was the beginning of the concept of martyrdom. The feast of Hanukkah, the feast of the purification of the temple after its desecration by the Greeks is one result of this period.

At last the Jews had risen up in force under the Maccabees to win their independence, which they kept for 130 years, from 164 B.C. to 63 B.C., when they were conquered by the Romans. Under Roman rule, Jewish institutions such as the temple, the priesthood, and the ecclesiastical council received a large measure of autonomy. But pious Jews wanted a society in which the Mosaic Law was strictly enforced; they wanted the complete rule or "kingdom of God." Other Jews, less pious, were glad to practice Judaism with moderation and to give thanks to Yahweh for Hellenistic culture and the Roman rule of law.

These groups hated each other. According to the Jewish historian Josephus, who lived in the time of Christ, the Jews of that time divided into four parties, described below in the order of decreasing acceptance of Hellenistic culture under Roman law. First, the Sadducees, a conservative urban party formed about 200 B.C., of priests, leading families, and wealthy merchants. They were in charge of the temple and sacrificial cult, which they held in high regard. They accepted *only* the written Law, the Torah or Pentateuch, the five books of Moses, Genesis, Exodus, Leviticus, Numbers, and Deuteronomy. They rejected the oral law which had been built up in Babylon. They did not believe in life after death of any kind, including the resurrection of the body; and they rejected the existence of angels, beliefs that the Jews had apparently picked up in Babylon. They were hated by the common people for their external, minimal religion and for their obvious partnership with the Romans.

Then came the Pharisees in about 140 B.C.. The Pharisees were the most popular party. They strictly observed both the written and oral laws, trying to adapt them by ingenious interpretations to changed conditions. Their attitude was obsessively legalistic, but they tried to split hairs in such a way as to make life on earth possible. They introduced the institution of the synagogue, which could be set up anywhere, in which there were no sacrifices, but simple readings, prayers, and sermons. Under them the study of the law became a duty of every Jew. The authority on the law, or Rabbi, was a Pharisee institution. They believed in angels, in the literal, physical resurrection of the dead, and the last judgment, beliefs which they may have gotten from the Zoroastrians while in Babylon, who also had precisely these beliefs. It is hard to believe, however, how they could have absorbed so much Zoroastrianism and tailored it to Judaism in so short a time.

Then there were the Zealots founded about A.D. 6 , who advocated violence and terrorism to overthrow the Roman occupation. They looked for a military Messiah to lead them. Then came the Essenes[11] who also had their origin about 140 B.C. They emphasized ritual purity to an extreme degree. They seem to have engaged in continual ritual immersions of a baptismal nature, and seem to have advocated communal property and possibly celibacy. It seems likely that John the Baptist had something to do with these people. Most scholars identify them with the people of the Dead Sea Scrolls at Qumran.

It was during this period that Christianity arose as a fifth sect among the Jews. Within a generation it had partly split off from Judaism. But before the split was complete, the Jewish world was once again shattered. Increasing tensions in Judea, caused partly by Roman tyranny and partly by growing messianic fervor among the Jews, led to a confrontation. The Romans decisively crushed a Jewish revolt in A.D. 6 . In A.D. 70 they captured Jerusalem, destroyed it amid a scene of unbelievable slaughter, and burned and razed the temple. Only one wall was left standing, the so-called Wailing Wall. It has remained the holiest place for Jews to this day, and of course something else has been built on the scene, the Dome of the Rock, one of the holiest shrines in Islam. So again, there's total confrontation, a recurring part of the role of religion in history.

The Zealots held out and holed themselves up in the fortress of Masada, where in A.D.73 they committed suicide in order to avoid being killed or captured by the Romans. Meanwhile, the Romans took the sacred paraphernalia of the temple to Rome, where they carried it in triumphal procession, an event commemorated in the Arch of Titus in Rome, which may still be seen today.

A final revolt occurred in A.D. 132 under a man named Simeon bar Kochba, who proclaimed himself the Messiah and fought the Romans for three years. After he was defeated, the Romans banned all Jews from Jerusalem and they built on its ruins another Roman city, Aelia Capitolina.

In spite of these colossal defeats, the Jews reformed their lines in exile and became a worldwide religion, on an ethnic basis, but open to any proselyte ready to live under the increasingly difficult Jewish law. In A.D. 69 a learned academy was founded at Jabneh on the coastal plain, also called Jamnia, and this academy fixed the number of books of the Bible. This is the beginning of what is called *normative Judaism*, when you have a written down rule on which there is general agreement by the whole community and everybody is expected to live by it. The body of authoritative commentary called the *Talmud* was completed in Babylon by A.D. 500. Since that time Judaism has had a rich history, but its essential philosophical and religious position has remained the same.

Now, let us consider the essentials of the Judaic position in a kind of philosophical overview. Like Hinduism, it is a religion of a people, but it is not the product of a slow growth of customs and institutions like Hinduism. Instead, like Buddhism, it contains a coherent message, something proclaimed as a new way of life. The message proclaimed is—"Hear O Israel: The Lord our God is one Lord."[12] This message is addressed to one people, the chosen ones. They are to leave behind them the flesh pots of the goyim, of the Gentiles, and to lead a pure life following a strict law. If they do this, they will survive as a group—but in a peculiar sense of "survival as a group." What is guaranteed is not the survival of all Jews as individuals, but that there will always be Jews, descendants of the present Jews, plus some proselytes, thoroughly scrubbed down. But also, if they follow the law, that means they will be persecuted. So if they don't follow the law, the foreign people will attack them, if they do follow the law, they will be persecuted for it, as every prospective proselyte is warned. Therefore, every Jew is damned if he does and damned if he doesn't. And if persecution ceases, that means the Jews must be assimilating and Jewish identity is being lost. *The essential thing seems to be the survival of certain traditions and practices.*[13]

Now let us look at Christianity. The question of the origin of Christianity is a matter of intense controversy. The storm center of the controversy is the central figure of the religion, Jesus. Did he even exist and if so, can we say anything definite about him? If he never existed, how can we explain the origin of Christianity? And even if he did exist, how would *that* explain the origin of Christianity?

Immense resources of scholarship have been brought to bear, pro and con, on these questions. The overwhelming majority of scholars hold that Jesus did exist and that we can know at least a few things about him. A tiny, unconvinced minority hold that he never existed and that therefore there is nothing to know about him except that he is the central character of a myth. Some of the reasons for this difference of opinion lie in the ideological premises of the scholars who study the documents, but others seem not to be so motivated. Obviously you would expect those who are Christians to argue for the existence of Jesus and those who are non-Christians to be glad to consign the whole subject to the sphere of mythology. But this is not entirely the case. The vast majority of non-Christian scholars hold that Jesus really existed, but a very few professedly Christian scholars have expressed doubt or disbelief about his existence, holding the quasi-Kantian position that what matters about Jesus is not whether he existed or not but the question of his value, not the fact.

All this should lead us to suspect that there are genuine problems in framing the right questions, in gathering and selecting the data and in assessing the evidence, and this I think is really the case. All historians, especially ancient historians, know how difficult it is to decide between hypotheses as to exactly what must have happened to explain the existence of such and such historical data. My *present* opinion is that, in the case of Jesus, we simply do not know for certain anything about his biography, not even that he existed. Nevertheless, we have to explain the origin of Christianity, and in so doing we have to choose between two alternatives. One alternative is to say that it originated in a myth which was later dressed up as history. The other is to say that it originated with one historical individual who was later mythologized into a supernatural being.

The theory that Jesus was originally a myth is called the Christ-myth theory, and the theory that he was an historical individual is called the historical Jesus theory. My present position is that the Christ myth theory is less probable. I think it is more probable that Christianity started within the milieu of relatively orthodox messianic Judaism and later developed into a mystery religion whose theology was more convincing than the rest precisely because it had an historical base and always took this base for granted.

At any rate, the Gospels say that the public career of Jesus began with his encounter with John the Baptist, a figure whose existence is historically authenticated by the historian Josephus.[14] John, according to the Gospel, was another prophet in the long desert tradition. He came dressed in camels' hair and subsisting on a diet of locusts and wild honey, baptizing people in the Jordan saying, "Repent, for the kingdom of heaven is at hand."[15] (It does you no good to be Jews, you've defiled yourself as much as Gentiles, so in order to be saved from the wrath to come, you must be given a purificatory bath here in the Jordan just like the proselytes, and you must live a completely different life.) "What then shall we do?" the people asked John. John answered, "He who has two coats, let him share with him who has none; and he who has food, let him do likewise."[16]

So we had the notes of the kingdom of heaven (or God): essentially an egalitarian, nomadic tribe ruled by an invisible God; the bringing in of this rule, not by Joshua and his legions, but by a supernatural apocalyptic force, a sort of religious science fiction. The message was repentance, in the sense not only of being sorry, but of radically reforming one's life; immersion, or baptism, to use the Greek word, now an act apparently imposed on all its members by the Dead Sea sect whose great settlement was in the desert close to where John was preaching; and finally, primitive communism of the tribe, a major ideal of the Judeo-Christian ethic.

Now, John said that he was preparing the way for the kingdom to come. The Gospels say that John was, at the same time, declaring that one mightier that he would come after him. Whether he said this or not is a question. Then Jesus arrived and was baptized by John. After his baptism, Jesus went out into the wilderness where he endured temptations and visions, thus repeating the pattern of the primitive shamans, as Moses had, as the monks of the desert would after him. Then, after he had heard that John the Baptist had been arrested for sedition, Jesus went into his home province of Galilee, where he began to call disciples. Then he began to teach in the synagogues, preaching "authoritatively," that is, on his own authority, and not as a mere expositor of the Law. Then he began to act as an exorcist and healer, claiming the power to forgive sins. He ate with nonobservant Jews and tax collectors, explaining he had come to call sinners. He said that his disciples did not fast because he was present with them. Like some other claimants to the messianic role, he excused his disciples and others for violating the Sabbath rules, saying that the Sabbath was made for man. He appointed twelve envoys to send out among the Jews to do the same work he was doing. The relevant question here is what was he doing? Or, what did he think he was doing? There is no question that he thought he was a divine agent, that he was the unique agent of Yahweh sent to bring in the kingdom of God. He would do half the job, God would do his half. Jesus would demonstrate, by his conduct and bearing, what it was like to live the spirit behind the law as he interpreted it.

As I understand it, what he was advocating and trying to show by his example was unlimited, unconditional, totally self-abnegating love for others, called, in Greek, *agape*, undeserved love, groundless love, love above all for those who don't deserve it. And this on the ground that, on principle, there is no such thing as deserving. On principle, all are equally at fault because Yahweh necessarily demands the impossible of man: total purity of motive and intention. "You have heard that it was said, 'An eye for an eye and a tooth for a tooth.' But I say to you, Do not resist one who is evil. But if any one strikes you on the right cheek, turn to him the other also, and if any one would sue you and take your coat, let him have your cloak as well."[17] "But I say to you that every one who looks at a woman lustfully has already committed adultery with her in his heart."[18] So, don't cast the first stone, because no one has ever been able to live up to this ethic, for it is not made to be lived up to in this world. The kingdom of God is already invading our world and it is time to begin acting like this, I will show you how it can be done.

Now, every Messiah is supposed to be successful. Such an ethic cannot be successful, for it leads to extinction, not to survival. But suppose that God were to step in and restructure reality so that values of this kind lead not only to survival but to *triumph*. That would indeed be the kingdom of God. *Worthiness to live would be rewarded by survival and happiness.* All Jesus would have to do would be to live his values to the bitter end. There was an old Jewish principle that said that the Messiah would come on the day that the whole law was observed throughout Israel. Jesus determined himself, in his own person, to observe the spirit of the law as he understood it for one full day, Good Friday.

At Passover, probably of the year A.D. 30,[19] he decided to go to Jerusalem to lay down a challenge to the Saducean establishment there. He would call all the Jews gathered for the feast to a decision between his ethic and that of the temple priesthood. He entered Jerusalem, apparently to some popular acclaim, but in the next few days he seems to be hesitant and even ambivalent. For instance, he staged a demonstration to clear the money changers out of the temple courtyard, supposedly in order to purify it. But then he uttered a cryptic remark saying that he could destroy the temple and rebuild it in three days. Apparently he believed that his symbolic actions would set in motion a kind of cosmic change; that God would intervene miraculously and set him up as Messiah. Or perhaps he had a more complex belief. But the expectation was not fulfilled; God did not intervene. If one shoots a lion one must shoot to kill. The lion, that is, the priesthood, had him apprehended swiftly in the night and turned him over to the Roman authorities on the charge of claiming to be the king of Israel. And so, he was executed by the Roman method of crucifixion. His disciples were left despondent. But shortly thereafter, his tomb was reported empty, and word got around that he had risen from the dead and was appearing to his disciples. The disciples were also searching the scriptures and finding texts that seemed to prophesy that the Messiah would die before coming in glory.

A few weeks later, an assembly of disciples gathered to celebrate the Jewish holiday of Shavuot, which marks the wheat harvest and the Sinai Covenant. They broke out suddenly into ecstatic "speaking with tongues" and they went into the streets to proclaim the "good news" of the suffering and resurrected Messiah who was soon to return and set up his kingdom. They made a sizable number of converts and soon began to form a community, a large number of whose members were poor. These poor members had to be supported by the whole group who were awaiting the return of Jesus in glory. So the more prosperous members sold their property to make this support possible. The whole group were very observant Jews, and so were, at first, tolerated. In fact they were a Pharisaic sect. The role in history of such a sect could not have added much to the contribution of Judaism unless its nature was thoroughly transformed. And transformed it was.

The community left by Jesus must not be conceived as anything like the later Christian church. It was as we have said a sect of Judaism, and of Pharisaic Judaism at that. We must repeat and underscore this point for emphasis.

It accepted the Law of Moses *in toto* and observed it quite strictly. It sided with the Pharisees against the Sadducees in accepting the doctrine of the resurrection of the dead. They differed only in their belief that Jesus was the Messiah, that he had already risen from the dead, and that he was about to return in glory.

They did not teach his divinity, for if they had they would have been immediately excommunicated from Judaism and regarded as pagans. On the contrary, they attended the temple together daily[20] and were defended by Gamaliel, a leading Pharisee and teacher of the Law.[21] There is no evidence that they taught that the birth of Jesus was anything but natural. And, attending the temple as they did, they must have accepted the whole system of the sacrifice of animals for the forgiveness of sins. So they could not have taught that Jesus had died as an atonement for the sins of the world. Nor did they teach that Jesus had abolished the Law. So they were in every way what are today called Orthodox Jews. The only difference was that they believed that the Messiah was Jesus and that he had made a preliminary visit to the earth and had been killed "by the hands of lawless men."[22]

If asked their view of the role of Judaism in history, they would no doubt have answered that it was destined to remain as God's chosen people to be ruled over by King Jesus until the end of time.

That there was such a sect within traditional Judaism in the middle of the first century A.D. may be regarded as a fact established by modern biblical criticism and confirmed by the existence, after the fall of Jerusalem, of communities of believers in the Near East who espoused roughly the same doctrinal position we have ascribed to the post-crucifixion Jesus sect. Such communities were called by such names as Nazarenes or Ebionites (poor men). Their existence is attested in the writings of such Church fathers as Justin Martyr (second century), Irenaeus, Hippolytus, Tertullian (end of the second and first half of the third centuries), Origen (middle of the third century), and Jerome (fourth century). These Nazarenes or Ebionites repudiated the Catholic or Orthodox Church of official "Christianity" together with its characteristic doctrines such as the divinity of Jesus, his supernatural birth, his blood sacrifice on the cross for the sins of the world, the Trinity, and so on.

We can only suppose that the fall of Jerusalem in A.D. 70 was followed by a split in the Jesus sect, the larger part of which was transformed into Catholic Christianity with a predominantly Gentile following, and the smaller part of which remained in intention part of Judaism—although they were apparently excluded from the synagogue as heretics and followers of a failed Messiah, about the end of the first century.

Meanwhile, the larger part of the Jesus sect underwent a massive transformation in its rapid evolution into Catholic Christianity. This transformation involved the attraction of a primarily Gentile following and the doctrinal changes brought about primarily by Paul.

Paul was one of the most important men in the history of the world, for it was he who later transplanted the Jesus sect from its Jewish base to the Gentile world, transformed it from a Jewish sect into a new and powerful world religion, Christianity, and by these actions brought about the eventual destruction of the Greco-Roman pagan civilization.

Paul, or Saul, as he was originally called, started out as a zealous Jew. He was against the Jesus party, because no matter how orthodox they were in practice, he thought they were a threat to the survival of Judaism. Now, why were they a threat to the survival of Judaism? Because of the situation they faced in spreading their movement. Gentiles were being committed to belief in Jesus. Now, the practice of the Jesus party in Jerusalem was to accept such converts only if they first converted to Judaism, were circumcised and observed the law; only then were they baptized in the name of Jesus. But now a problem arose. The Hellenistic synagogues had an institution known as the God-fearers, or "fringe of the synagogue." These were Gentiles, who, although attracted to Judaism, did not want to be circumcised or to obey the dietary laws. They were allowed to become honorary Jews and attend the synagogue provided they observed a simplified form of the Law. They were allies and friends, but not for intermarrying and not for sharing all foods. Now, many such honorary Jews were attracted to the Jesus-preaching for obvious reasons. They noticed that Jesus was represented as one who had preached the spirit, not the letter, of the law, that he wasn't a stickler for points, that he had been persecuted by the establishment both Gentile and Jewish, that he had been a friend of outcasts. Such Gentiles wanted to join the new movement. They began to speak with tongues too, and the leaders of the Jesus sect had to do something about all these non-Jews speaking with tongues. They agreed to baptize, finally, all Gentiles who would live by the "law of the God-fearing."[23]

But there was a problem—this problem was at the very center of the new sect's life—with the communal meal, the Lord's Supper. At first the leaders tried to enforce *separate tables* for this rite, but the pressure was growing. Saul must have seen the problem clearly. A Jesus sect completely open to Gentiles in the Lord's Supper was impossible, for the law would be breached, the Gentile members would soon overwhelm the Jewish, so one or the other must go, so the Jesus sect must go if Judaism was to survive. So Saul participated vigorously in the persecution of this sect, but unconsciously he must have realized that he had leapt too quickly from the premise that one or the other must go to the conclusion that *the Jesus sect* must go. Great tension built up in his mind, and one day he had a vision of the risen

Jesus saying, "Saul, why persecutest thou me? It is hard for thee to kick against the pricks."[24] Implying, of course, that Saul's persecution of the Christians was a defense mechanism. Saul was immediately baptized and was henceforth known as Paul, but he did not associate with the leaders in Jerusalem, the leaders of the Jesus sect; he remained isolated. He stayed for some time in an Arab vassal-kingdom to the east of Damascus. Then he returned to preach his distinctive theology, which, in effect, transformed the Jesus sect into Christianity as we know it.

Many scholars have sought for the origins of Paul's theology. Much of their search has involved the assumption that Paul simply reproduced in his thought the religious tendencies existing around him in his time. It is my view that the influence of such ideas upon Paul varies a great deal in weight depending on which ideas we are considering. Furthermore, I hold that Paul, insofar as he may have utilized such sources, or was unconsciously affected by them, wove them into his own original synthesis, a synthesis powerful enough to shape the course of civilization. And that synthesis was an answer, a solution to the problem of transforming messianic Judaism into a universal religion. Finally, it was the answer to a personal problem of Paul's: the appeal of the person of Jesus to him versus the integrity of Judaism in his own life.

By the time of the early Christians, the Hellenistic world which surrounded them was not exactly characterized by undiluted happiness. The individual felt that a burden pressed upon him, in his deepest soul he felt that he was in the hands of alien powers. These powers might be the stars pursuing their fateful course across the heavens or it might be *ananke*, impersonal necessity, or it might be heartless, capricious chance. None of these could be influenced by the prayers of a poor mortal. Man was "alone and afraid in a world he never made," as A.E. Housman would say. His soul lay in the prison of the body and could not free itself. Therefore, said some, enjoy the good things of this world, for afterwards your soul will perish with your body. This answer was to be found, and is still to be found, in inscriptions on gravestones all around the Mediterranean. Others agreed, life is full of pain and sorrow. Where have we heard that before? In Buddhism. It was the same cry that life was worthless that had gone up in India, it's the Great Disgust period now of the Western world. Just as many people preached the message of alienation and disgust, many of them preached about redemption or salvation. This message was preached in the religious movement known as *Gnosticism*.

It's impossible in a short space to chart out the various strands in Gnosticism, but a few words perhaps can summarize. They preached the doctrine of redemption, they taught that the soul of man was of divine origin, had in fact originally been part of God, but that some ancient crime had plunged it into the lower world. The lower world was the world in which we live, and it was created and controlled by the evil Jewish god who had given the Law. But a divine savior had descended, the Messenger of the true or "unknown" God. He was incarnate only in appearance. He was the bearer of revealed knowledge which he imparted secretly to his disciples. This knowledge, called *gnosis*, would allow man to outwit the hostile powers, to mount up through the seven celestial spheres and be reunited with the good God who lived beyond the outermost sphere. To do this, one had to respond to the "call" of the divine savior, receive his teachings which were secret, experience the influx of his strength, receive the benefits of his heroic work, and become a member of the religion. Since the body is a part of matter, and since matter is by nature controlled by the hostile powers, salvation requires *extrication* from the body. It is not enough to die, it is necessary to die a good death. This was foreshadowed in the Platonic doctrines. According to Plato, the body is the prison of the soul, and philosophy, the love of wisdom, is the preparation for death. Such doctrines are worked out to a logical conclusion in the teachings of the different Gnostic sects, one variant of whose theological position I have just summarized in compressed form.

According to some of these sects, proper preparation for death requires complete abstinence from wine, meat, and sex. At the other extreme, some of them abdicated and practiced orgies because they regarded the moral law as part of the repressive establishment. As for the cosmos, it was hostile, it was evil. Now it was in the face of these Gnostic sects that Paul preached his faith.

For the new Gentile Christians, the Jewish concept of Messiah had no emotional meaning. Without *abandoning* the concept of Messiah, Paul *identified* the concept of divine *savior*, which he found at hand in the Gnostic doctrines, with the Jewish concept of Messiah, using the term *Christ,* the Greek for "anointed," using it as part of a personal name, Jesus Christ. He then made an original contribution to the interpretation of Jesus' death and resurrection. Christ, he declared, was a divine being, but he had humbled himself and come down from heaven and assumed a real human body, not to impart a secret message, *but to die on the cross as a sacrifice for the sins of the world.* Thus he had triumphed over sin. But death was the penalty for sin, and *in his resurrection Christ had triumphed over death also.* He was now sitting crowned at the right hand of God, and all who had faith and identified with him would come to participate in his death and resurrection and so *with him* gain victory over both sin and death.

Now by this rethinking, Paul captured the sympathy of the pagan Gentiles. To drive his point home, Paul gave a new theological interpretation to the practices of baptism and the Lord's supper, practices already engaged in by the Jesus sect. By the mystical experience of baptism, he taught, those who believed may identify themselves with Christ in his death and resurrection. Going down into the water in baptism is an act of identification with his death, while emerging from the water is an act of identification with his resurrection. By this death in Christ, sin and death are wiped away and the newly baptized Christian lives a new life. This is obviously a revival of the primitive initiation ceremony in which the initiate is made to undergo a ritual death by cutting off some part of his body. Then he is made a full member of the tribe and is reborn to a new life.

Now, here's the crux of the matter. The question arises: of what tribe is the initiate made a member? The answer which Paul gives is, the Christian Church, which he identifies with the body of Christ. I pointed out, in my remarks on Judaism, that the identification with the tribe is the basic idea there, not identification with God. I also said that in a mystery religion the identification with the god is the important thing. In his new interpretation, Paul merges the two ideas. Christ's body means both his literal body and the church, the new tribe. In order to weld together the two parts of this ambiguous concept, a unifying theme is introduced: we become one body by eating him. Now since the broken bread symbolizes broken body, and the wine the blood, it's obvious that this eating and drinking is the participation in the sacrifice of the cross. The Eucharist is a meal on the body of the slain victim. The Christian appropriates the strength of the victim and becomes one body with him. Paul had thus revived, in his doctrine of baptism, the very primitive concept of initiation, and in his doctrine of the Eucharist, a very primitive doctrine of feeding upon a sacrifice, in this case a human sacrifice.

It must not be thought that Paul is mechanically borrowing from the Gnostics. As a matter of fact, the latter do not have the unique power and force of his conceptions. What Paul has done is to create, working largely on Jewish but also partly on Gnostic materials, a new universal religion which dominated Western civilization from the fourth century to this day.

Paul's theology was essentially a syncretism of several elements. *First*, there was the teaching and practice of the Jesus sect centered in Jerusalem. Paul did not repudiate this sect, but collected money for its support. He claimed to be an apostle equal in position to the leaders of the sect whom he identifies as "James and Cephas [Peter] and John."[25] According to him, James, Peter, and John had recognized his unique status as apostle to the Gentiles and extended to him "the right hand of fellowship."[26]

On his side, in addition to the financial support he brought the leaders of the Jesus sect, he accepted their teaching that Jesus was the Messiah of Israel, had risen from the dead, and was soon to return to establish the Kingdom of God and to judge the living and the dead who were all to be resurrected in turn. He also accepted the practices of baptism, the laying on of hands to receive the Spirit and the Lord's Supper as a memorial of Jesus' death (for the last, see 1 Corinthians 11:23-6). Thus the continuity was maintained between the largely Gentile communities Paul had founded and the Jewish messianic sect centered in Jerusalem.

The *second* basic element in Paul's theology was the influence of *Gnosticism*.[27] Gnosticism was a widespread religious movement that extended eventually from the Atlantic to China. It was characterized by rejection of both the classical Greek outlook and the Jewish outlook.

The classical Greek outlook and the Jewish outlook shared a positive evaluation of the world and man as *good*. The fundamental difference between them was that the Greeks went beyond this and regarded the cosmos as divine and the realm of men and gods as overlapping. The Jews on the other hand, postulated a sharp discontinuity between man and God.

Now, the typical Gnostic declared that the cosmos was fundamentally evil[28] and created by the Demiurge, an evil God. Man was imprisoned in the cosmos. Nevertheless man had a spark of the divine in him, a spark of a *good* but *unknown* God existing far outside the cosmos. This good God took pity upon men and decided to save as many of them as possible. To bring about this salvation it was necessary to communicate to man the knowledge (gnosis) that his spirit (pneuma) was essentially divine and that to rescue this spirit it was necessary to liberate it from the animalistic flesh (sarx) in which it was imprisoned. The communication of this knowledge was entrusted to a Divine Savior or Messenger who would, so to speak, leap down from the heaven and appear disguised as a man to deceive the Demiurge and all the evil powers of the world, but ready to proclaim to men the message of salvation.

The Gnostics firmly rejected Judaism as an earthbound false religion which taught that man could save himself by obeying the Law of Moses, which was in fact, given to Moses by the Demiurge. The Gnostic religion is the ancestor of the New Age movement of today.

We must now compare Judaism, Gnosticism, and Pauline Christianity. Here we are entering a highly controversial area and I must warn readers to whom this material and these topics are new, that the available data may be interpreted in different ways.

I have made a certain option, namely to treat the Judaism from which Paul *diverges* to be *approximately* identical with the rabbinical or normative Judaism whose outlines become indisputable about A.D. 100, that is shortly after the time of Paul.

As for Gnosticism, I treat it as a religion that is almost parasitic upon Judaism at first and soon thereafter upon Christianity so far as its mythology goes. This parasitism is paradoxically associated with the fact that it is at the same time violently anti-Jewish and anti-Christian in the orthodox senses of these two faiths. Temporally speaking, it antedated the final form of Rabbinical Judaism while developing symbiotically with Christianity. Most Gnostics called themselves Christian, but the Church became *"Catholic"* only in the process of differentiating itself from the Gnostics. As a result of these distinctions, I treat the Jerusalem Jesus sect as a form of classical, Second Temple Judaism and I treat Pauline Christianity as a kind of mutation of this classical Judaism into a unique and mild form of Gnosticism.

This entire manner of construing the evidence is *one* of the ways accepted by scholars today, but there are other schools of thought on the subject. For instance, most scholars accept a greater continuity between Jesus and Paul and between the Jesus sect and Paul. And they see some Pauline doctrines as genuinely those of Jesus, citing certain

Gospel passages in confirmation of those conclusions. I have contrariwise given great weight to the undisputed fact that the Gospels were written later than the Pauline Epistles, and have used this fact as license to interpret the "Pauline" passages of the Gospels as largely the teaching of Paul put in the mouths of Jesus and his immediate disciples in an attempt to reconcile the Jewish and Gentile parties in the early church.

As for the Dead Sea Scrolls, the chorus of divergent views is so great that I have refrained entirely from any interpretation of them. Progress in their decipherment and interpretation has been so slow that treatment of them in the context of this book would risk the intrusion of arbitrary views into what I regard as opinions that have a considerable degree of probability in their favor.

Let us look then at Judaism at the time of Jesus and the immediately following Jesus sect, the whole religion being interpreted in the sense of the normative Judaism of about A.D. 100. It was strictly monotheistic and defined by a covenant between God and his people, the Jews. The covenant bound the Jewish people to observance of *Halakhah*, the elaborate body of commandments and practices governing worship and everyday life. Every such commandment is called a *mitzvah* (the plural is *mitzvoth*). The whole system we will call the *Law*; acceptance of it and commitment to its performance *is* Judaism.

Religious virtue consists in the performance of mitzvoth; sin is disobedience to the Law. No reason can be given for the Law; it simply defines the special manner in which man stands before God. Although the *subject matter* or *content* of the Law is life on earth, it cannot be proved by showing that conditions on earth demand it. Man's everyday concerns are therefore governed by demands upon him that are transcendental and unexplained.[29] Now survival and success in the world demand a certain selfishness, aggressiveness, and even exercise of roughness and ruthlessness, certain unworthy emotions such as envy. These are all necessary to "climbing the corporate ladder," yet Judaism and, as we shall see, Christianity, regards them as unworthy.

According to rabbinical Judaism, there are two basic inclinations in man, the evil inclination (*yetzer ha-r'a*) and the good inclination (*yetzer ha-tov*). Both inclinations are created by God; the evil inclination is present from birth and the good inclination from about the age of thirteen. Were it not for the evil inclination, nobody would build a house, marry and beget children. Therefore Scripture says, "Then I saw that all toil and all skill in work come from a man's envy of his neighbor. This also is vanity and a striving after wind."[30]

Now it is worthwhile to recall at this point the Objectivist position that a fundamental moral fallacy lies at the heart of the Judeo-Christian tradition, the illegitimate split between *ability to live* and *worthiness to live*. We are encountering it here in its *Jewish* form. This is *Jewish ethical dualism*. Shortly we shall compare it with Christian ethical dualism. But remember here that the Jewish teaching holds that God has created both inclinations and that a man is *oriented in opposite directions* from about the time of his bar-mitzvah on. One of his urges is selfishness; this is the basis of civilization. The other is unselfishness; this is the basis of humanitarianism, amounting at times to self-sacrifice.

Man has free will in the Judaic tradition. He may sin or be righteous. His natural tendency is toward unrighteousness. But God has provided him with a powerful aid to righteousness. This is the Torah, the Law. When tempted by the evil inclination, a man should "drag it to the house of study." Continued and intense study of the Law can overcome the evil inclination. Even so, man is likely to sin. If he does, the remedy is repentance and reparation, especially on "the Days of Awe" culminating in Yom Kippur, when forgiveness is solemnly proclaimed (animal sacrifice was included in the time of the Temple). Second Temple Judaism minus the animal sacrifices is normative Judaism.

In the Jewish scheme of things there is an unbridgeable gulf between man and God, *not* between flesh and spirit. "For my thoughts are not your thoughts, neither your ways my ways, saith the Lord."[31] "The Lord gave, and the Lord hath taken away; blessed be the name of the Lord."[32] Just as incarnation is impossible, so God cannot be questioned by man. Man can be "justified" (accounted righteous) only by good works (mitzvoth). Faith is complete obedience to God, and the defining symbol of Judaism is Abraham's readiness to sacrifice his son Isaac humbly and obediently without questioning God. The true spirit of Judaism lies in its readiness to accept the Law without questioning. True religion is man's service of God, *not* God's action in satisfying human needs.

Gnosticism is the opposite of this. First the physical universe is regarded as fallen, and man as entangled in the Fall. One way of expressing this is to say that the creation and the fall are one. The cosmos, far from being divine as the Greeks taught, is a kind of trap or prison. The stars are hostile to all that is good. The celestial sphere and the rest of the physical universe were created by Yahweh, the Jewish god, *who is evil* (he is also identified with the Greek Demiurge). Thus the Gnostics are opposed to *both* the Greeks and the Jews. The true God is the Unknown God who exists beyond the outermost spheres. The early Gnostic doctrines, as well as most of the later ones, hold that man has a spark of the true and Unknown God which dwells within him. Some sort of cosmic catastrophe, a sort of theological Big Bang, caused men to be separated or emanated from the good God. Man is thus alienated from the universe. He is a creature of flesh (*sarx*) whose cravings and desires inevitably dominate him. He thus has no free will. However, there is hope. Some men in whom the divine spark predominates are predestined to restoration of their unity with God. To save these men a Divine Messenger or Divine Savior approaches from above, deceiving the hostile powers and dominations who rule the planets. The Divine Messenger lets out a *Call* to which the more spiritual men respond. This Call consists of the revelation of the Gnosis or knowledge that one is a spark of God (which knowledge when developed as self-revelation is automatically saving). Those who accept the revelation fully are known as *pneumatics* (spiritual men and women) and are automatically saved, that is, they will at death be reunited with God. Those who obey the revelation without fully understanding it are known as *psychics* (men and women in whom the element of *soul* predominates). These emotional adherents are basically ignorant and believe on faith, which is inferior to knowledge. They may eventually progress to the pneumatic level. Those who reject the revelation are called *sarkiks* or *hylics* in whom raw materialistic or fleshy impulses predominate. They have no chance of salvation.

The most salient and arresting characteristics of Gnosticism are its metaphysical dualism of spirit versus flesh (with its unstable intermediate element of soul), its rejection of the cosmos and the world of everyday activities for what others would call a kind of romantic dream world, its hatred of the Jewish God, whom it makes into a kind of Satan, its rejection of the whole element of law in life, its denial of free will, its radical separation of power (which it regards as evil) from moral virtue and innocence, and its solution of the whole problem of evil by denying that the true God is omnipotent. Then, following from its rejection of law, is its rejection of justice in favor of mercy. This last teaching only became fully developed in the teaching of the *Marcionites* which emerged around A.D. 140 claiming to preach the correct interpretation of Paul.

Gnosticism also exhibited paradoxical extremes of teaching and practice with respect to sex. Some of them tried to renounce the flesh entirely by subduing it via harsh ascetic practices, such as extreme fasting and the renunciation of marriage. Others claimed to be so free from fleshly desires that they could indulge them indifferently and nonchalantly, which they proved by putting on orgies (this attitude is called *antinomianism*, or being above the moral law.) Being moral is for psychics or people on a still lower rung of religion.

Now, since the flesh is evil according to the Gnostics, the Divine Savior could not have become incarnate. He only *appeared* to become flesh. This doctrine is called *Docetism*. And therefore he did not die on the cross, but only appeared to. Indeed the whole idea of his dying on the cross is blasphemous. He redeemed man simply by giving him the knowledge (Gnosis) that he (man) is a spark of God. The person having knowledge will be able to extricate himself from the body by becoming indifferent to it and all earthly things. Indeed the attitude of the Gnostics was such that "if called upon to sacrifice to the pagan gods they would do so, for such action would be a matter of indifference. Their freedom through knowledge gave them freedom from constraints, from ignorance, from the Law, and from fears of the coming or of judgment."[33]

Pauline Christianity can be understood only in terms of Paul's unique situation as the founder of Gentile churches and the claimant to apostolic authority equal to that of the leaders of the Jerusalem church. He made sizable money collections for the poor of the Jerusalem sect anxiously awaiting the second coming of Christ, which was expected month by month. On their part, the leaders of this church probably recognized the legitimacy of his apostolate to the Gentiles, but were divided over his claims concerning the extent and meaning of freedom from the law in the Gentile communities which he had founded. But there is no doubt that it was Paul's intention to supplant the law with some other criterion of identity in these new churches, churches that were now called "Christian," a term used to designate the first disciples in Antioch.[34]

From the sociological point of view, Paul's basic aim was to create a new corporate society—the church—which would unite the monotheistic ideal of Judaism with the universalism of Hellenistic civilization. Such a society would inevitably be *urban*[35]: the universal society, the Church with a capital "C" would be encapsulated in each local church with a small "c" or holy *polis*, just as Hellenistic civilization was. And such a society would have to be both non-ethnic—"neither Jew nor Greek"—and yet in some fundamental sense exclusive. All previous barriers would have to be lowered while some new barriers would have to be erected. This holy entity, the "new Israel," would have to stand distinct from both the pagan "world" of sin and the old Israel of Law.

Two layers in Paul's thought may be distinguished, the first concerned with abrogation of the Law of Moses as the criterion of identity, and the second concerned with the substitution of a new mystical ideology of participation in the "Body of Christ." From these two acts of abrogation and substitution has emerged the idea of a *Christian* civilization.

The first layer came first chronologically in Paul's thought. It was the essence of his early Gospel or Good News: "If you confess with your lips that Jesus is Lord and believe in your heart that God raised him from the dead, you will be saved."[36] As for being *saved*, it consisted of being swept up in the glory of the coming cataclysmic end of the world: "For the Lord himself will descend . . . with the sound of the trumpet of God. And the dead in Christ shall rise first; then we who are alive, who are left, shall be caught up together with them in the clouds to meet the Lord in the air; and so we shall always be with the Lord."[37] As for *belief* in the Lordship of Jesus, this was to supplant the Law of Moses as the sole precondition of salvation. Although the believer is still in his sins, his faith is "accounted to him for righteousness." And what made faith the key to righteousness? The death of Christ on the cross, which was the sin offering for all mankind. Here we come to the link between the first and second layers of Paul's teaching. It was what, more than anything else, marked the ideological split between Judaism and Christianity. This was the doctrine of the crucified Messiah offered as a sacrifice for the sins of the world

The Messiah in Jewish thinking was, and still is, supposed to be a glorious and triumphant figure. "Jesus cannot be the Messiah, for he has been crucified by his enemies" was the reproach leveled by normative or Pharisaic Judaism against the adherents of the Jesus sect in

Jerusalem. The answer of the adherents of the Jesus sect was that Jesus had proclaimed the coming of the kingdom of God and the necessity of national repentance without effect, and had then suffered vicariously for the whole Jewish people, just as Moses had, and just as the Suffering Servant of Second Isaiah had.[38] God had answered by resurrecting him, bringing him to heaven and crowning him Messiah soon to return to take the throne of David.

This teaching made a profound impression on Paul, who is likely to have had knowledge of two extra-Judaic bodies of myths which bore a distant relationship to it, however repellent to the mind of an Orthodox Jew. The first such body of myths was, of course, Gnosticism with its doctrine of the Divine Savior who descended to earth in order to redeem lost humanity from the bondage of demonic powers. The second such body of myths consisted of the teachings and practices of the ancient mystery religions, whose central figures went down into the underworld and were then resurrected to the joy of their followers who were then said to gain eternal life through identification with the god. Paul may have had knowledge of the cult of Attis, a handsome young god who was whipped to death under a pine tree, died, and was resurrected (he was called "the Hanged god"). His resurrection was a great springtime feast and the day of its occurrence (March 25) was called "Hilaria." Any influence on Paul of the *mystery religions* remains quite controversial and indeed the details of the religions themselves are very much open to dispute, but Paul's awareness of and use of *Gnostic* concepts cannot be denied. At any rate extra-Judaic concepts provide an important link between two layers of Paul's thought, the *eschatological* layer which identifies the foundation of Christian life as justification by faith in his resurrection and messianic status, and a more sensational layer yet to come.

This second layer begins with a darker view of sin. No longer is it the result of the evil inclination recognized by rabbinical Judaism. It is now a powerful demonic force which is the result of a primeval Fall, and which is cosmic in its ramifications. The whole creation now "groaneth and trevaileth"[39] under the power of the rulers of darkness. There are now two Adams, the historical Adam and Christ. Sin entered through the first Adam, and the result of sin is death. Christ was a divine savior who descended in order to redeem man. In this respect he was like the Gnostic Divine Savior. But unlike the Gnostic Divine Savior he was really incarnated. He became man. And, unlike the

Gnostic Divine Savior, he really did die on the cross. His death was the death of a completely innocent victim, the first perfect sacrifice. It reversed the sacrificial paradigm of Judaism, the sacrifice demanded of Abraham, wherein God requires a man to sacrifice his beloved son to God for no other reason than the fact that a command had been given. The new Christian paradigm is this: that *God* sacrifices *his* beloved son in order to satisfy human needs, specifically the need of redemption. This is the basis of Paul's difference with Judaism, the doctrine of "amazing grace," an act of mercy transforming a "wretch like me" into a new creature. This is the doctrine of being "born again." It is appropriated by *faith*, not knowledge, as the Gnostics claimed. And it differs as well from the Jewish concept of justice by its claim that the total innocence of the victim (Christ) satisfies the demand for otherwise impossible justice, and releases a torrent of mercy upon sinners. Christ thus occupies the role of the scapegoat in primitive religion (a scapegoat was actually used on the Jewish Day of Atonement during the Temple period which was about to end when Paul was writing.)

The idea of the perfect victim implied the *divinity of Christ*, a doctrine which drove a further wedge between Christianity and Judaism. The accompanying doctrine of the incarnation nullified the absolute gulf between God and man. This nullification occurred not merely in the person of Christ, but in the person of the Christian who *identified* himself with Christ in what were later called sacraments or *mysteries*. In Baptism, for instance, according to Paul's teaching, when the believer is immersed, he goes down to the grave with Christ, and when he emerges from the water he is being resurrected with Christ.[40] And in the Eucharist he eats and drinks in a mystical way the body and blood of Christ proclaiming "the Lord's death until he comes."[41] A new urban subculture has been born and stands in stark contrast to the majority culture which the early Christians called "pagana" (rural). What is non-Christian or non-Jewish is rural, folk religion, however distinguished and urbane its imperial or senatorial representatives might be. Each such *polis*-church soon organized itself into a mini-state, hierarchically differentiated into "orders" or ranks. In a large church we would have first the monarchical bishop, then priests, deacons, subdeacons, acolytes, exorcists, readers, doorkeepers, confessors (those who had suffered in the persecutions), virgins, widows, orphans, "and all of God's holy people" (the laity). Meanwhile economic dependents were provided for. Is it any wonder that the Roman state was suspicious of such a network of elaborately organized societies?

The Jews, of course, had already had a network of such communities all over the Roman empire, and like the Christians, they accepted converts. But conversion to full Judaism meant for males circumcision, a practice looked upon with horror and derision by Gentiles, and for all converts it meant living by complicated dietary and cleanliness laws (later to be codified at 613) that prevented easy socializing with non-Jews. The Christians naturally won out in this competition for converts.

But if living by the Law of Moses (*Halakhah*) was the criterion of the true Jew, what was the governing principle, the criterion of the true Christian? Once we identify this, we shall have identified the nature of specifically Christian civilization. It was (externally) undergoing the *ceremony of initiation* (Baptism) and then continuing to live *in communion with* the local bishops. This communion (*koinonia*) had its price: the willingness to undergo martyrdom for one's faith, avoidance of bloodshed, avoidance of sexual intercourse outside marriage, in other words apostasy, and idolatry, adultery (in the very broad sense), and murder. If any of these sins were committed after Baptism, one was "excommunicated," deprived of communion, and, if one had publicly confessed, finally after a long period of penance, restored to communion. But such forgiveness ("the last plank in the shipwreck") was not even generally allowed until the third century A.D.

Apart from the avoidance of these heinous sins, an early writer named Hermas defined the positive Christian life in the following words: "To minister to widows and the destitute, to be hospitable . . . to resist none, to be poorer than all men, to reverence the aged . . . to preserve the brotherhood, and not to oppress poor debtors." It is obvious that these words do not reveal a *major* difference between the Jewish and Christian ethics. In what, then, does the difference lie?

As we have seen in the Jewish conception there are two basic inclinations in man, the good inclination and the evil inclination. The evil inclination is present in man from birth. It is a kind of vitality, aggression and competition. It is a kind of roughneck, unscrupulous, bully-in- the- schoolyard attitude. It is not nice. Its worst manifestation is envy, says Ecclesiastes. But in spite of its drawbacks, it is necessary for individual survival and for the material aspects of civilization. The good inclination is created in a person about the age of thirteen, the

age of bar mitzvah. It inspires *via study of the Law* to deeds of cooperation, charity, generosity, and kindness. It helps one to avoid the
cardinal sins of idolatry, unchastity, bloodshed, and slander, essentially the same sins singled out as "grave" or "mortal" by Christianity.
These definitions seem to point in the same direction, indicating a
common "Judeo-Christian ethic." So we must ask again, wherein lies
the difference?

The difference is metaphysical. It lies in a different view of the
nature of the universe and of man. In the Christian view, derived, we
have surmised, from Gnosticism, there are two mighty cosmic powers,
God and Satan. (The ultimate source of this idea may have been Zoroastrianism). These two powers are good and evil, respectively. Good is
identified as Light, evil as Darkness. "The light shines in the darkness
and the darkness has not overcome it,"[42] says the Gospel of John.
Light and Darkness are substances and they divide man between them.
Light appears in man as *pneuma*, or spirit; Darkness as *sarx*, or flesh.
The spirit and the flesh ever war against each other. There are two
types of men, the Sons of Light and the Sons of Darkness. Those who
are saved and become Sons of Light, are saved by *grace* operating
through faith. This grace is *mercy*, canceling the just sentence that has
already been pronounced against man. This is made possible by the
substitutionary death of the Divine Savior.

It is obvious that, compared to Judaism, the will of man is less free
and justice is less important. Charity and mercy and forgiveness indeed to the point of total self-sacrifice are considerations that override
justice. St. Francis is the ideal after Jesus. And this is an *other-worldly*
ethic. The good life is seen as surrounded by a supernatural halo and
by a kind of mystical love between the devotee and the Savior. It may
justly be said that Christianity evokes a more other-worldly, more
mystical sense of the ethical life than does Judaism. One might say
that Judaism is an ethic for life in this world, Christianity for life in the
next world. The ethical dualism is far less pronounced in Judaism.
However, this point must be made with reservations. In Judaism, God
creates both the good and the evil inclinations. It is precisely the
values of the *evil* inclination that make us able to survive and prosper
in the world. And it is precisely the values of the *good* inclination that
give worth and meaning to life. Obviously Judaism has its ethical
wires crossed here. If the world in which we live is *good*, how is it that
in order to survive and prosper in that world, evil inclinations and evil

values like envy are necessary? Is this world in which we are "making it" metaphysically evil? If not, where is the connection between fact and value?

On the other hand, consider the still greater predicaments of the Christian. At his Baptism he renounces "the world of flesh and the devil," embraces an ethic of complete unselfishness and then walks (or is carried) out of the church doors to face the business of survival and prospering in the very world he has just renounced, by practicing the values he has just embraced.

It must be understandable that these two religions have played a role in history that has created and accentuated the inner tensions of mankind.

Notes

1. Exodus 3:6 RSV
2. Exodus 22:20, 22:18, 22:25 KJV
3. Exodus 22:26–27 RSV
4. Exodus 22:29 RSV
5. Exodus 20:5–6 RSV
6. Amos 6:4–6 RSV
7. Amos 5:21–24 RSV
8. 2 Kings 21:6 RSV
9. W.K. Lowther Clarke, *Concise Bible Commentary*, New York: The MacMillan Company, 1953, p.18.
10. *Ibid.,* p. 19.
11. Josephus, *The Jewish War* 2.8.2 120–21; *Jewish Antiquities* 18.1.5, 18–22
12. Deuteronomy 6:4 RSV
13. The world outlook involved in these traditions and practices will be dealt with in ch. 5 where it will be studied necessarily within the nexus of a review of the historical material set forth in the present chapter.
14. *Jewish Antiquities* 18.5.2, 116–19.
15. Matthew 3:2 RSV
16. Luke 3:10–11 RSV
17. Matthew 5:28–40 RSV
18. Matthew 5:27–38 RSV
19. Here I follow the recent calculations of John R. Meier, *A Marginal Jew: Rethinking the Historical Jesus*, New York, Doubleday, 1991, vol. I, ch. 11, especially p. 406.
20. Acts 2:46 RSV
21. Acts 5:34 RSV
22. Acts 2:23 RSV
23. In Maccoby's illuminating explanation, abstinence (1) from all food over which "grace" had been said to a pagan god, (2) from adultery, incest, sodomy, and bestiality, (3)from anything strangled, and (4) from murder. See Hyam Maccoby, *The Mythmaker: Paul and the Invention of Christianity*, San Francisco, CA, Harper and Row, 1987.

24. Acts 26:14 KJV
25. Galatians 2:9 RSV
26. Ibid.
27. The best systematic treatment of Gnosticism is *Gnosis, The Nature and History of Gnosticism*, by Kurt Rudolph, translated by Robert M. Wilson, San Francisco, CA, Harper and Row, 1987. The reader is also referred to the brilliant earlier work, *The Gnostic Religion*, by Hans Jonas, 2d rev. ed., Boston: Beacon Press, 1963.
28. For an example of a *pagan Greek* attack on Gnosticism see "Against the Gnostics" by the neo-Platonist philosopher Plotinus (c. A.D. 250) in his *Enneads II*, 9, translated by A.H. Armstrong, Cambridge, MA, Harvard University Press, 1966.
29. My approach here is essentially that of Yeshayahu Leibowitz, *Judaism: Human Values, and the Jewish State*, Cambridge, MA, Harvard University Press, 1992.
30. Ecclesiastes 4:4 RSV
31. Isaiah 55:8 KJV
32. Job 1:21 KJV
33. W.H.C. Frend, *The Rise of Christianity*, Philadelphia, PA, Fortress Press, 1984.
34. Acts 11:26 RSV
35. Cf. Wayne A. Meeks, *The First Urban Christians: The Social World of the Apostle Paul*, New Haven, CT, Yale University Press, 1983.
36. Romans 10:9 RSV
37. 1 Thessalonians 4:16–17 RSV
38. Isaiah 53: 3–7 RSV
39. Romans 8:18–22 KJV
40. Romans 6:3–4 RSV
41. 1 Corinthians 10:16; 11:23–30 RSV
42. John 1:5 RSV

4

Islam

Islam is an Arabic religion. The Arabs were a Semitic people who had become relatively isolated from other Semitic people; a larger proportion of them had remained nomads than was the case with other Semites. And yet there were many inhabitants of Arabia that lived a settled and urban life in the south and around Mecca. Still, among the urban Arabs, the influence of the old desert life was very great and you had the same conflicts that you had in Judaism. A good part of the values were old tribal desert values and these conflicted with town living. Islam, in part, sought to bring about the revival of these desert values. But we cannot say simply that Islam is a religion of the desert any more than we can say that of Judaism. To understand either of them, we must see the clash between desert values and urban values.

The nomad of the desert is not a natural monotheist, he is a worshipper of stone pillars, trees, groves, sacred bushes; he propitiates serpents and hyenas, he is an animist. In the time of Muhammad, the nomads were basically polytheistic in their attitude, yet there was a contrary factor: the presence of wandering hermits with a monotheistic tendency—these were called Hanifs—desert hermits who were monotheists and who worshipped the God of Abraham even though they were not Jewish.

Mecca was an important trade center on the way from India to the Mediterranean Basin, but it was famous for more than that. It was famous for its shrines, especially the Kaaba, the central shrine in Mecca. In prehistoric times, a great black meteorite had fallen on the future location of Mecca, and, when people moved in and founded a town there, they built a shrine around the meteorite. There you have the connection between extraterrestrial events and religion very concretely brought out. They were stone worshippers, and it was natural for them to do this. They put the meteorite in a big box, the meteorite being exposed in the southeast corner. The box had inside it the idols of three goddesses. One Meccan tribe was made the guardian of this shrine and there was an annual all-Arabian pilgrimage, which was a major festival, and brought in much money for the people who ran Mecca. The pilgrimage to Mecca, therefore, was an institution which preceded Muhammad.

Now let us look at the early career of Muhammad. He was born in Mecca in 570 of a poor family of the tribe that was the guardian of the Kaaba. He was orphaned at an early age and was sent out with a nurse to live with a nomadic tribe in the desert, so he knew both the desert values and the values of the city. He felt very keenly that, being an orphan, he was deprived of his inheritance. This is the origin of a very important feature of Islam, the high valuation placed on taking care of orphans. In time Muhammad was taken under the care of the head of his clan, and he began to go on trade journeys, camel journeys, to Syria.

At the age of twenty-five, he was in charge of the merchandise of a wealthy widow of forty named Khadija, and she became interested in him, and eventually, married him. She later bore him six children, two boys and four girls. This marriage was the turning point of Muhammad's life. Had it not been for Khadija, there might have been no Islamic civilization. She set him on the road and saw to it he remained on it. After their marriage, Muhammad had sufficient capital to invest in mercantile activities and he became well known as a businessman of ability.

At this time, Mecca itself was becoming more and more urban. The old tribal values were breaking down. Individual merchants more and more pursued their own individual interests, disregarding the ancient tribal injunctions that they were to share their wealth with the poor and unfortunate and especially with the orphans. Muhammad had lived under both tribal and urban conditions and he was torn between the two sets of values. At about age forty he suffered the loss of both his sons, and he went into a sort of mental depression and began to look disheveled and to spend more and more time out in the desert. His friends joked that "our Muhammad is becoming a Hanif."

One night when he was out in the desert he had a vision of a majestic being who said to him, you are the messenger, (*rasul*) of Allah. Allah was the same being, the same high God, I mentioned as bearing the name "El" in the Hebraic tradition. Muhammad rushed home and told his wife he thought he was going crazy and she said, "You're not going crazy, Muhammad, just have a little more self confidence, maybe you *are* the messenger of Allah." She took him to her Christian cousin who listened to the verses and the Christian cousin said this sounds like the laws of Moses to me. You are *naabi* (the word for prophet.) From now on, at frequent intervals, Muhammad would go into seizures during which he would sweat profusely and receive what he regarded as revelations. With the help of his Christian relative, he came to interpret these messages as, in general, identical with those given to Jews and Christians. Soon he gathered around himself a group of followers who joined him in worship that culminated in an act of prostration toward Jerusalem. They touched their heads to the ground in acknowledgment of the majesty of Allah.

In about the year 613, he began to preach publicly. Now, the people of Mecca, in general, took religion very lightly. Although they worshipped a number of gods and idols, they depended on rational planning for the conduct of their lives. They ardently pursued wealth and the enjoyment of life. They did worship Allah as a kind of high god, but regarded him as distant, having no more than honorary status, nothing like the important goddesses that dwelt inside the Kaaba. They were perhaps willing to go so far as to say "In Allah we trust," but they didn't take him very seriously.

The earliest revelations of Muhammad call on the people of Mecca to acknowledge that their prosperity was due to Allah alone—this is a very important concept—their prosperity is due to Allah and not to themselves. Gratitude to Allah for prosperity should be expressed by sharing one's wealth with the poor. These points are driven home with a threat; everyone will appear before Allah on the last day to be judged for his deeds.

In all this we can see the same phenomenon that we saw in the case of the Hebrew prophet, John the Baptist, and Jesus. A man of the town goes out in the desert and receives revelations which he is commanded to preach. Repent, repent, turn from your evil deeds and do good deeds; God will punish or reward you according to the choice that you make. Now to make statements like this implies that your hearers already agree with you to some extent, that to some extent they share your values. By contrast, if someone had appeared wandering among the igloos of the Eskimos and saying "repent, repent," they would not have known what he was talking about.

Muhammad had gathered around him about seventy young men before opposition began. These young men were of the wealthy class, and most of them were people who were second and third sons and who were cut out of their inheritance (as orphans often were).

There was implicit in Muhammad's teaching a critique of the conduct and values of the rich merchants of Mecca. Muhammad's revelations constantly denounced the mistreatment of orphans. He was an orphan himself and not, by law, allowed to inherit his father's wealth, since he was a minor when his father died. Now the rich merchants of Mecca began to get worried by this preaching. They tried to soften his criticisms by offering him a fuller share of trade and a further marriage alliance with one of the wealthiest families. Muhammad refused. Economic pressure was brought to bear on his followers. His doctrine of the resurrection of the body was questioned, as was his monotheistic teaching; his condemnation of idolatry was probably also feared. Why would his monotheism be feared? What did they have to lose there, commercially? The Kaaba, with the goddesses inside. How was monotheism going to be fitted in with the Kaaba? The several goddesses were venerated by the use of idols inside the Kaaba, and religious pilgrimages to the Kaaba brought in much cash. Muhammad was accused of planning to become politically supreme in Mecca, while depriving the city of a main source of its revenue.

In 619 his wife died and his own clan withdrew their protection of him; a petty persecution began. By petty persecution I mean that the other Meccans began to deposit pots of excrement outside his door. This was the first opinion that they had of Islam, in Mecca. Things have changed since then.

Then in September 622, Muhammad fled to another city, a northern city called Medina. And this flight to Medina is called the *Hijrah*, sometimes called *Hegira*. Now, from this flight, the whole Muslim calendar is dated. This was the Year One of Islam. The first day of the year in which this took place, 16 July 622, was the beginning of Islam. On arriving at Medina, Muhammad made an agreement with the eight Arab clans there, in which they acknowledged him as the prophet. They heard he was doing a good job down in Mecca trying to preach against warfare. Now, they had a lot of tribal warfare up there so they welcomed him as mediator. They agreed to refer serious disputes to him. The Jewish clan refused to recognize him as a prophet, but they got in on the deal by negotiating associate membership with the Arab clans. Muhammad's power was limited to matters judicial, but he did promulgate several revelations giving legal rules to the Medinans.

In January 624, an important thing happened. Now one of the major customs in old Arabia was the *rasiah*: where you're up behind a dune with a lot of men and you see a camel caravan coming, you decide that they're fair game, swoop down on them, kill the people in the caravan, and loot the goods. *Rasiah* is a raid. In January 624, Muhammad's followers successfully conducted a *rasiah* on a caravan which was under the protection of the Meccans. Now, Muhammad had been teaching that these *rasiahs* are bad, but if somebody initiates aggression against you, a *rasiah* is all right. The Meccans suddenly became aware that Muhammad was a threat to them. At the same time, Muhammad, alienated from the Jewish clans who continued to reject him as a prophet, veered away from his previous pro-Jewish policies and ordered his followers not to face Jerusalem anymore but to face Mecca during prayer.

In the same year, he defeated in battle a much larger force of Meccans during another *rasiah*. Some people in Medina had satirized him, and they were soon assassinated. He made a minor disturbance in excuse for expelling the Jewish clan that ran the market. The remaining Arab dissidents then became his followers.

In 627, a great army of 10,000 men from many Arab tribes marched against Medina to stop this new, increasingly strong threat. Muhammad exhibited brilliant military, economic, and political strategy. He saw to it that the crops were all harvested before the besieging army arrived, he had a large trench dug around the city, and he sent agents to sow dissension among the attacking tribes. After a night of wind and rain, the enemy melted away.

Muhammad then turned to his chief enemy in Medina, and he became reconciled with him. This was a man who had seriously slandered him. Then they agreed to attack the Jews who had been intriguing to overthrow Muhammad. They executed all the men and sold the women and children into slavery.

This was the beginning of a new policy for Muhammad; this is how he began to build Islam: divert the feuding of the Arabs outward, make peace with your lesser enemies, and go against your greater enemies. He saw the tremendous energy the Arabs spent on bloody feuds, killing somebody whose great-grandfather had insulted one's own great-grandfather. This was something special to the Arabs, something they did not share with the Jews. If only this energy could be united into one force and directed outward, it could be used for conquest. How to unite them? By offering them his religion as a platform of unity and by making every kind of diplomatic concession, including offers of economic advantage, to the tribe.

In a dream Muhammad saw himself performing the annual pilgrimage to Mecca, and in March he set out with only a few men, driving sacrificial animals before them. This was more of a demonstration on his part; it was similar to some of the demonstrations we see today. The Meccans stopped him in front of Mecca and said you can't come in, and Muhammad said: "Okay, if we can come back next year." And they murmured and debated among themselves and they finally agreed to let him come back the next year and make a big pilgrimage to Mecca provided he wouldn't attack them. In this piece of brilliant strategy, Muhammad had stooped to conquer. He saved face for the Meccans at the same time, but he still had to deal with the feelings of his followers, so he said "Let's attack some Jews."

They attacked the Jewish oasis of Kibar, north of Medina. The Jews surrendered, but this time Muhammad was in full control of himself and he made terms with the defeated Jews, allowing them to remain exactly as they had been, in uncontested possession of their oasis provided they sold half of their date harvest in Medina. The Jews agreed. Muhammad then married the two daughters of two Meccan opponents, so he had two fathers-in-law working for him in Mecca, and thus assured himself of inside support when the time came for the march on the city.

So finally he came to besiege Mecca with ten thousand men, his fathers-in-law came out to meet him, and submitted with their followers. Muhammad then promised a general amnesty. He entered Mecca without resistance, he pardoned most of his enemies, and he gained the allegiance of most Meccans. He did not insist that the Meccans become Muslims, but many soon did. He did insist, however, that Islam become the public religion of Mecca. The Kaaba was cleansed of idols. To relieve the poorest of his followers, some of the wealthiest Meccans were forced to grant them loans.

Muhammad was now the strongest man in Arabia, and delegates

from tribe after tribe came to swear allegiance to him. Generally, in dealing with the nomadic tribes, he began to insist on conversion to Islam. Arab states and Yemen in the Persian Gulf soon thereafter turned to Muhammad because their former protector, the Persian empire, had been defeated badly by the Romans recently.

By 630 Muhammad's power extended all the way up to the Syrian border. Muhammad personally led the now completely Islamic pilgrimage to Mecca in March 632. In the beginning of June, he fell ill in Medina, and he died within a few days.

Now, I want to examine the teaching of Muhammad under three headings: (1) a return to tribal values; (2) a set of rewards and punishments sanctioning a return to tribal values; (3) a religious and social setting, fusing into one community, all those who obeyed Muhammad's call.

First, the return to tribal values. In Mecca, there had been, before Muhammad, a change from a pastoral, nomadic economy to a mercantile one. The Meccans had retained some of their tribal customs, such as clan solidarity and the blood feud, but these were in conflict with the business ethic. By this I mean, if you find your business partner's great-grandfather has insulted your great-grandfather, you cannot simply walk into his office and shoot him dead; it's bad for business. The new business ethic, however, now meant the businessman was no longer in a position to protect the weaker members of his clan, for his wealth was no longer derived from tribal raids and looting, but from his own shrewdness in business. This was the great Semitic conflict of values, and it was seen wherever desert nomadic tribes settled down to do business. Blood brotherhood, feuding, protection of the weak, had to go by the board. So did the old concept of tribal honor. According to this older concept, the meaning of life, the sense of being a worthy person, is bound up in how one appears to one's tribe.

How does one appear worthy? By recognizing that one is one's brother's keeper, by helping him when he's in trouble, by defending his honor. Brotherhood is all important to the tribal ethic. This is how the nomadic desert tribes survived, and the individual survived, or failed to survive, with his tribe, for, once the tribal connection was broken, one would wander in the desert without helper or protector; one bore the mark of Cain, so to speak. The tribeless man—in modern terms, is the man without a country.

Now, the merchants in the town had found a different way to survive: it was by individualistic free enterprise and rational planning. They found that one could survive and live well through the accumulation of wealth. This became the great goal in life. Those who were successful were full of pride and self confidence, yet many of them were filled with guilt because they remembered those old tribal values from out on the desert. Inwardly, they had not rid themselves of those values. Others were frustrated because they failed to make it in the wealthy establishment, and this played on their guilt. They began to wonder if they should have ever lived the city life. So there was social conflict in Mecca.

In the midst of this conflict, Muhammad appeared, preaching a return to tribal values, but touting it as a return to *general communal* values. Instead of the values of *our* tribe, it is going to be the values of *the whole community of Islam.* For what he wished to see was not return to primitive tribes, but the establishment of one great universal tribe. Similarly to St. Paul, Muhammad's message begins with a declaration that man is puffed up with a pride that is not justified. Man, he preaches, is fundamentally a metaphysical dependent. Here he harks back to the experience of the nomad. True, the survival of the nomad does depend on his reason and the sharpness of his mind, but there is another factor and this factor is what the old nomads, the old pagan nomads, had called *time.*

Suppose that a man starts out on a camel journey one Saturday morning, and rounds a dune at 11:00 rather than 11:10 when he should have rounded it; suddenly he meets the brother-in-law of a man he had insulted nine years ago, there is a fight and one of them is killed.. He lives twenty years rather than the seventy he would have otherwise lived. His *time* has come. Everything has a fixed time.

So there came to the nomad a belief that time was some kind of fate that accounted for all the chance factors, and within a certain context, this belief had a certain survival level, for a great many things were really out of the control of the nomad, *really* out of his control; sandstorms, the sudden discovery of a cave for shelter, or of a hidden spring, or a cave wherein someone had deposited some wealth, some diamonds, or something else. Recall the Arabian nights and Aladdin's journey into the cave, if you will.

Now suppose a given nomad, is a worrier, an obsessive worrier, always rushing around the backside of dunes to see if an enemy of his is there, or always poring over genealogical tables, to find whom his grandfather's brother-in-law has cursed. Such a man would never have the time or the energy to control what is controllable. The belief in fate will relieve him of such worry, and therefore, is a kind of metaphysical, psychological defense mechanism that promotes his survival. Within the limits of the nomad's very limited world and in the absence of a rational alternative, it aides him in moment-to-moment survival. The Arab, therefore, scorns the man who is always obsessively trying to control everything. His hero is not the nomad, who lives his life worrying, but Aladdin, who suddenly stumbles on a cave full of diamonds, a pile of diamonds with a beautiful girl sitting on top of the pile. It is the decree of fate, or they began to say in Islam, it is the will of Allah. Did the diamonds turn out to be fake and the girl faithless? It is the decree of fate, the great allotter. As a poet said, go your way without getting angry until it becomes clear what the allotter allotted to you. In other words, don't look backward and think of all the possible different things that could have happened to you.

Now what Muhammad did was to take this belief in time or fate and turn it into the eternal decree of Allah. Allah is good, he has the whole world in his hand. Man is dependent on the inscrutable decrees of a God who is, by definition, good, but whose goodness one is not allowed to question. As the Qur'ān says, "Have you considered the seed you spill, do you yourself create it or are we the creator? Had you considered the water you drink? Did you send it down from the clouds or did we send it? Have you considered the fire you kindle? Did you make the timber grow or did we make it?" Now, since man is dependent on God, it is the height of presumption to think that he can control his destiny. The denial of dependence on his part is the sin of pride.

God is the author of those old tribal values of brotherhood and help to the poor. These values arose from metaphysical dependence. Those who pursue wealth and oppress the poor deny these values of dependence, so they commit the sin of greed. But, they go further, and they deny their dependence, and this is the sin of pride, which is the greatest sin. God had prepared for them the punishment of hell. For those who observe the old values, on the other hand, he has prepared paradise. These are the sanctions that are very important in Islam.

Let us now look at the religious and social systems welding these values into one community religion. The religion is called Islam, which means *surrender.* An adherent to Islam is called a Muslim, which means "one who surrenders." What you have surrendered to is the will of Allah, who is the one God. This one God is the creator, the sustainer, and the restorer of the universe. He revealed himself to a whole line of prophets from Noah through Moses to Jesus; Muhammad is his final prophet. The revelation to Muhammad consummates all previous revelations and cancels them.

The basic belief is expressed in the formula of faith, which you should learn and repeat to the angel who wakes you up the last day— "there is but one God and Muhammad is the prophet of God." From this essential belief are derived belief in angels, commandments, the series of prophets, the Qur'ān as the final statement of God's revelation, the doctrines of the resurrection, the last judgment, Heaven and Hell, and the Five Pillars of Islam. The Five Pillars of Islam are as follows: (1) to say from one's heart, and, sincerely, the profession of faith. (2) the five daily prayers, including congregational prayer on Friday; (3) the welfare tax; (4) fasting; and (5), the pilgrimage to Mecca.

Let us look at the doctrine of God. There is one God, a necessary being, one person only, omniscient, omnipotent, all good, pure consciousness. He has no partners. There are no intermediaries between him and the created universe. The created universe is contingent, created out of nothing by God's simple command, "Be!" He is utterly transcendent, he does not dwell *in* anything, but he's around, he's closer to you than the vein of your neck, Muhammad says. He's ready to punish you in case you step out of line. While all-just, he's at the same time compassionate and merciful. He's ready to forgive at his whim. Everything happens by his command. *He decrees each individual unique event.* Now, in a certain way this, by its influence on certain Western medieval philosophers, notably Nicolas of Autrecourt, c. 1350, paved the way for Hume, because each event can be conceived as existing by itself, apart from all other events, and each event is separately decreed by God. Do you see what happens to scientific law then? God might have called into existence any of an infinite number of universes. He might have commanded the separate events to fit together in an infinite number of other possible ways. So, you can never know what is going to happen.

Only angels and men are capable of departing from the order decreed by Allah. Dogs will always act like dogs. Allah never willed that a dog suddenly climb a tree or anything like that, he puts them in their proper order, to be sure, but angels and men can depart from that order. The devil rebelled because of pride, and he persuaded Adam, the first man, to join him. Adam, however, repented and was forgiven. His sin was not inherited, but man remains frail and susceptible to sin.

Every other creature accepts its limitations and dependency, man alone regards himself as self-sufficient. He is full of pride. He becomes guilty of ascribing to himself partnership with God, the basic heresy (*sherf*) is to say that God has a partner in power, me or anyone else. Instead of associating a creature with its creator, what is needed is faith in the unique transcendent being and total submission to him, total absolute prostration. A modern Islamic theologian, Frithjof Schuon, a Swiss convert, says, "Islam is the meeting between God as such and man as such, and they're totally different in nature."[2] Now, conversion from pride to submission may be made at any moment; God will be compassionate and merciful; he will forgive.

Now let us look at eschatology, the doctrine of the final things, the things that are to come. Islam gives you a vivid picture of the end of things. Islam, while dualistic about the relation of God and his creation, is not dualistic about the mind's relation to the body, holding that they can exist only together. Body and soul (or mind) are fundamentally one; thus if there is to be any after life it has got to be resurrection of the body—unless you believe in reincarnation, but the Semites did not have that belief.

Why must there be an afterlife? To reward the just and to punish the unjust. "The trumpet will sound on the last day," I'm quoting from the Qur'ān now, "the earth shall shake and quiver and the mountain crumble away and scatter abroad into fine dust." "The dead shall rise and appear before the throne of God, who will accept no excuses: I sent you the prophets didn't I?" He'll divide them into two groups of people, those on the left and those on the right. Those on the left will go to hell. "They shall dwell in pitch black smoke among scorching winds eating bitter fruit and drinking boiling water." But as for those on the right, I quote from (chapter four) Sura 56, "Upon close-wrought couches reclining upon them... set face to face . . . immortal youths going round about them with goblets and ewers and a cup from a spring (no brows throbbing, no intoxication) and such fruits as they shall choose, and such flesh of fowl as they desire, and wide-eyed houris . . . a recompense [for that they labored] . . . spotless virgins chastely amorous like of age . . . " Now, obviously if you have a chaste woman as a reward for your deeds, she presumably does not remain a virgin, but he says, "we created the houris and made them virgins, *loving companions for those on the right.*" The real meaning apparently here is that these houris, to satisfy the impulses of the Arab, are perpetually "revirginated." That seems to be the implication involved. What happens to the good Muslim wives? Well, tradition holds that after death they are transformed into houris. And so, you have an addition to this, the vision of Allah, the beatific vision. You can see his face, so it is not all finite, bodily pleasure; but you can see that there is a lot of the latter for the good Muslim.

In spite of Muhammad's doctrine of the left and the right, he has a doctrine of social service—expending one's wealth for the sake of others. This is an integral part of Islamic teaching. It is Satan who whispers into men's ears that by spending for others, you will become poor. God, on the contrary, promises prosperity in exchange for such expenditure, which constitutes a credit with God. Usury is forbidden; give to the poor and you will become rich—this seems to be the doctrine. Usury, even to outsiders, is forbidden.

Now we come upon the conflict with Hellenism. The forces of Islam quickly conquered the southern and eastern Mediterranean basin. There they encountered the Hellenistic culture which was already absorbed into Christianity. Translations of Aristotle had been made into Syriac in the sixth century by Eastern Christians, and these translations were in turn translated into Arabic in the ninth century. Other writings in Greek philosophy also became available. The Greek viewpoint was at first admired in Islam, (unaware of what they were getting into), and it was advocated up to a point by a party called the Mutazilites, the pro-reason party in Islam. Greek philosophy, however, especially Aristotle, contradicted the whole Islamic viewpoint. The points of conflict were the following:

The Greek point of view was based on reason, the Islamic, on faith and revelation. Greek philosophy regarded all of reality as knowable— this was true even of divine beings like the Prime Mover—knowable by reason. Whereas Islam believed that God was transcendent and unknowable. That is the second conflict. First is reason versus faith, secondly is the knowability of divine beings. Third, the Greeks believed the universe was fundamentally orderly and subject to regular law, but the Muslims believed that each event was separately decided by God's arbitrary predestination. Fourth, the Greeks believed in an ethics and politics based on reason. For the Muslim, ethics and politics were based on the Qur'ān and sacred tradition.

Those who subscribed to any Greek philosophy, especially that of Aristotle, were soon in deep trouble. This is especially evidenced by the fate of the largely pro-Greek party, the Mutazilites. The sect of the Mutazilites represented a strong pro-reason reaction against the traditional doctrine of Islam. The traditional doctrine about the Qur'ān was that it was part of the mind of God and therefore co-eternal with God. The real meaning of this doctrine is that it is a blasphemy to raise the slightest question about the Qur'ān. The Mutazilites rejected this doctrine, and they said that it is making the Qur'ān into a second God to make it unquestionable. The Qur'ān, they said, is a creature just like a beast of the field, therefore it does not necessarily express the essential nature of God any more than a cockroach does (they didn't put it that way). The Qur'ān must be subject to the interpretation of reason. If we find that a given thing is irrational and seems to be taught in the Qur'ān, we conclude that God didn't intend it this way; he merely talked obscurely at that point. If anything in the Qur'ān seems contrary to reason, we must then reinterpret it in accord with reason.

This had an influence on the Christian Middle Ages. In this Mutazilite doctrine, we do not erect a second God and, at the same time, reason is saved. This is called the *doctrine of the unity of God*; it is really the doctrine of the priority of reason. Secondly, we apply this immediately to sections of the Qur'ān which seem to teach predestination. Now predestination takes away moral responsibility and man, the Mutazilites said, is morally responsible. A good God would not reward or punish eternally unless man were morally responsible. This the Mutazilites called the doctrine of the justice of God and presented themselves as defenders of the justice of God. But of course it was really the assertion of man's free will. These two pro-reason doctrines were accompanied by a strong emphasis on moral virtue and uprightness.

The Mutazilite position began to make some headway when, unfortunately, their own zeal proceeded to fanaticism, as does indeed happen sometimes with people advocating a reason, as well as anything else. While advocating reason the Mutazilites were trying to control the reason of others. They sabotaged their own cause. They came into power and issued a requirement that all public officials swear that the Qur'ān is created and not divine. Some who refused this doctrine were put to death. This is sometimes called the Muslim Inquisition, from

830 to 845 (ironic in that the only real inquisition in Islam was initiated by the pro-reason faction). Of course there was a religious reaction and the Mutazilites were thrown out of power.

Now I want to discuss another sect called the Kharijites. This will
help us to understand the fanaticism often involved in Islam. The
name of these people means "the seceders"; they broke away from the
rest of Islam in the seventh century. Their secession was on a fundamental point: granted that the principles of Islamic morality are correct, how shall they be applied in practice? Now the principles of
Islamic morality do not necessarily cover all eventualities, and therefore it follows that to apply them is going to be difficult.

How *shall* they be applied in practice? All Muslims agree that one
should do good and refrain from evil but, they added, this must be
understood under the condition that one takes circumstances into account. The *Kharijites*, who were mostly nomads, rejected this condition. They insisted on good conduct as defined by the Qur'ān; avoidance of sin as an absolute duty to be performed in and out of season,
even at the cost of life itself. Anyone who fails to do this is not a true
Muslim and should be excluded from the community. The gate of
paradise, they said, is open only to those who believe and live an
upright life; they are the only true Muslims, they are the people of
paradise, all others are the people of hell. This is a parallel here, to
Augustine's city of God and city of man, except not an exact parallel
because Augustine thought the two cities were intermixed in the church.
A person who has broken any commandment of the Qur'ān has for-
feited his membership in Islam; he belongs to the people of hell. First,
exclude him. Next, does any leader hesitate to exclude him? Assassi-
nate the leader, he is no guardian of the purity of Islam. So much for
anyone who tried to be a moderate Kharijite.

Naturally a doctrine like this resulted in more and more splintering
and more and more killing. The Kharijites began to break down into
small bodies of men varying from thirty to a hundred in number, each
body claiming to be the pure people of paradise. They camped near
cities or trade routes. The doctrine eventually became—"*the only true
Muslims are the people camped here.*" Well, here comes a caravan,
and lo and behold the hundred good men, the true Muslims, return
with a good conscience to the pre-Muslim ethic of raids on all cara-
vans: everyone is fair game, let's kill them and rob them.

The fundamental roots of this fanaticism can be found in the phe-

nomenon of the break-up of tribes. In a primitive tribe you have absolute certainty, in a nominalistic sense. As a matter of fact, you *get to
know* your fellow Kharijites and you watch their body language and
you know how they don't want the flap of their tent disturbed, and so
on; to understand *that* you don't need precise theological principles
involved. When these people were taken out of their tribal life and
thrown into the vast body of Islam and given the general principles of
Islamic law, they began to get scared because they were unsure of the
proper interpretation of the principles. And so they began to try to
apply the principles in the most literal and wooden way possible, and
the result was the return to this primitive sporadic aggression.

After the Kharijite revolt, the Muslim position on virtue became
formulated. The orthodox doctrine became the following: all Muslims
will go to paradise (they still believe this today); nevertheless, there
are some big sinners among Muslims, who will be punished for a time
in the next world, perhaps very severely, but all will ultimately go to
paradise. They thus made a very clever compromise. Thus, the *Sunnites*,
the main body of Islam.

Now I want to deal with the Shi͞'ites. They are a surviving major
sect in Islam, about whom we are hearing more and more today. The
Shi͞'ites reject the whole idea that disputed questions are to be decided
by the consensus or majority of Islam. They believe in a kind of pope,
a member of Muhammad's family, descendants of his son-in-law Ali.
Ali's own son, Hussein, was treacherously killed in 680, and from
then on the Shi͞'ites have venerated him. On the anniversary of his
death, thousands of men march in procession whipping themselves,
cutting themselves with razor blades and so on. It's like the Penitentes
of New Mexico reenacting the death of Christ.

The supreme head of Islam, according to the Shi͞'ites, is the Imam.
Rather, he *should* be, because the last supreme Imam disappeared in
the twelfth century! According to them, he is actually alive though,
but hiding somewhere; in one of the caves in Mesopotamia. He is
called "the hidden Imam." His recent representative is well known: the
Ayatollah Khomeini. The Imam himself is not only *infallible*, but
without sin (*impeccable*)—not even the pope claims that. There are
also schools of thought that believe this Imam is a kind of emanation
from God. They have introduced some neoplatonism into the equation.
The Shi͞'ites are today among the most fanatical Muslims.

I pass to the next sect now, the *Assassins* (c. A.D. 1200). This sect was led by a mountain chief called "The Old Man of the Mountain." The Old Man of the Mountain surrounded himself with an army of fanatical youths. Their training included the following as a finale of their "Paris Island" experience; they all got completely stoned on hashish, from which we get the word assassin. They were then led to a hidden cave where they enjoyed all sorts of delights, the wine, the women—everything, for a month. Then they were put to sleep and taken back to the barracks. Back in the barracks they were told they had been in paradise. "And how do we get back there?" would be the question of the youths. "Go out and die in a holy war against the enemies of Allah and you'll wake up again in paradise where you were." This made for indomitable fighters, and the principle still works today even without the use of the cave and props.

I will offer some conclusions about Islam. It is a religion born out of tension between nomadic life and urban life. Muhammad saw that Meccan life was corrupt, then retired to the desert to gain instruction from God. Finally, the instruction came. The message was not a simple call to return to the traditions of tribal life, but a call to create a *new tribe based* on a set of *principles* rather than tribal customs. These principles called for the protection of orphans, the poor, and the weak, backed up by a threat—if people did not do this they would go to hell—and a promise—if they did this they would go to paradise. A theology to support this, absolute monotheism, derived from the Jews. The doctrine of the last judgment, derived from the Jews and the Christians, told people to submit absolutely to this message, and, if they did so, offered them entrance into a new super-tribal Islam. This allowed men of all races, without distinction, to come in, turning intertribal warfare and caravan-raiding outward against those who attacked Islam, integrating all of the above into an unbelievably simple and articulate code.

The ensuing history involved the conquest of the two decadent and corrupt civilizations of the north, the Zoroastrian and the Christian—both of whom were involved in fanatical and interminable theological disputes sects always fighting with each other—but never wholly conquering their rivals. These moves were carried out by Muhammad and his successor with unbelievable skill and diplomacy, and they resulted in the creation of a new civilization, the Islamic. But the fierce spirit of the tribal caravan raiders was never fully subjected to the needs of civilized living. The result was the continual outbreak of waves of fanaticism by people who were uncertain of the proper interpretation of Islam, or uncertain of what to do next. Fratricide, continues to this day. It was Muhammad's desire to bring Arabs together, and to a certain extent he did, but then they began to quarrel over the theology, over the principles. When the use of force became the available means for the solution of these quarrels the result was fanaticism, just as it was among the Jews and the Christians.

There are some general conclusions to be drawn about the role and function of religion in human history, which is the topic of this volume.

First I wish to call your attention to a point in my definition of religion; that religion rests on the assumption that certain human needs can be satisfied by resort to the supernatural. This of course, leaves open the possibility that some of the needs may not be real at all. Some of the needs we may want to satisfy may be merely subjective needs, pseudo-needs, such as the need that everyone should love me. That is a subjective need, not a real need.

As a man passes from primitive to highly civilized society, his objective and true needs are increasingly met by technology and medicine. But this control is far from perfect and so certain objective needs remain. Take, for instance, the need to predict the path of tornadoes, which is presently fraught with a good deal of inaccuracyt—an objective needs not yet taken care of. That is where the preachers enter praying, giving thanks that we have not been destroyed by this tornado even though most of our relatives and friends have. They sayit is the inscrutable will of God. So religion partly claims to be in control of these events, or at least to submit these events to the will of God, namely certain events impinging on objective needs, like security from tornadoes.

But then there are certain subjective needs, certain illusory needs, like the need to be loved by everybody. In an advanced technological society, religion continues to appeal to such needs: "what a friend I have in Jesus," "somebody up there likes me" . . . So there are then, these two classes of needs which remain to be satisfied by religion, real objective needs not yet taken care of by man's control over his environment, and many illusory subjective needs. Religion will always be with us, as long as it is assumed that any need, real or illusory, can be met by appeal to the supernatural. The model is the child-parent relationship. This is the main reason for the survival of religion in modern civilization and this is the question that we addressed at the beginning of chapter 1, the reason for the survival, for the continuing strength of religion.

But one may object, why the continuing primitive content? Why the emphasis on dietary laws? On original sin? On being washed in the blood of the lamb? On eating the body and blood? And so on. Why are the religions with large amounts of primitive content so much stronger than sanitized religions like Unitarianism and Reform Judaism? Liberal religions, people who merely believe in the fatherhood of God, and the brotherhood of man, and the neighborhood of Boston? Why doesn't this form of religion become stronger? When the Second Vatican Council liberalized to some degree the Catholic Church, attendance at Mass and confession began to fall off.

Why then do the primitive elements continue to appeal more? First, because they claim more supernatural power. No Unitarian minister can claim that his vestry is full of supernatural power or hewould be laughed out of the pulpit. But the conservative churches promise more—and threaten more. You never hear a Reform rabbi warning that you may wind up in hell. Secondly, they appeal to unresolved emotional conflicts that remain from childhood. They promise a true father, a really loving father, not the possibly insensitive clod who raised you. A true mother, not one that tells you to go and clean your room or else. A warm and caring family. Total forgiveness, as in the hymn, "what a friend we have in Jesus," or, as a nun might sing, "what a lover I have in Jesus." You see, these things cannot be offered by the diluted forms of religion. Thirdly, these traditional religions tie us to our ethnic and ancestral identities. They bring with them the approval and support of our real families, our uncles and our cousins and our aunts. The God-father becomes God the Father. Ultimately these ties lead back to a distant past, with which we may feel proud to be identified, and the ties lead forward to a continuation of the tradition in the future. Not to pass on the tradition is to be some kind of traitor. It's like not continuing a chain letter, but with much more convincing sanctions. All of these things help to explain the function of religion in history. But the child-parent model does not work for adult living—and adult living is the precondition of civilization.

Excursus on the Qur'ān

The Qur'ān is the holy book of Islam. It is the unique and ultimate religious, moral, and political authority of the community. It establishes Islam as a revealed religion, that is, a religion based on instructions allegedly given by a deity to mankind. In the case of Islam this deity is the same as that of Judaism and Christianity, El Elohim or Yahweh. Furthermore, the founder of Islam claimed to be a member of a long line of Jewish and Christian prophets stretching from Abraham through Moses to Jesus. But he was, he insisted, the last such prophet, crowning and sealing once and for all the entire process of divine revelation. This process of revelation, moreover, was written down in the form of sacred scriptures intended to be read aloud. Indeed the very word for his own revelation, Qur'ān means "reading" or "recitation."

But a major difference between the scriptures of Judaism and Christianity on one hand and Islam on the other is that while each of the former consisted of several books (Bible=Biblia=Books) written by many authors, the latter was a single book written by one author. Indeed the difference in time span between the writing of the Jewish Bible and the Qur'ān was that of one thousand years to about twenty years.

This difference in the composition of the scriptures did not seriously affect their function in the three religions. The Jewish Bible, the New Testament, and the Qur'ān were accepted as divinely inspired by each of their religious communities, and had as well the role of settling all controversies of creed, code, and cult. In addition, as "reading" or "reciting" in the mosque, the Qur'ān duplicated the function of the scriptural lessons read in the synagogues and churches. In time the Arabic of the Qur'ān became the liturgical language of the mosque just as Syriac did for the eastern Christians and Hebrew did for the Jews.

Muhammad sharply distinguished between the non-Islamic "people of the book" on one hand who had a sacred script and confessed one God, and the pagans on the other hand who were polytheists and lacked a liturgical script. Pagans were to be persecuted or forced to become Muslims, whereas "the people of the book" were to be tolerated, although taxed at a higher rate than Muslims. But this higher rate was often lower than the one they had been paying to the Christian

Roman empire, so it is understandable why many Christians welcomed the Muslim conquerors.

Islam, then, is a religion of written revelation in the form of one book, the Qur'ān. It consists of a series of such revelations given from time to time as guidance to believers in specific situations. It is, as a matter of fact, composed of 114 chapters called *suras*. Each sura states a religious belief, dictates a prayer, regulated rituals and pilgrimages, tells a story, distinguishes true believers from hypocrites, identifies enemies, appeals for funds, issues rules for industry, finance and trade, marriage, inheritance, treatment of women and children, and speaks on all kinds of subjects, some concerning general principles, other concerning merely passing topics.

The revelations of Muhammad were often dictated while he was in a trance, and simply memorized by his followers. After his death different visions appeared. Around 650 Caliph Utman, the head of the Muslim community, ordered leading scholars to produce an official version which is known as the Utmanian Recension, and is still the orthodox text today.

The Qur'ān is regarded as so holy that it is forbidden to imitate its style. It is significant that the most important theological controversy in the history of Islam was the debate, which we have described earlier in this chapter, between the orthodox, who maintained that the Qur'ān is eternal and uncreated, and the Mu'tazilites who denied this. After the victory of the orthodox the Qur'ān became an object of veneration surpassing all other religious books.

Note

1. Frithjof Schuon, *Understading Islam*, translated by D.M. Matheson, Baltimore, MD, Penguin Books, 1972, p.13.

Part II

Ethos of the Judeo-Christian Tradition

5

Judaism and Its World Outlook

Every civilization is characterized by a set of fundamental ideas and an ensuing sense of life that is the result of those fundamental ideas. The set of fundamental ideas is passed on from generation to generation, and for this reason it is called a tradition. Our civilization, Western civilization, is almost unique in a sense of being based on two very divergent traditions, the Greek and the Judeo-Christian.

I am using the term "Greek tradition" to refer to the predominant strain in Greek culture which stood for the view that the universe or cosmos, as the Greeks called it, is intelligible and hospitable to man, and that man is potentially a being of *Kalok'agathía* (beauty and nobility) whose destiny it is to find happiness in this cosmos by the use of his rational faculty. The most consistent proponent of this Greek tradition was Aristotle, and it is to this great thinker that we are indebted for its most lucid articulation and its most unwavering advocacy.

In identifying the Greek tradition as rational, I am not denying that there was also an irrational strain in ancient Greece. Indeed, this irrational Greek strain was also swept up into the Judeo-Christian tradition, and later helped the Judeo-Christian tradition to gain its foothold and finally rise to a predominance that lasted for centuries. By "the Judeo-Christian tradition," I mean a common set of ideas generated in the Jewish and Christian religions. These religions are in many ways quite different from one another, and their modes of expressing the ideas and values are somewhat divergent. Yet as I shall argue, the areas of agreement are far more important than the areas of divergence.

We now will attempt to describe, analyze, and evaluate the Judeo-Christian tradition. Chapters 5 and 6 will supply the indispensable historical framework, chapter 5 being devoted to Judaism and chapter 6 to Christianity. Chapters 7 and 8 will analyze and evaluate the *content* of the tradition, chapter 7 being devoted to fundamental teachings in ethics, politics, and economics, and chapter 8 largely to sexual precepts and practices. The final chapter will offer a summary of the basic theses or positions of Judeo-Christian ethics, and will conclude with an estimate of the future of the tradition, in effect the estimate of the likelihood of the tradition continuing to maintain its strong grip on our culture.

I now come to the matrix of the Judeo-Christian tradition, which I place during the period 400 B.C.–A.D.100. It was in about 400 B.C. that the scribe Ezra, backed by the police power of the king of Persia, imposed upon all the inhabitants of Judea the now-completed code of regulations known as the Jewish Law, the practice of which would fully and irrevocably segregate the Jews from all other people. And it was about A.D. 135 that a prayer was inserted into the synagogue liturgy, "May the Nazarenes and the heretics be suddenly destroyed and removed from the book of life," marking the decisive act of throwing the Christians out of the synagogues. It was about this time also that a council of rabbis, meeting at a place called Jamnia (now called Yibna, about thirteen miles south of Tel Aviv), laid down once and for all the basic structure of *normative* or *rabbinical* or *Orthodox* Judaism. During this period of five centuries, the Judeo-Christian tradition, in its two alternate forms of Judaism and Christianity, had finally crystallized.

For our purposes, Jewish history may be divided into the following periods. The first period was 1800-1000 B.C. It was characterized by semi-nomadic life on the fringe of the Fertile Crescent, tribes wandering back and forth between Babylonia and Egypt. The second period is called the period of the First Commonwealth, and it lasted from 1000-577 B.C. This was a period of Jewish statehood, of settled life, both rural and urban, ruled by kings. The third period was 577-500 B.C., a period of only seventy-seven years, during which the leading Jewish families were exiled in Babylon. The fourth period is called the period of the Second Commonwealth, when once again there was a Jewish state. This lasted from 500 B.C. to A.D. 70. When I say "once again a Jewish state," I mean a state under either native or foreign rule, but if the latter, then at least with Jewish under-administrators. The fifth period is a period of the completion of the Diaspora of the Jews. "Diaspora" means the dispersion or scattering of the Jews around the world, and this became complete about the year A.D. 70 and lasted to A.D.1948, when the state of Israel was established and many Jews returned to the land of their ancestors.

The Judaic tradition can only be explained in terms of the situation which gave it birth, the invasion of the rich agricultural and urban civilization of Canaan—that is to say, Palestine—by a semi-nomadic, highly tribalized people called the Israelites. This invasion took place between 1200 and 1000 B.C. To understand the critical nature of this confrontation, let us look at the two societies involved. First let us look at the civilization of the native peoples of Palestine, the Canaanites.

Canaanite civilization was the civilization of a settled, urban society. Its economy was based on agriculture and trade. It was made up of small city-states, each ruled by a king with absolute power. The king was also regarded as a priest, the mediator between his people and the gods. The society was not based on tribal blood relationships. It was a feudal society, with land or privileges conferred in exchange for military service. The land was worked with the conscripted labor of peasants. The state's main source of income was trade, and the king was the chief trader. There were also some very rich, private businessmen and others who amassed wealth as business agents of the king. It was a relatively prosperous mixed economy.

The Canaanite religion was polytheistic; they had many gods. Each piece of land had its own landlord-god called a *baal* who had to be propitiated in order to ensure a good rainfall and a good harvest, and in order to ensure also the fertility of the farm animals and the fertility of the human family living on the land. Each local *baal* granted or withheld fertility at will. He died each year with the drying up of the soil at the beginning of summer and people mourned his death, weeping and tearing their hair. He was reborn with the autumn rains, and his rebirth was greeted by singing, dancing, and orgies designed to encourage him to restore fertility to the farm.

Each city had a temple in honor of its patron *baal*, and since these cities were built on dominating heights, their shrines are referred to in the Bible by the name "high places." The image of the god inside his shrine could be dimly seen by the worshippers, and outside the shrine stood a *mazeppa* or pillar, a large phallic symbol. Sacrifices were offered and eaten in communion meals. Temples were served by sacred prostitutes, including homosexual prostitutes.

At the head of all the *baal* was the great *baal*, a youthful, vigorous storm god incessantly fighting monsters. Children were sacrificed to the great *baal*. There was also a great female *baal*, named Ashterot or Astarte, goddess of fertility, who was usually represented naked. She was also the goddess of vengeance. When either side of her nature got out of control, she really was something to deal with. She sometimes grabbed a sword, sprang naked on a horse, and rode forth to slaughter. In the fertility festivals in the autumn, she represented the soil, and *baal* the storm god was supposed to fertilize her by his rain.

The word for god, any god, was "el," and at the top of the hierarchy was (capital) El or God, a remote being regarded as the creator of heaven and earth and all the other gods. From the word "El" was derived the Arabic name "Allah."

It is obvious that the religion of the Canaanites was a nature religion. Divinity permeated all nature and was concerned with keeping natural processes going. The religion of the Canaanites was also a cyclical religion, being tied to the cycles of life and the seasons. Sexuality and aggression were sacred forces pervading all nature. There was nothing really outside nature. The universe was regarded as a vast conglomeration of gods and men, wildly wheeling around. The world outlook of the Canaanites was not rational, but it was in a sense secular, in the sense, that is, of affirming the goodness of all natural processes, the enjoyment of life, sex, health, wealth, and so on. Being irrational, it had some gruesome and monstrous sides, such as child sacrifice.

It was this civilization which the Israelites faced when they invaded Canaan. They confronted it with a world outlook that was vastly different from the Canaanites. The Israelites were breeders of small cattle—sheep, goats, and asses. They were semi-nomads. Part of the year they moved around with their flocks in the unsettled grasslands on the borders of Canaan. Then, when their flocks had consumed all the available fodder, the Israelites negotiated grazing rights with nearby farmers whose fields had already been harvested.

Sometimes they settled down and planted some crops, As a result, they developed an ambivalent attitude toward settled life. On the one hand, they dreamed of a promised land flowing with milk and honey, where they could eat, drink, and enjoy all the good things of civilization. On the other hand, they wanted to preserve the tribal ties of desert life. *The understanding of this ambivalence helps us to understand the ambivalence of the Jews throughout history*, who have alternately been attracted to the individualist life of urban centers, on the one hand, and the communal life like that of the *kibbutzim*, on the other hand; to the joys of worldly living, on one hand, to the strict observance of the Torah or Law, on the other. The invading Israelites of 1200 or so B.C. felt this ambivalence keenly.

Let us look for a moment at the tribal tradition of the Israelites to see how different it was from the non-tribal tradition of the Canaanites. The tribal way of life of the Israelites depended on blood relationships. Families named after the father extended into larger units called clans, named after a remote ancestor. Clans extended into still larger units, called tribes, named after a still more remote ancestor. The whole group of Israelite tribes were supposed to be descended from a very remote ancestor named Israel, or Jacob; his father Isaac; and his father Abraham. Jacob had lived about five centuries before, and the various tribes were descended from him, some tribes by his first wife Leah, six tribes; some by her maid Zilpa, two tribes; some by his second wife Rachel, one tribe; some by her maid Bilpa, two tribes.

Whatever god or gods they worshipped, they were united in the worship of a god called El-Shaddai, which means "the god of the plains" or possibly "the god of the mountain." Let us call him the god of the plains; that is the most widely accepted interpretation today. This god was also called the god of the fathers. He was a nomadic deity who had revealed himself to a remote ancestor, Abraham. God adopted Abraham and his descendants, promised land and posterity to them, and was now accompanying and guarding the whole group, deciding where the people should go, and keeping them safe on their way.

Now some of the southern tribes crossed the border into Egypt, where they were conscripted for forced labor. These must have included the tribe of Levi, a so-called Leah tribe, the only tribe that later bore Egyptian names. At any rate, among these tribes in Egypt arose a great leader with the Egyptian name of Moses. Moses had experienced a revelation in which a god had appeared to him. This god announced that his name was Yahweh, the meaning of which we do not know, but it may mean "he is," or "I will be who I will be." According to one component document of the Bible, Yahweh is recorded as having said to Moses, "I am the Lord [Yahweh]. I appeared to Abraham, to Isaac, and to Jacob as God Almighty [El-Shaddai], but by my name the Lord [Yaweh] I did not make myself known to them. I also established my covenant with them, to give them the land of Canaan. . . Say therefore to the people of Israel, 'I am the Lord, and I will bring you out from the burdens of the Egyptians, and I will deliver you from their bondage. . . and I will take you for my people, and I will be your God. . . And I will bring you into the land which I swore to give to Abraham, Isaac, and to Jacob; I will give it to you for a possession. I am the Lord.'" [1]

Moses, armed with this message, persuaded the enslaved Israelites to follow him, and he then led them successfully out of Egypt in a feat, according to the Bible, teeming with miracles. He brought them to the foot of a mountain.. We don't know just which mountain it was, but it is referred to as Sinai. Yahweh called to Moses from the top of the mountain: "Thus you shall say to the house of Jacob, and tell the people of Israel: You have seen what I did to the Egyptians, and how I bore you on eagles' wings and brought you to myself. Now therefore, if you obey my voice and keep my covenant, you shall be my own possession among all peoples; for all the earth is mine. . ."[2]

Moses told the people of the offered covenant and they agreed to it in advance. Moses went back and told Yahweh that his offer, which couldn't be refused, had been accepted. Yahweh then said to Moses, "Lo, I am coming to you in a thick cloud, that the people may hear me when I speak with you, and may also believe you for ever. . . And you shall set bounds for the people round about, saying, 'Take heed that you do not go up the mountain or touch the border of it; whoever touches the mountain shall be put to death; no hand shall touch him, but he shall be stoned or shot; whether beast or man, he shall not live . . . ' When the trumpet sounds a long blast, they shall come up to the mountain."[3] So Moses went down from the mountain and told the poeple to be ready in three days and in the meantime not to have sex.

When the third day came, there was thunder and lighting and a dense cloud on the mountain. Moses led the trembling people to the foot of the mountain. Yahweh came down on the mountain in fire, smoke arose from the mountain as from an oven, and the whole mountain trembled violently. The blare of the ram's horn grew louder and louder. Whenever Moses spoke, Yahweh answered him with the sound of thunder. Meanwhile, Moses kept warning the people back, warning them they would die if they caught a glimpse of Yahweh's face. However, Yahweh did relent and allowed Moses' brother Aaron and a select few to come up and view Yahweh from a safe distance for a moment. Then Moses came down from the mountain, built an altar, sacrificed some bulls, threw half their blood on the altar, and sprinkled the other half on the people to signify the covenant.

Then Moses read to the people the terms of the covenant—in other words, the Mosaic law. The earliest edition of the Mosaic law, which is the basis of our Judeo-Christian tradition, is contained in the book of Exodus, chapters 20–24. At the core arc the famous Ten Commandments. The Ten Commandments are supposed to be the ethical base of the Judeo-Christian tradition. When we look at the Ten Commandments, it is easy to see that they fall into two groups, the last six and the first four. The last six are "honor your father and mother," "do not commit murder," "do not commit adultery," "do not steal," "do not bear false witness," and "do not covet what belongs to others."

I want to say two things about this group of six commandments. First of all, their content is not unique to the Judeo-Christian tradition. Such moral principles and the values lying behind them have been shared by many ethical and legal systems and by many other societies. Secondly, however, there is a difference. These commandments are absolute. They contain no provisions for exceptions. There are no situations in which it is permitted not to honor one's father and mother, for example. These commandments are given in the form that Immanuel Kant was later to call "apodictic." It means "unyielding," "unconditional," "absolutely necessary," "in the form of absolute, categorical imperatives." Other moral codes contain provisos for special situations or for mitigations; these commandments do not. Now, why do they have this absolute form? Because they are revealed. Because the nature of the revealer is hidden from the scrutiny of reason, and because the revealer *refuses to entertain any questions* as to the premises behind the commandments or behind any of his actions. His answer is always, "Because I say so."

This is clearly brought out when we examine the other group of commandments, the first four commandments. "I am Yahweh your God. You shall have no other gods before me." "You shall not make a carved image of me or any natural object, or bow down to such an image, for I, Yahweh your God, am a jealous God." "You shall not use my name lightly." "You shall not do any work on the seventh day, the Sabbath." Now these commandments are unique to the Judaic tradition. They deal with attitudes and actions to be taken up by those who accept the last six commandments—attitudes toward the revealer of the commandments, Yahweh. First, Yahweh is to be the only object of reverence. He openly says he is jealous. Secondly, he is not to be represented as having any form. Now "form" is what you can scrutinize with your senses or examine by your reason. "Form" means "identity," but Yahweh is beyond form, beyond identity, beyond identification. If you ask him what he is, he answers, "I am inscrutable." Now, all nature has form. Yahweh is therefore beyond all nature, beyond the universe. Just as "apodictic" is the correct word for his commands, so "transcendent" and "inscrutable" are the correct words for his nature. Transcendent: he is hidden, he is beyond our scrutiny. Thirdly, his name must not be used lightly. Later the Jews elaborated this commandment as to prohibit the very pronunciation of the name "Yahweh." There is thus a prohibition of *perceiving* Yahweh. There is a prohibition of *framing a concept* of him, and finally a prohibition of *naming him*. All the elements of a proper (in the Objectivist sense) epistemology are thus violated. (A good account of these elements is to be found in Ayn Rand's *Introduction to Objectivist Epistemology*.) Finally, there is the consecration of a special day to Yahweh, a day on which man's productive activities must come to a complete halt, in order to acknowledge the fact that Yahweh is the supreme creator.

Besides the famous Ten Commandments, there are many other commandments in this earliest document of the law. Among them are statements such as we saw in chapter 3: "He that sacrificeth unto any god, save unto the Lord only, he shall be utterly destroyed." "Thou shalt not suffer a witch to live."[4] Realize that this is not merely an ethical code. It is at the same time a political code, a system of criminal law. All ethical prohibitions are to be enforced by the police. "He who strikes his father or mother will be put to death." (Calvin, a Christian continuator of the Jewish tradition, is said to have ordered a young child to be decapitated for striking his father in Geneva in the sixteenth century.)[5] Among other prohibitions is one against lending money at interest to a fellow Israelite. This prohibition of so-called usury was to have many repercussions in history. Some of the prohibitions go rather far. The prohibition against nakedness is so extreme that it is forbidden to build an altar on steps lest presumably some voyeur peer up the priest's vestments as he ascends the steps. This is the first trace of the extreme obsessiveness that later grew to such enormous proportions in the rabbis' interpretations of the law.

The law of Moses was generally stricter than the laws of other peoples. For instance, the Mosaic code was far stricter in matters of sex. In other codes, a husband may forgive an adulterous wife and her lover. The law of Moses orders both the wife and the lover to be put to death. Why? Because the act is not just an offense against the husband, but against God. All "irregular" forms of sex were banned. Incest was regarded as particularly horrible. This whole attitude toward sex was passed on by Judaism to Christianity and Islam, and we know the results.

(I might here mention the fact that so-called crimes against property were played down. This was an expression of the tribal, nomadic sense of communal possession and the belief in economic equality.)

So much for the oldest forms of the Mosaic law. It was accepted from Moses by the southern tribes who had been in Egypt. After Moses' death, another great leader named Joshua persuaded the northern tribes to accept the religion and the Law. The tribes were now merged into a great confederacy and began to invade the land of the Canaanites with full military force, with the Ark of Yahweh going on before. Soon they would conquer all of Canaan and their religion would confront that of the Canaanites.

We have already seen what the religion of the Canaanites was: we have characterized it as one of very mixed values, at once worldly and irrational. We have spoken of it as a nature religion, and as cyclical in its point of view. One generation was pictured as following the same pattern of the previous generation in a yearly round of agricultural festivals, propitiating the gods who seemed interested only in these natural cycles.

The religion of the Israelites, on the other hand, was not at all concerned with the cycles of nature. It was concerned with what had happened in history, what was happening, and what would happen to the whole group of people called Israel. Together this people had gone through rough times. They had received an offer from the god of their fathers of a promised land. They had been enslaved in Egypt, then they had been liberated. But then the God of the fathers, revealing himself under a new name and as a warrior god, had miraculously redeemed them from slavery and was now leading them on into the promised land. He had initiated them to be his chosen people, and they agreed to abandon the worship of all other gods. He would lead them into the promised land, defeating all their enemies, provided they followed his law and worshipped him alone. He would reward them by giving them land, children, and flocks in abundance.

The acceptance of Yahwism by the Israelites meant, therefore, the adoption of a linear or straight-line view of history, as opposed to the cyclical view of history characteristic of the Canaanites. What interested them were the events along the straight line: creation, going down to Egypt, being liberated from Egypt, promises by their god, miraculous deliverances, improbable victories, and so on. It was a whole philosophy of history that was to influence all Western civilization through the spread of the Jewish and Christian religions. This is the philosophy of history that we are to see later in Augustine, in Hegel, and in Marx. In this scheme, the field of history is pictured as a battleground in which some are chosen, be they Jews, Christians, Germans, the proletariat, or what not—chosen to be the agents of order and light against chaos and darkness.

The invading Israelites regarded themselves as chosen people united in the covenant. They were to keep Yahweh's law, and if they did, they would be rewarded by lands and children. It was a two-way street. God had to do his part, too. Now this is a very brittle position for any religion, for what if it turned out that the wicked—that is, those that did not keep the law—prospered? They did. And what if it turned out that those who did keep the law suffered misfortune? They did. This is what happened again and again throughout all Jewish history. So it set the stage for the so-called problem of evil.

In time, the invading Israelites captured Jerusalem from the Canaanites and completed the conquest of the country. They settled down to an agricultural and urban life. They had kings for the first time, great kings, David and Solomon. But in the very process of settling down, the Israelites underwent great tension between the new life and the old social values they had brought in from the desert. First of all, they had to be farmers now. But remember that in Canaan, every patch of land had its *baal* or fertility god who had to be propitiated with sacrifices and orgies—if, according to the local edition of the *Farmer's Almanac*, the crops were to grow. Some of the Israelites thought this was great, and took to the orgies like fish to water. Also, just to be on the right side of things, they worshipped Yahweh as well.

What was emerging was what we call a "syncretistic" or "mixed" religion. The kings added to this syncretism. David brought the Ark with its stone tablets of the law to Jerusalem. He set it down in a shrine, made it stationary, something it had never been before. Then he and all Israel performed Canaanite dances before it, accompanied by harps and lutes and tambourines and cymbals.

Soon David proclaimed that Yahweh had made a *second covenant* with him personally, parallel to the original covenant he had made with Israel—a covenant that channeled divine benefactions through the king and his dynasty to the people. From this time on, the belief took hold that the king of Israel must be in the line of David, the "son of David." Later, when Israel was under foreign domination, the people looked for someone that was a descendant of David to appear and redeem the nation from its oppressors. This coming redeemer was called the "anointed one" or the "Messiah"; the corresponding Greek term, of course, is "Christ," a fateful concept indeed.

Solomon, David's son, succeeded him in 965 B.C. He brought the kingdom to wealth and power. The local Canaanite population was largely absorbed, and Solomon allowed the worship of the fertility gods to flourish alongside that of Yahweh. To Yahweh he built a great temple in Jerusalem, in the Phoenician style, to house the Ark of the Covenant. The Ark was placed in a dark central room called the Holy of Holies. And right around in the neighborhood of the temple, Solomon built temples to the gods of many of his non-Israelite wives.

I now want to say a few words about the origin of the Bible. Every religious cult requires a sacred story to explain the meaning of its ritual acts and festivals. So now a cult official or maybe a committee of cult officials began composing the first document of what we now call the Hebrew Bible, or what Christians call the Old Testament—the book which became the main literary source of the Judeo-Christian tradition. The writing of the document, which was done in many places, took about eight hundred years, from about 965 to 165 B.C., and was made official for the Jews at the council of Jamnia, about A.D. 100, at the beginning of the final dispersion of the Jews.

Following Solomon's death, the ten northern tribes seceded from the south and set up their own kingdom of Israel in the north. The remaining kingdom in the south was called Judah, with the capital at Jerusalem. The kingdom of the north was called Israel, with the capital at Samaria. The kings of Israel severed all religious ties with Jerusalem and set up a shrine in the north with the old totem image of the golden bull to stand for Yahweh. In both kingdoms, the amalgamation of the two religions, Yahwism and the fertility religion of the Canaanites, continued. In both kingdoms, the kings and their hangers on lived luxuriously on heavy taxes and enforced labor in the royal mixed-economy style of other kingdoms of the Near East.

And then along came the prophets. In both kingdoms, there arose prophets of Yahweh, who denounced the decadence, dishonesty, seizure of property by the kings, and so on. But in the message of the prophets, there was a kind of package deal. People were being asked to choose between two false alternatives: on the one hand, a whole list of values, including urban life, luxurious living, breaking contracts, expropriation of private property, the worship of fertility gods; on the other hand, a list of values, which included honesty, decent upright living, the life of the poor shepherd, retreat to the desert, living in tents, and sincerely worshipping Yahweh. The coming of this prophetic religion marked the definitive appearance within the Judeo-Christian tradition of protest in the name of, what has been called ever since, "social justice." This kind of protest is addressed to the rich man who feels guilty because he is rich, but who has tried to get rid of his guilt by contributing to his local church or synagogue—endowing chapels, buying splendid vestments for the clergy, and so on. This is the kind of compromise policy that has supported establishment religion ever since the beginning of the syncretism between the Israelite and Canaanite traditions.

It is against this establishment religion that the radical prophets were protesting. They were protesting in the name of a standard of values derived generations before from the nomadic tribes of the desert. So the rich temple-going city dweller is being recalled to the values of his great-great-great-great-grandfather. Consider again the lengthy exhortation of Yahweh, speaking through the mouth of the prophet Amos, that I quoted in chapter 3: "Woe, woe to the city dwellers lolling on their ivory divans, sprawling on their couches, dining off fresh lamb and fatted veal. . ."[6] We thus see a conflict between ideals derived from a pastoral life and ideals derived from a settled life. As I pointed out, this conflict existed from the beginning of Israelite history, but now it became exacerbated by the preaching of the prophets.

The old story of the Tower of Babel was recalled, the moral being that the attempt to build a skyscraper is a challenge to God, and he had punished men for so doing. The story of Cain and Abel was also recalled. God had preferred the gifts of Abel, who was a herdsman, over the gifts of Cain, who was a cultivator of the earth. Cain slew Abel because he believed Abel was unjustly favored. Then, when God asked Cain where Abel was, Cain answered, "Am I my brother's keeper?" The implication is that by the ideals of pastoral, tribal life, all men are brothers and all are responsible for their brothers. Many Israelites, as I said, were ambivalent between the two sets of ideals, pastoral versus settled. But there were some of the pastoralist party who carried their viewpoint to the extreme, and they were called Rechabites. Now, these were an ultra-orthodox cult dating back to at least 800 B.C. The Rechabites made three solemn vows: not to sow fields, or possess vineyards; not to build houses, but to remain tent dwellers all their lives; and not to drink wine. Here we find a group of Israelites regarding themselves as pure and more observant than the others, and approaching in their attitudes those of the pure nomads of the desert.

Here we can mark the entry into the Judeo-Christian tradition of such tendencies as moral and religious puritanism, and neo-primitivism—tendencies which we can trace later in the Dead Sea sect, Christian monasticism, Christian puritanism, and Islam; and all of them philosophically in Rousseau and all the varieties of socialism in the nineteenth and twentieth centuries.

So the message of the prophets may be summarized in this way: Yahweh alone is to be worshipped. Agricultural and urban modes of life breed injustice. Tribal values and desert ideals are models of justice. And if the Israelites continue in their corrupt way, Yahweh would bring woe upon them, which meant they would be conquered by foreign powers. The message of the prophets evoked much popular sympathy because of its nationalism. Yahweh was like the flag, the God of the nation, and the nation was in danger of attack. The message also contained a threat that if the pure worship of Yahweh were not reestablished, Yahweh himself would bring foreign powers to conquer the Israelites.

Now, if Yahweh could control the foreign powers, he must be sovereign over all nations; in effect, the only God. This was an age in which all the people of the Middle East were hungering after one God to establish peace throughout the region. In fact, they were tending toward monotheism. Now the Israelites had in their national God Yahweh the jealous God, the one who could be most easily transformed conceptually into the one and only God, the controller, even the creator, of the universe. The Israelites therefore became the first nation that permanently adopted monotheism, the doctrine that there is only one god.

Soon after the message of the prophets came the fulfillment of the threat of woe. In 722 B.C. the northern kingdom was conquered by the Assyrians. In reaction to this disaster, a party of religious reform arose in the southern kingdom, and came to power under King Josiah. Josiah suppressed the fertility cults, centralized the worship of Yahweh in the temple in Jerusalem, and established a purified religion based on a new edition of the Law. And it was expected that now that it had cleaned up its act, the southern kingdom of Judah would be saved from the fate of Israel; but it was not to be. In 587 B.C., Nebuchadnezzar, the King of Babylon, captured Jerusalem, destroyed the temple, and deported 5000 of the leading educated Jews to Babylon, where the whole group of them remained for about seventy-five years. While prospering in business, they remained as a distinct community, growing ever more exclusive and concerned with the preservation of their own identity. "What has happened?" they asked. "The reforms of King Josiah have apparently failed to appease Yahweh's wrath. What is the explanation of all this evil?"

A prophet named Ezekiel came along, who preached that the suffering of the Jews was due to the fact that even after the reforms, some Jews had retained heathen practices. "What the Jews need," he said, "is to purify themselves absolutely, to become strictly observant." "If we will only do this," continued Ezekiel, "God will restore the Kingdoms of Israel and Judah." So here we have one solution: the reason for all your sufferings is you are not pure enough. Rid yourself of impurities and victory is sure.

This solution, which I will call the Ezekiel solution, has recently been advanced in an extreme form by a certain rabbi, Yakov Homnek of Chicago. I quote from Rabbi Homnek: "Especially is the Holocaust a proof of God's justice, coming as it does at the climax of a century in which the vast majority of Jews, after thousand of years of loyalty in exile, decided to cast off their yoke of the law." This remark was made in the course of a debate with the late Sydney Hook, who replied: "The Rabbi cannot be unaware that the vast majority of the Jewish victims of the Holocaust were as orthodox as he is. And even if they constituted only a minority of world Jewry, where is the justice of *their* punishment or in that of their wives and children?"

A more radical solution was proposed by a writer in the Babylonian captivity called Second Isaiah. Second Isaiah vividly portrays an individual called the Suffering Servant. The Suffering Servant was a symbol of the Jewish people. The Suffering Servant, though innocent, is horribly persecuted for his obedience to the will of God. Why does he suffer? It is for the sins of others, vicarious suffering. "He was despised and rejected by men; a man of sorrows and acquainted with grief. . .But he was wounded for our transgressions, he was bruised for our iniquities, upon him was the chastisement that made us whole, and with his stripes we are healed. . . and the Lord has laid on him the iniquity of us all. He was oppressed, and he was afflicted, yet he opened not his mouth; like a lamb that is led to the slaughter, and like a sheep that before its shearers is dumb, so he opened not his mouth."[7] This Suffering Servant was identified by rabbinical commentators with the Jewish people, who are suffering for the sins of others. Of course later this text was applied by Christians to Jesus.[8] Here then we have the second solution to the suffering of the Jewish people. The first was that they had not observed the law strictly enough, and that they should clean up their act: this is the Ezekiel solution. The second solution, aware of the objection that most of the sufferers are innocent, openly proclaims that it is precisely their innocence that makes their suffering valuable in the eyes of God. Their innocent suffering creates a treasury of merit from which God dispenses rewards to those who have earned nothing, like the nonobservant Jews who did not observe the simplest ethic. Another principle has now been added to the Judeo-Christian tradition, the principle of a vicarious atonement, with its corollary of the transfer of merit from those who have earned it to those who havenot. It might be called the redistribution of spiritual resources.

A third solution is the solution given in the book of Job, dating from perhaps 500 B.C. Job is a very wealthy man, rich in lands, possessions, and children. He is a devoutly observant man in religious matters, and otherwise upright in his life. Satan suggests to God that maybe the reason Job is so virtuous is in order to earn all these rewards from God. God becomes disturbed at this suggestion, and he allows Satan to conduct a controlled experiment to see if this is so. First Satan kills all the flocks of Job, then he kills Job's children in a tornado. Job's only response is, "The Lord gave, and the Lord hath taken away; blessed be the name of the Lord."[9] Then Satan smites Job with a disease whose description sounds something like AIDS. This then begins to get to Job, and he examines his conscience to see if he has done anything to deserve this. Finding himself innocent, he questions God, "Why are you allowing this to happen to an innocent man? Why? Why?" Then comes a second tornado. God answers Job, "Who are you to dare to ask questions? I will ask questions and you will answer. Where were you when I laid the foundations of the earth? Do you understand lightning, thunder, the movements of the tides? Do you understand how animals are constructed? Can you draw out Leviathan from the sea with a hook? Are you trying to instruct me? He who dares to question me the Almighty had better be prepared to answer for it." Job replies, in effect, "I guess I was presumptuous to question things beyond the power of my reason. I'm sorry. I know that you are the Almighty. I repent in dust and ashes." Then the Almighty was very pleased and he gave Job back everything that he had lost. (Not the same children, but ten brand new children.)

Now, the Book of Job is a departure from the previous Israelite tradition. The old tradition had been that the Lord rewards the just and punishes the unjust. One could even argue with God, reminding him of his promises under the covenant. With the book of Job comes a new message, a twofold message: don't dare to question God, because he is beyond human comprehension; and his benefits are not necessarily earned by any human standard. The same goes for the misfortunes he sends. This is a foretaste of Islam and, it should be added, of Saint Augustine's doctrine of predestination. So just as puritanism entered Judaism with the Rechabites, so now does this accompaniment, the doctrine that God's decrees are inscrutable, enter as well.

The Jews in Babylon accepted the Ezekiel solution, namely that their failure to observe the Law exactly and precisely was the cause of their misfortunes. So their young men devoted their spare time not to sports or to chasing girls, but to the study of the Law. And the Law itself was steadily becoming more complicated. Fences were being built around the Law, extra prohibitions against touching something that had touched something that had touched something that was unclean. Eggs laid on the Sabbath were declared unclean. And needless to say, in accordance with immemorial taboo, the ways in which women could become unclean were much more numerous than the ways in which men could become unclean. The Law kept growing and growing into a massive, obsessive system. Complicated dietary regulations evolved. It became difficult to socialize with non-Jews and impossible to marry them. The Jews in Babylon became, in a period of seventy-five years, more and more exclusive and more and more isolated—more and more what I would call "Law cadets," a variety of "space cadets."

Suddenly in 538 B.C., Babylon was conquered by Cyrus the Great of Persia. He allowed those Jews who wished to do so, to return home. A minority of them did. They were not welcome. The inhabitants had experienced a time of religious liberty. Now, however, they were placed under a regime of religious authoritarianism such as they never before had to endure. The temple was rebuilt, although on a more modest scale. Around the year 400, the fanatical scribe named Ezra arrived, armed with the authority of the King of Persia to publish the elaborate version of the Law we now have in the Torah, the first five books of the Bible. As mentioned in chapter 3, Ezra called an assembly of all the Jews who had not gone to Babylon and read them the Torah, ordering them under penalty of Persian law to divorce their non-Jewish wives.

This year—400, in round numbers—marks the birth of classical Judaism, as I have called it. By "classical Judaism," I mean the religion demanding the observance of all the laws in the first five books of the Bible, including animal sacrifices in the temple, all the dietary laws, circumcision of infant males, and so on.

After the overthrow of the Persian Empire by Alexander the Great in 333 B.C., the Hellenizing of the Near East began. Call to mind the profound antithesis between the Hellenistic and the Jewish spirits. Hellenism was a great enlightened civilization that had spread throughout the Mediterranean basin. It was rational, empirical, open to new knowledge, critical. It was relaxed, harmonious, open to the joys of both the mind and the body, both of which it prized and trained. Its gods were anthropomorphic, subject to rational criticism. It was a man-worshipping civilization. The Jewish spirit, on the other hand, exalted God above man's understanding or reach. It did not even raise the question whether God existed. God was assumed on faith. Did man's reasoning have any place? Yes. But only to figure out exactly what God wanted—poring over the law endlessly, seeking to perform the rituals exactly, and to avoid contamination by the foods or practices of the Gentiles, which they abhorred.

The Greeks in turn were horrified at the Jewish dietary laws, at the

Jewish practice of circumcision, and at the Jewish taboo on nakedness. Before long many Jews, admiring the Greek point of view, became thoroughly Hellenized. In 175 B.C., there was a high priest calling himself Joshua Jason, who scandalized the observant Jews by leading his priests in gymnastics, clad only in the Hellenistic equivalent of golf caps. Armed opposition broke out, which the local Greek dynasty put down severely, even at one time installing a statue of Zeus in the temple. This the Jews called the Abomination of Desolation. Many Jews died as martyrs in the struggle against the imposition of the Greek customs and style of life, which as mentioned marked the entrance of the concept of martyrdom into Western civilization.

However, outside of Palestine and all around the Mediterranean basin, Jews were settled in large numbers. They may have composed at one time about ten percent of the Roman Empire. These Jews adopted the Greek language and many aspects of Hellenistic civilization, while continuing to observe the main points of the law—the Sabbath, dietary laws, circumcision. They worked out a system by which they could sit at a table with Gentiles while not sharing all the same foods, and they solved the marriage problem by converting the non-Jewish partner to Judaism. In addition, many other Gentiles were on their own part converted either partly or wholly to Judaism, being attracted by the monotheism and the stricter moral code. Educated Jews began to regain their pride in their religion, and defended it by using the resources of Greek philosophy. They thus effected the next step in the history of the Judaic world outlook, its entrance into European culture.

The main agent in this step was the philosopher Philo of Alexandria, who is a much more important person than most histories of philosophy seem to be aware. He lived about the time of Jesus, and he was a Platonist. He was in fact called the Jewish Plato. His aim was to present Judaism as a school of philosophy superior to Greek philosophy and in every way intellectually respectable. His method was to take the main points of the Judaic worldview, state them in Greek concepts, argue for them from Greek premises, and finally conclude that Judaism was the best, the most cogent, the most unassailable intellectual position, a position which Plato, Aristotle, and the Stoics had only dimly foreshadowed. They had dimly foreshadowed Judaism in the sense that they, the Greek philosophers, had discovered by their own reason the existence of a supreme being whom they called God or ho Theos. Plato had called him the world architect, Aristotle had called him the Unmoved Mover, and the Stoics called him the Mind of the Universe. The divine being had, claimed Philo, been discovered by the unaided human reason, but (and here is the crucial point that reverberated down the halls of the history of philosophy) only God's existence had been discovered, not his essence or nature.

Philo was the first to introduce the claim that there is a distinction between the existence and the essence of God, and then to claim further that knowledge of God's essence was unattainable by the human reason. In other words, we can discover *that* he is, but not *what* he is. What the Greek philosophers had discovered without knowing it was Yahweh, the Jewish God, said Philo. God is, in fact, Yahweh, and Yahweh is God. But the Greek philosophers were sadly mistaken in imagining that they had understood the nature of the being they had discovered. In his essence, God is ineffable, indescribable.

Here Philo introduced three new terms to refer to the essence of God: *árretos*, ineffable; *akatonómastos*, unnameable; and *akatáleptos*, incompehensible. Only from Philo onward were these names used in Greek philosophy when referring to God, including Neoplatonism. Previous Greek thinkers had regarded God as knowable, as intelligible. But, claimed Philo, that was because they had mistakenly conceived him as having form, and therefore as finite. Actually, God is without form and infinite, as the Bible implies. Now the Greeks had always believed that the infinite was incomprehensible, and so most Greek thinkers had denied that there was any actual infinite being. But Philo, while agreeing that the infinite was incomprehensible, taught that there was an incomprehensible, an infinite God, Yahweh, who could not be understood or described.

Philo had another modification to offer to Greek philosophy. Greek philosophy taught that God acts out of inner necessity, that he must fashion the world because "he is," said Plato, "not jealous, and wishes to share his being." Philo replied that this is all a mistake. God freely chooses to create; he is not compelled by his nature to do so. As a matter of fact, he added, the Jewish God, who is the true God, *is* jealous. He is not going to share his divine nature with anyone. So God is a being of arbitrary will, for in the exercise of this will, there is no impelling reason to serve as a motive for action. Philo also taught that God is concerned with men's destinies. He introduced the notion of *particular* providence. Whereas the Greeks had thought that God was responsible for the major features of the universe, or at least for some of them, they did not think that he concerned himself with such trivial matters as the fate of individual human beings, or the course of history. But now Philo taught that he did.

The next doctrine that he introduced was that God had created the universe out of nothing. This was a new doctrine of creation. According to Philo, God both created the universe out of nothing, and gave it certain unvarying laws. Before the creation, God could have refrained from creating at all, or he could have created another universe governed by different laws of nature. So Philo originated the idea that our universe is only one of a number of possible worlds. That our universe exists and that the laws of nature are the ones that they are—this is an arbitrary fact selected by the will of God. They are brute facts dependent upon God's original caprice. The necessity of the laws of nature is further limited by the fact that God can turn them off if he wants to; he can suspend them. This is known as a miracle, of course. Philo repeats often the statement that all things are possible to God, a view he draws directly from the Book of Job: "I know that thou canst do all things, and that no purpose of thine can be thwarted."[10]

To these changes in the Greek metaphysical point of view, Philo adds an epistemological change, namely that knowledge comes in part by revelation: the revelation on Sinai, the written law, the utterances of the prophets, the inspired interpretations of the rabbis constituting the oral law. This revelation has to be grasped by faith. It corrects the discoveries of reason, and it adds to them; it revises them when necessary. By revelation, for instance, we know that the universe is not eternal, that it was arbitrarily selected by God out of a number of possible universes, and that it had a beginning. By revelation, we know that God is good in spite of all the evil in the world, for God has his own standard of value unknown to us. Again Philo is paraphrasing the Book of Job: "Can you find out the deep things of God? Can you find out the limit of the Almighty?"[11]

All these changes in Greek thought were of course radical transformations, affecting the very substance of the Greek outlook, and negating that outlook in content while accepting its conceptual framework. Philo thus advanced the cause of the Judaic world outlook by putting at its disposal the weapons of Greek philosophy.

But he did more than that: he prepared the way for Christianity. He did this by introducing into his philosophy the concept of the *Logos*, or the Word of God. As a good Platonist, he had to believe in the

Platonic forms; but as a good Jew, he could not believe that the forms could be eternal, since only God was eternal. Philo therefore declared that God had created a second quasi-divine being, the Logos, whom he called the first begotten son of God. The Platonic forms were all ideas in the mind of the Logos, and as a vast system of ideas formed what Philo called the intelligible world. God then used the Logos as his agent or intermediary in creating the sensible world in which we live. There is therefore a *mediator* between God and man.

For centuries, the Jews had looked for the coming of a Messiah, an ideal, anointed king. By the first century A.D., the normal Jewish concept of Messiah was that of a human leader who would drive out the occupiers, set up an independent Jewish state, bring an era of peace, justice, and prosperity for the whole world, ruled, at least indirectly, by the Jews.

Some Jews, however, thought otherwise. They saw their nation as an impossibly weak one, crushed by the weight of mighty empires around them. They thought that only a tremendous divine intervention could free the Jews from oppression. They expected this divine intervention to be coming ever sooner as things got worse and worse. In other words, the worse things got, the better the prospects. These people were called apocalypticists, because they believed in books called apocalypses (revelations). These books taught that after wars, famines, and plagues had nearly destroyed the world, and the Jews were at their low point, the Messiah would come on the clouds of heaven. The wicked world would rise up under an Anti-Messiah. The Messiah, invested by supernatural power, would then destroy the Anti-Messiah and all his armies. Jerusalem would not simply be cleaned up, it would be replaced by a celestial New Jerusalem, prefabricated on high and let down to earth for Messiah to reign in. In and around this celestial city, the Jews, no longer scattered, would dwell in their ancient glory, in that golden age of happiness promised in the covenant. And finally would come the resurrection of the dead.

These doctrines, revealed in the apocalyptic writings, played a continuing underground role in the Judeo-Christian tradition. In the secularized Judaism of the nineteenth century, a strong attraction to socialism was one result. And then in the twentieth century, Protestant Christianity produced the social gospel, and Catholic Christianity what is known as liberation theology.

By the time of Jesus, there were four sects among the Jews: the

Pharisees, the Zealots, the Sadducees, and the Essenes (or the Dead Sea sect). The Pharisees were the majority party. Not only did they accept the written law, they added a much more elaborate oral law. Esteemed for their piety and earnest prayer, they were generally popular. They accepted the doctrines of the immortality of the soul, and the resurrection of the body, and rewards and punishments after death. They also believed in a qualified doctrine of free will, which chose between good and evil inclinations. They believed in the existence of angels. They took a passively disapproving attitude toward the Roman occupation. They looked for a Messiah to deliver them.

Then came the Zealots. They accepted the legal standpoint of the Pharisees, but they took up an aggressive attitude toward the Roman occupation. They despised all Jews who sought peace and conciliation with the Roman authorities. Extremists among the Zealots resorted to terrorism and assassination, and became known as dagger men, frequently haunting public places, seeking to strike down persons friendly to Rome. They played a leading role at the battle of Masada in A.D. 73, where the defenders of the fortress committed suicide rather than surrender to the Romans.

Then there were the Sadducees. The Sadducees were the priestly party in charge of the temple. They accepted only the written law of the Bible. They denied the immortality of the soul, the resurrection of the body, the existence of angels. They apparently believed in a full doctrine of free will. They accepted Roman rule, and were generally wealthy and prosperous. They were the nearest equivalent in their day to the modern secular Jew.

Finally the Essenes, the Dead Sea sect, numbered only about 8000. They lived in communities in the east, apparently holding property in common. They were meticulous ritual purists, refusing to have anything to do with the temple, which they regarded as polluted. They lived ascetic lives of manual labor and seclusion, taking their communal meals in silence. Their scrolls were only discovered in the 1940s. They tell the story of their own persecution, set forth in great detail the rules they expect their members to observe, and they predict a coming war of the sons of light against the sons of darkness.[12]

Finally, in A.D. 66, the Jews revolted against Rome. The war lasted four years, from A.D 66-70. The Romans besieged Jerusalem, led by the general Titus, with 60,000 men and the latest siege equipment. The Jews had 25,000 men, divided into factions as usual, but fighting bravely. The Romans, of course, took the city, burned the temple, massacred thousands, and then held a victory procession in Rome, in which the most sacred objects of the temple were paraded in the street. (Titus's triumphal arch commemorating this event still stands in Rome.) To the Jews was left the fortress of Masada, on a rock 1300 feet high, which had been captured by their hero Menachem. But Menachem himself was murdered in a factional struggle, and the Romans attacked the fortress, which held about 1000 men, women, and children. The result was inevitable, granting the systematic siege methods of the Romans. Eleazer, the new leader, either forced or persuaded the defenders to engage in an act of mass suicide, leaving storerooms full of food to prove the point to the Romans that they had died voluntarily. Two women and five children survived.

In A.D 135, the Jews again revolted against the Romans, and this time the Romans decided from their vantage point that they had had it. They destroyed Jerusalem, building on its ruins a new city called Aelia Capitolina, in whose center was the temple of Jupiter. Thus at least militarily, the Hellenistic spirit triumphed over the Judaic spirit.

But before the Jews suffered this defeat, they had given birth to a child, Christianity.

That will be the subject of the next chapter.

Notes

1. Exodus 6:2–8 RSV
2. Exodus 19:3–5 RSV
3. Exodus 19:9–15 RSV
4. Exodus 22:20, 22:18 KJV
5. Philip P. Schaff, *History of the Christian Church, The Swiss Reformation*, vol. 2, (Edinburgh, n.p., 1893), p. 491
6. Amos 6:4–6 RSV
7. Isaiah 53:3–10 RSV
8. The first generation Christians, faced with the problem of how the Messiah could be put to death, identified Jesus with the Suffering Servant.
9. Job 1:21 KJV
10. Job 42:2 RSV
11. Job 11:7 RSV
12. The identification of the Dead Sea sect with the Essenes is disputed by a minority of scholars.

6

Christianity and Its World Outlook

In the first century A.D., a new religion arose partly within Judaism and partly around its periphery. This religion adopted and used the Hebrew Bible, which it called "The Old Testament." To this Bible it added gradually a corpus of documents that it called "The New Testament." According to this new religion, the Old Testament was a record of a temporary covenant made between God and the Jewish people through Moses. The New Testament, however, was a record of a new and final and everlasting covenant, made between God and the whole human race, through the intermediacy of a figure who had allegedly lived in the early part of the century, whom it called Jesus Christ. This new religion was Christianity. Its central figure, Jesus, it claimed, had presented himself to the Jews as their expected Messiah at the end of the third decade of the century. He had preached what they claimed was the final and complete theological and ethical revelation. But, according to Christian accounts, the Jewish establishment had rejected Jesus and persuaded the Roman authorities to put him to death. He had, however, risen from the dead, and ascended into heaven and was soon to return in glory to preside over a universal messianic kingdom. Meanwhile, he had left his disciples instructions to preach the gospel, in other words, the good news among both Jews and Gentiles—gathering them both into a new Israel, a universal community to await his return in glory.

The most careful and exhaustive analysis of the available documents and records surviving from the period has yet to reveal the real story behind the origins of Christianity. In round numbers, the period of origins is from the year A.D. 30 to the year A.D. 135. We can identify with certainty two significant events within the period. About the year 30, a Jewish prophet named John the Baptist appeared proclaiming that the kingdom of heaven was about to be inaugurated. Then, sometime between A.D. 90 and A.D. 135 the orthodox Jewish authorities excommunicated from the synagogues the sect, which they called the Nazarenes, the followers of another prophet named Jesus, who was alleged to have been associated in some way with this same John the Baptist. I quote the final cursing, "May the Nazarenes and the Minim (that is the heretics) forever be blotted out of the book of life." And from that time on, the Jewish Christians were not allowed to attend the Synagogues.

What had happened in between? What is the evidence for the existence of this new sect and for its teachings? We must look first at their literature. This literature centers around a person, whether mythical or real, who was called by the Greek name of Jesus, to which is added the title "Christos," or "anointed." The name and title are a translation of the Hebrew Yeshua Mashiah (Yeshua the Messiah).

The literature is divided into two main strata. The first or *earliest* stratum is known to have existed from A.D. 50–90 and consists mainly of letters or epistles, most of which are written to urban communities founded by the authors who are called "apostles," those who are "sent out"—in other words missionaries. The chief letter writer is named Paul. These letters treat Jesus as a real person, but show little interest in his biography or his teachings. Instead they treat him mainly as a divine or semi-divine personage who descended from heaven, died at some unspecific date at the hands of "the powers of this world" as a sacrifice for the sins of mankind, rose again, ascended into heaven and will soon return to judge the living and the dead and inaugurate a millennial kingdom on earth.

The second or *later* stratum of the literature, dating from A.D. 90–135, consists of (at the minimum) certain pseudo-letters of the apostles plus the writings of the "apostolic fathers" of the church, Clement Ignatius and Polycarp. These documents, while not rejecting the characterization of Jesus given in the earlier stratum, describe him also as a teacher and miracle worker who was crucified under the Roman governor, Pontius Pilate, who ruled Judea from A.D. 26 to 36.

Into this later stratum must be inserted three of the four gospels, Matthew, Luke, and John. The generally accepted dates of the four gospels are Mark c. A.D. 70, Matthew and Luke c. A.D. 90, and John c.

A.D. 100. The word "gospel" means "good news." The real authors of the gospels are unknown; the purpose of their composition was to flesh out the life of Jesus, giving him the lineaments of a real man, with the ultimate end of being read in churches and used to answer the questions of those being instructed in Christianity. They are founded in oral traditions and hypothetically in previously written documents. It is amazing that the biographical picture of Jesus that they give appears quite unknown to the authors of the documents of the first and oldest stratum. That the gospels reflect the life of a real person is largely dependent on the early dating of Mark at A.D.70, which places it in the older stratum. Since Matthew and Luke utilize Mark as a main source, this means that they are probably founded on an account of the life of a real person. On the other hand, if the date of Mark is pushed forward to about A.D. 90, as a few scholars think it should be, the evidence for the historicity of Jesus is accordingly decreased.

To explain these data, theories abound. It is possible to maintain that Jesus never existed at all, but in that case one has to resort to complicated theories to explain what happened. In my mind it is easier, using Ockham's razor, to postulate the existence of one person who was crucified and whose memory was transformed into a cult. But on either theory, a certain unique personality is portrayed in the first three gospels, a certain set of events, and a certain set of teachings, which as part of the Judeo-Christian tradition, have had an enormous effect on Western civilization.

Assuming then Jesus' existence, his public career probably lasted only through the years 28–30.[1] It began with his encounter with John the Baptist, a figure for whom there is evidence from outside the New Testament. John was a prophet preaching in the wilderness east of the Jordan in the area of the Dead Sea sect from which he possibly had emerged. He was a rather wild-appearing individual, dressed somewhat like a first-century "street person." He ate nothing but locusts and wild honey. He kept crying out (I am paraphrasing), "Repent, repent, for the kingdom of God is at hand. I have come to make clear the way before God's coming. It does you no good to be Jews. You're living lives as defiled as Gentiles. You need to be washed. In order to be saved from the wrath to come, you must repent and undergo a purifying bath or baptism (complete immersion) in the river Jordan, and then you must turn around and live a completely different kind of life." "What kind of life?" he was asked. "Well," he said, "anyone with two shirts must share with him who has none, and anyone who has food must do the same."

So it was the old message from the prophets of the desert, but with a new emphasis on the term "kingdom of God." Kingdom of God means the reestablishment of Yahweh over Israel. He had been king once before when they were nomads. Yahweh was their portable king whom they carried around in an ark. His will had been interpreted to the people by judges. But when they settled down to be an agricultural people, they had demanded an earthly king, and the judges had reluctantly consented. Saul was made King first. Then David, then Solomon. But life under the kings became corrupt. Why? Because the kings oppressed the people by their absolute rule, by heavy taxes and confiscations of property. So many pious Jews dreamed of the return of the kingdom of God. God would bring this about through the agency of a Messiah, or anointed leader, who would do away with all human kingdoms. But as to what would happen then, there was no settled opinion. John the Baptist, for instance, suggested the complete sharing of property, and he himself, as I said, may once have been a member of the Dead Sea sect.

I have said there is external evidence for John the Baptist. One piece of evidence is ancient. It comes from the great Jewish historian Josephus. Another piece of evidence I am going to mention in just a moment. It is contemporary, it is living twentieth-century evidence. But let us first mark the association of Jesus with John the Baptist. The gospels of Mark and Matthew assert unambiguously that Jesus began his public career by being baptized by John in the River Jordan. This would ordinarily mean accepting his teaching and becoming his disciple, and there is no reason to doubt such testimony. But John was soon arrested by Herod, the Roman puppet ruler of the area, on the ground that he criticized Herod's divorce and remarriage. John was eventually executed. Herod had John's head brought in on a tray for his stepdaughter at the latter's request. At this time, Jesus began to preach and many followers of John were swept up into the movement Jesus was starting.

Now, I noted that there is some living, twentieth-century evidence for John the Baptist. There exists today, in Iraq, a sect called the Mandeans, the best description of which is in a book by Kurt Rudolph called *Gnosis*.[2] The members of this sect claim to be disciples of John the Baptist, and their history truly seems to go back to the first century. They curse Jesus as an impostor who stole John's disciples. They likewise curse Moses, and (very quietly) curse Muhammad (and this is Iraq).They are violently anti-Christian, violently anti-Jewish, and also anti-Islamic. They claim to have come from Jerusalem in the A.D. 60s, and they claim that Jerusalem fell to the Romans because the Mandeans were persecuted by the Jewish establishment.

Some of the Mandeans living in the southern Euphrates area are very poor, and they are continually baptizing people in ditches. Can you imagine what they call the ditches? "Jordans." You see how a religious practice will sometimes remain for a millennium, after the people have lost the original meaning behind the practice. That is the nature of religion. Other Mandeans are very rich who have made fortunes from their control of the gold and silver markets of Baghdad. *They* baptize people in tiled swimming pools, which *they also* call "Jordans."

Now let us look at the preaching of Jesus. After the imprisonment of John the Baptist, Jesus started preaching in the villages of Galilee, his northern homeland. He taught in the synagogues and also in the open air. He taught with authority, not by appealing to the text of scripture or to tradition; he taught in parables, metaphors, proverbs, appealing directly to everyday experience and common sense. His manner of behavior was highly informal and he went about with many persons who would not ordinarily be found in the company of a Jewish religious teacher.

Like John the Baptist, Jesus preached that the kingdom of God was in the immediate future. But at present, the world was under the domination of satanic powers. How then, was the "Kingdom of God" to be established? Jesus rejected the idea of the Zealots, that it would be brought about by a military insurrection lead by a soldier-Messiah. He rejected also the idea of the Dead Sea sect, that the Kingdom of God required withdrawal into the desert, and preparation for a war of the sons of light against the sons of darkness. He did teach that the coming of the kingdom would be a supernatural event initiated by God and accompanied by earthquakes. But this supernatural event would only occur as the follow-up to Jesus' actions as Herald. Jesus' actions would consist in proclaiming the coming of the kingdom, healing the sick, and driving out demons.

The exorcisms were of great importance, since they were the sign that God had begun the process of redeeming the world from the power of Satan. But there was another vital task which Jesus regarded as part of his mission. This was to teach the ethics to govern those awaiting the coming of the kingdom. These ethics were to become the basic Christian ethics, but they were in no way contradictory to Jewish ethics. In fact, they consisted of a radicalization, in very compact form, of the Jewish ethics, a stripping of the latter doctrine down to basic premises, and the drawing out of consistent conclusions from these.

Jesus was a peripheral member of a Jewish school of thought called the Pharisees. The Pharisees, as we saw in chapter 1, believed not only in the written law of the Bible but in a larger oral tradition, adapting the commandments of the Bible to special circumstances. That Jesus belonged essentially to this school of thought, there can be no doubt. But he regarded the Pharisees as too observant on small, picky points, and not sufficiently observant on the large points. He said, Matthew 23, "The scribes and the Pharisees sit on Moses' seat; so practice and observe what they tell you, but not what they do; for they preach, but do not practice."[3]

As a Pharisee, Jesus also believed in an immortal soul, the resurrection of the body, divine punishment of sin, and the existence of angels. But Jesus belonged to a sort of informal subschool of pharisaism, which had its own special emphasis. These teachings apparently arose out of an attempt to solve the problem of evil. You will remember that problem from chapter 3. How does it happen that the man who follows the Jewish ethic is often the least successful in life? And how is it that the wicked prosper? Now, this subschool had an answer. If virtue inevitably led to success and happiness, people would be virtuous in order to succeed, and be happy. In other words, they would be virtuous in order to reap the rewards and avoid the punishment, and this would be wrong, for virtue should be practiced *as an end in itself,* as an intrinsic good. I will quote from a Jewish sage from the second century B.C. This is from a work known as *The Sayings of the Fathers,* "Be not like slaves who serve the master on condition of receiving remuneration, but be like slaves that serve the master *not* on condition of receiving remuneration." To put it another way, treat the commandments of the law as unconditional, commands which one obeys merely out of the pure motive of obedience, not out of the expected benefits of the covenant.

This is a strange foreshadowing of Kantianism. If Jesus had read

Kant, he might have said that the righteous should suffer in this world as a necessary part of the divine plan. For God does not want to make the rewards visible, in other words, God does not want to let the rewards appear in the "phenomenal world."

As a matter of fact, this is, in a nutshell, the complete Kantian formula. Man must act out of the pure devotion to duty, if he is to be moral, and any reward that he earns need not be apparent, that is, need not accrue to him in this phenomenal world. And the obligations of morality are unconditional or categorical imperatives. This doctrine is clearly taught by Jesus, when he says in Luke 17, "Does he thank the servant because he did what he was commanded? So you also, when you have done all that is commanded you, say, 'We are unworthy servants; we have only done what was our duty.'"[4] Actually, Jesus out-Kants Kant, for he says *we deserve no credit*. Even Kant says we deserve credit and should receive happiness in the next world.

I think we can see here the ancestry and source of the basic line of thinking that ultimately emerges in Kant. The first note that Jesus sounded in his ethics was that of unconditional obligation. The second note followed directly, a tremendous emphasis on the inner state or intention of the agent as opposed to the outer act. For instance, he attacked the performance of good deeds, (or *mitzvoth.* as they are called in Judaism) in order to gain a good reputation, or a reputation for piety. Third, and closely connected with this, he put great emphasis on the emotional state of the person he was morally evaluating. This led him to regard a person who merely had the urge to do something unlawful as just as evil as if he had actually committed the deed. I am paraphrasing: "You have heard that our forefathers were told, do not commit adultery. But what I tell you is this, if a man looks on a woman with a lustful eye, he has already committed adultery with her in his heart. You have heard that our forefathers were told, do not commit murder. But what I tell you is this, anyone who nurses anger against his brother must be brought to the Judgment."[5]

In making these statements, Jesus was only putting in the sharpest form the ideology of his own school of thought which as early as 200 B.C. had already condemned wrath and anger as in themselves sinful. I quote from another Jewish document at 185 B.C., the book called Ecclesiasticus, which is contained in the Septuagint, the Greek version of the Bible. "Wrath and anger, these also are abominations. If a man cherisheth anger against another, doth he seek healing from God? On a fellow man the man hath no mercy, and doth he ask forgiveness for his own sins?" All of this should be sufficient evidence that the germs of Christianity were already present in Judaism, and that Jesus thought of himself as merely radicalizing the demands of the Jewish law, drawing out what was implicit in it and demanding that people follow this stricter version of the law as a condition to their admission to the kingdom of heaven.

Now, I have mentioned as a first point of Jesus' ethics, his teaching that morality was unconditional and an end in itself. And as a second point, his emphasis on the intention of the agent as opposed to the external act. As a third point, his evaluation of the person as good or evil in terms of the latter's emotional state, such as lust or anger, rather than the act itself. I should like to add as a fourth point that he made some of the commands of the law concerning external actions, stricter. "Whoever divorces his wife and marries another commits adultery against her." The dominant feature in the teaching of Jesus is that God is pleased with those who adhere to the spirit of the law rather than to its letter. Some people would, he said, "strain at a gnat, and swallow a camel."[6] They were picky about small infractions, while losing sight of the good of the law. Jesus, however, introduced a new note which is only to be found in the smallest germ in the Old Testament. Whereas the Old Testament said love your neighbor,[7] including your non-Jewish neighbor, Jesus said, "love your *enemies*."[8] "If anyone strikes you on the right cheek, turn to him the other also; and if any one would sue you and take your coat, let him have your cloak as well."[9] Now all of this, of course, is the insistence on mercy, even to the most extreme sacrifice of justice.

As a matter of fact, Jesus is saying even more. He is saying—mercy *is* justice. Those who have ill treated you deserve your love more than those who treat you well. If you love only those who love you, what reward can you expect from God? Recall the "wilding" episode in Central Park: Cardinal O'Connor of New York paid a hospital visit to the woman who had been raped and beaten—but then afterward visited her rapists because he did not want to be partial. Now if mercy is justice, then what we have here is a new law, which Jesus obviously regards as the radicalization of Jewish ideas. "If your right eye causes you to sin, pluck it out and throw it away." (Some of the rabbis are supposed to have answered him, "Suppose one has only one eye?") "Verily I say unto you . . . " Jesus said, "there be eunuchs, which have made themselves eunuchs for the kingdom of heaven's sake."[11] Verily. The ideal is unlimited, unconditional, totally self-sacrificing love for others. It is called by the Greek word *agape*, unconditional love especially for those who don't deserve it, and it is different from two other kinds of love, *philia*, which means essentially benevolence, and *eros*, which means desire, erotic love, that grows out of some kind of need or instinct, urge, or impulse. This teaching of Jesus *seems* to go against the very essence of Judaism, which claims to be a religion of justice. Now, if it really *did* go against the essence of Judaism, it would make nonsense out of the very title of this chapter, "The Judeo-Christian Tradition."

The term *Judeo-Christian tradition* supposes a common essence shared between Jews and Christians. Does this teaching of Jesus negate the idea of a common tradition? I decided to consult a Jewish commentator on the New Testament. If it did, after all, wouldn't we expect the Jews to seize the advantage at this point and say that the basic ethics of Christianity cannot work in this world, and that therefore Christian ethics do not represent the true ethical ideal, and that the Jewish religion has a more practical, realistic ideal? Well, what do you suppose I found?

Here is the comment of a well-known Jewish New Testament scholar, Hyam Maccoby.[12] I am slightly rewording his comment: "As for Jesus' recommendation that one should not seek compensation if injured, but should offer the other cheek, he certainly did not mean that one is free from any obligation to compensate for injuries that one may *oneself* have committed." In other words, Maccoby is saying that it is all right for me to turn the other cheek, but I can't expect the other person to do so if I slap him. I must compensate him. "In Jewish thought," Maccoby says, *"the Christian ethics is 'an option.'"* "And," he adds, in Jewish practice "the very person who was ready to waive his own legal right to compensation would be the first to uphold the right of others, especially if he himself had injured them. The words of Jesus cannot be applied universally, Maccoby adds, for that "would result in a society in which oppression and violence would remain unchecked." Jesus' law of love, therefore, could not have been meant this way. Rather it must be interpreted as a "counsel of perfection," moral perfection, and, as such, is an *option* for especially righteous individuals in Judaism.

In other words, if I wish to be morally perfect, I shouldn't sue for injuries. This is an ideal for *me,* but I cannot, at the same time, expect *you* to follow it. So it comes down to the issue of selfishness versus unselfishness. *Perfect unselfishness is my personal ethical ideal,* but I can't demand that you follow it too. As a matter of fact, I must unselfishly defend your right to be selfish. Now, in using the words "counsel of perfection," Maccoby is borrowing a term from Catholic theology. According to traditional Catholic doctrines, the Sermon on the Mount is a set of counsels of perfection. Those who choose to follow them would, in Catholicism, be well advised to enter monasteries or convents, because among other things they will need to be supported by those who don't follow these counsels.

So you see, Ayn Rand was quite correct in attributing the same basic ethical values to both Judaism and Christianity, and in endorsing the common term "the Judeo-Christian tradition." And she was also right in analyzing this tradition as an ethic of self-sacrifice. Jesus, then, preached a radical doctrine of self- sacrifice, but his message, while going against the grain of everyday Judaic rule-of-thumb ethics, was really an attempt to draw consistent conclusions from the *basic premises* of Judaism. And let it be said that he had some support in that tradition.

Another feature of Jesus' teaching, which he carried out in life, was his self-identification with the poor, the humble, the "meek," the lowly, with social outcasts of all types, including prostitutes, and, even worse, agents of the Roman equivalent of the Internal Revenue Service. As Jesus saw it, many of the Pharisees had formed themselves into a religious elite, who covered their lack of true righteousness with a show of religious observance. They spiritually oppressed the poor and simple Jews of the countryside, by demanding of them literal observance of the smallest points, while granting themselves all sorts of loopholes. Jesus condemned Pharisees of this type and called them "whited sepulchers." That is why he is pictured as rescuing the woman taken in adultery by challenging the man who is sinless to cast the first stone. In taking this attitude, Jesus was only developing the attitude of his own school of thought. This exaltation of humility was accepted in theory by the ordinary Pharisee, but the latter did not regard poverty as a literal virtue also. Jesus did, and apparently adopted from the Dead Sea sect, the doctrine that it was harder for a rich man to be saved than for a camel to go through the eye of a needle.[13] Meekness, humility, poverty, acceptance of persecution, all the virtues that identify those who will be first in the kingdom of God, these were the ethics preached by Jesus.

Now, how did Jesus mean this doctrine of self-sacrifice and humility to be taken? It is not absolutely clear, but at the very least, he did set it up as an ideal. This ideal became predominant in Western civilization as soon as Christianity became predominant. And the failure to attain such an ideal has made men feel guilty ever since. The neo-pagan comment on this guilt has been best expressed in the words which the poet Swinburne put in the mouth of the dying emperor Julian the Apostate: "Thou hast conquered, O pale Galilean, and the world has grown gray from thy breath." So then, Jesus conquered an entire civilization, the Greco-Roman civilization. How did he do it? By attempting to practice his ideals completely. And by producing in the minds of men unsure of their own values, a vast reaction of awe. What did he think he was doing? Conquering the Greco-Roman civilization? Not at all. He knew nothing to speak of of the cultures of Greek and Rome. What he thought he was doing was announcing that the kingdom of God was about to begin, and preparing the way by persuading the people to follow his new ethic. But by and large, his countrymen seemed to reject it.

So he decided to go up to Jerusalem for the Passover, probably in the year 30, and lay down a challenge to the establishment. He went into the courtyard of the temple and physically attacked the money-changers, overturning their tables. Then, after this challenge to the priestly establishment, he hesitated. Perhaps he had expected God to intervene and establish his kingdom. As we know, God did not intervene. But the priestly establishment did: they apprehended him and they brought him before the Roman governor as a rebel. The Roman governor had him executed, Jesus up to the last minute expecting divine intervention, but at last dying with the Aramaic words, "Eloi, Eloi, lama sabachthani," in his mouth, "My God my God, why hast thou forsaken me?"[14] This probably happened on the Passover of the year 30, on the seventh of April, the fourteenth of the Jewish month of Nisan.[15]

His followers were disorganized and discouraged. However, they couldn't believe that this was the end. Suddenly word got around that he had risen from the dead. His disciples began to have visions in which he appeared and talked with them. Soon, they began to believe he was the Messiah. Soon after that, they were searching the scriptures and finding texts which seemed to imply the Messiah was to be killed as a martyr, and then return in glory. A few weeks later, on the feast of the Revelation of the Law ("Shabuoth" or "Pentecost"), a whole assembly of followers of Jesus broke out suddenly into ecstatic "speaking with tongues" and rushed out into the streets to proclaim what they called the "Gospel" or good news of the suffering and resurrected Messiah. An authentic-sounding comment is recorded in the Book of Acts, "These men are full of new wine,"[16] the people who were standing around said.

They made a surprising number of converts. They decided to stay around Jerusalem and await the return of Jesus. Thus was founded the Jesus sect. Now, many of the converts were poor, and the poor brethren had to be supported, as they continued to live in the city. And so the more prosperous members were asked to support the whole group while waiting for the return of Jesus in glory. This practice of supporting the poor as a matter of duty became an important ingredient in later Christian ethics, and eventually evolved into the welfare system.

The Jesus sect was hardly taken seriously by the Roman authorities since it preached a *supernatural* revolution. It was tolerated by the observant Jews, because its members were themselves very observant. But soon a group of Hellenistic Jews, who had several synagogues of their own in Jerusalem, began to enter the sect. The Hellenistic Jews were, as we have seen, living in tension between their Judaism and their Hellenism, and they were seeking some solution of the problem. These people became caught up in the idea that the coming of Jesus indicated that the whole temple cult was about to be abolished, and that the wall of separation between Jew and Gentile was about to be torn down. Its followers were driven out of Jerusalem to take up their headquarters in Antioch in Syria, where they began for the first time to call themselves "Christians," after the Greek word Christos, which means anointed King, equivalent to Messiah. From this moment, what had begun as a small Jewish sect, the followers of a failed Messiah, began to spread slowly out over the Mediterranean Basin. Even though the full weight of the Roman state was thrown against it, Christianity conquered and became, within three hundred years, the established religion of the Roman Empire, and has long survived the fall of that empire. Such is the power of ideas.

Christianity would have spread anyway wherever there were Jews, as did every messianic sect. It could never have become a world religion unless it became attractive to non-Jews as well. But to Gentiles, the idea of a Jewish Messiah was irrelevant, the idea of his execution a significant refutation of his claims, and the idea of the resurrection of the dead, an idea for horror night at the movies. Christianity had to be totally restructured in its *theology* while retaining the *values* preached by Jesus. This restructuring was accomplished by Paul, whose original Jewish name was Saul, after the first king of Israel.

Paul began his career as a fanatical type of Orthodox Jew who saw a particular danger in the Hellenistic wing of the Jesus sect, in other words, in Christianity. He signed on as an agent of the priestly establishment in Jerusalem to persecute the Christians, and was dispatched to Damascus to counter their activities. Now Paul must have been in some kind of conflict over his observant Judaism, and must have felt an unconscious attraction to the figure of Jesus and the claims of the Christians—an attraction which he denied and compensated for by the reaction formation of persecution. At any rate, just as he was approaching Damascus, in his moment of truth, he fell into some sort of fit. In his fit, he heard the voice of Jesus speaking to him, saying, "Saul, Saul, why persecutest thou me? It is hard for you to kick against the pricks."[17] Paul went temporarily blind, and upon being led into Damascus, was baptized into the Christian community there.[18] He then went forth on missionary activity of his own, proclaiming Jesus as Messiah in the Hellenistic synagogues. And then, if he was ejected, as he usually was, he preached to the Gentiles. In the latter activity, he was very successful. He made many converts, and he founded over the northern shore of the Mediterranean communities called *ekklesiai*, assemblies or churches.

This activity posed a delicate problem for the original Jesus sect in Jerusalem, the problem of to what extent these converts to Christianity should be obliged to follow the Jewish law. Just what final agreement, if any, was reached has been lost in the mist of history. But we do know that Paul maintained that the Gentile converts should not be obliged to follow the Law of Moses. In the context of this controversy, Paul developed his peculiar theology and ethics, the theology and ethics which differentiate Christianity from Judaism.

You will remember the essential Jewish position in ethics, that all men whether Jews or Gentiles, are obliged to live up to a minimum law. And that in the case of Jews, they are under the much heavier obligations of the Law of Moses. It is difficult to live a moral life, and more difficult to live a Jewish moral life, because of the presence in man of an evil inclination called *Yetzer ha Ra*. Still, it is possible to live a moral life, because man has free will, and in case he sins, divine forgiveness is always available. Now, Paul presents an entirely different picture of man. He does not deny the possibility of living up to the commandments by strenuous effort as a few men do. He himself claims that as a Jew he was "as to righteousness under the law blameless."[19] Those were his exact words, so he claims to have succeeded in living up to the Law. But he says that even those who do lead the moral life are under the power of Sin, Sin with a capital S. Even though they avoid specific sins, with a small s, they are still guilty of Sin with a capital S. Let us call this "Basic Sin," ancestral to Original Sin.

What is Basic Sin? It is a basic repressed hostility against the God who gave us the Law. And it is pride in one's own achievements and power, including the power to keep the law. If I break the Law, I am guilty, if I keep the Law, I am guilty. *Any* man believing himself in such a situation would feel despair. Man in this state is lost, and has been lost ever since Adam. No efficacy can be ascribed to anything man does. He is in utter depression. Continual studying of the Law, and working to keep up to its demands—they make things only worse. So Paul substituted for the Gospel of the Jesus sect, another Gospel, and the basic theme of that Gospel is the concept of the descent of the divine Savior. If I call someone my savior, I imply two things: that I am in danger of disaster, and that he alone has the power to rescue me.

Philosophically, this depends on the assumption that there are two realms: the upper realm, which is the realm of light; and the lower realm, which is the realm of darkness. Mankind is imprisoned in the lower world. We do not belong here in the realm of sin and death, but here we are. We cannot avoid Sin, sin with a capital S at least. We are determined by the nature of our situation. This is *metaphysical* dualism. You will remember that I spoke of Judaism as a *moral* dualism, that is a doctrine that holds that good values are somehow inserted into a world of inferior values. But Judaism, in most of its schools, hangs on to the doctrine that "the world," that is, *this* world, is metaphysically under God's complete rule and blessing. Still there is occasionally to be found in Jewish writings the sentiment that, "the Olem is a Golem," (the universe is a monster), out of God's control. This is mixed with stories of man's having fallen from the realm of light into the realm of darkness. Where did this doctrine come from?

Well, on the periphery of Judaism there existed another religion called Gnosticism. Gnostics are people who claim you can "*know*," in the sense that the "New Age" people "know." This Gnosticism is a sort of photographic negative of classical Judaism. Gnosticism means reliance on a *secret* knowledge, the "channeling" concept. The fundamental idea of Gnosticism is that this is a malevolent universe in which we live. The universe is a monster, the Olem is a Golem. This is a malevolent universe created by a malevolent deity, who is the Jewish God, Yahweh. This evil deity gave mankind the moral law, in more precise terms, the Jewish Law. This Law created misery for man. Many Jews were inclined to agree, as well as Gentiles, and Gnosticism had many converts. But the doctrine continued, there is another God above the creator, a higher God, who transcends the transcendent God. He is the high God who had compassion for poor humanity. He sent humanity a messenger to teach them how to free themselves from their creator, the Jewish God. This messenger is a divine Savior who can free mankind by giving them secret knowledge, or gnosis. But in order to reach mankind, the savior must enter the evil universe, beginning with the outermost astronomical sphere. He must deceive the ruling spirit of each of the planets to let him through. Eventually he is to reach earth, where the powers of the world, meaning the princes of the world and the Jewish establishment, will try to obstruct his work. Now, the doctrine of Gnosticism went on to say that the Gnostic savior then communicates to the chosen ones the knowledge (gnosis) and passwords by which they can, at their death, rise up to heaven passing through the sphere of the moon, the sphere of Mercury, the sphere of Jupiter, and so forth, fooling each one of the ruling spirits, until finally they get through, whizz past Yahweh, and go up and join the God of light, love, and mercy.

Paul was aware of this doctrine, and his own teaching sometimes sounds like a watered-down version of it. He retained the Jewish doctrine that Yahweh was a good God, and that Yahweh was the creator of the world, and that Yahweh was to be loved and obeyed, but at the same time he preached the doctrine of the radical fall of man. Now, according to Jewish teaching, sin had entered the world through Adam, but the guilt of the sin had *not* been inherited, only the punishment of death *had* been inherited, and furthermore, there was no one who absolutely had to sin. As a matter of fact, some of the rabbis actually claimed that there were four men in the history of mankind who had avoided sin. Now, Paul changed this: he taught that all men had some-how become radically involved in the consequences of Adam's sin, from one generation to the next down through the centuries. And that Moses had given the Law to mankind, not in order to redeem and sanctify mankind, but in order to bring mankind into repentance, to hold a mirror up to them so they could see how dirty their faces were, and realize that they were sinners and long for a Savior. Then Paul went on to teach that Jesus was the divinely appointed Savior, who had come in from the world of light, who had come down and who had taken on himself the sins of the world, and who *was crucified as a vicarious atonement* for the sins of the world, and resurrected as the conqueror of death, which came as the consequence of Adam's sin. Now this doctrine was a doctrine, not of collective redemption, but of individual salvation. It was the doctrine of the salvation of each indi-vidual soul by their faith in Jesus, by their identification with him, by their incorporation into his body through baptism and communion. Thus Paul gradually fashioned the theology on which Christianity was based. His teaching distantly resembled the Gnostic, but diverged far less from Judaism. One major point of his was that the key to salva-tion was *faith*, not *knowledge*.

The early church grew out of the communities founded by Paul, and by indeed other missionaries who went out from the Hellenistic syna-gogues. The early Christians were persecuted by the Romans, largely for the reason that they refused to do the equivalent of saluting the flag. That is, they refused to offer incense as a sacrifice to the statue of the Roman emperor. The Jews were exempted from this. The Romans thought it was good policy, good diplomacy, to exempt the Jews from this in order not to cause trouble. Now here was this new sect coming along, composed of some Jews, but mainly of Gentiles, claiming the same exemption. In other words, everybody seemed to be refusing to salute the flag, and the Romans sensed the threat of a crisis of loyalty This was one of the reasons why they began to persecute the Chris-tians, and to make martyrs of them, throwing them to the lions. Many Christians felt that by becoming martyrs they were actually gaining crowns of glory in heaven. They were purifying themselves from all the idolatry of Rome and of all the dirt and the sin that went along with everyday life in the Roman Empire. And so the blood of the martyrs became the seed of the church.

And the church eventually increased in numbers and triumphed over paganism and was established as the favorite cult of the whole empire, in the early fourth century, by the emperor Constantine. Constantine himself did not become a Christian at first; as a matter of fact he wasn't baptized until he was on his deathbed. But he established the Christian church as his favorite cult in the empire. And the church, once established, changed its character considerably. So now as an established church, people found Christianity the "in" thing to belong to. In other words, the world flowed into the church, and the bishops were no longer such holy men, they were arrogant men, very often, and they were always quarreling and fighting with each other over small points of doctrine or over priority of rank.

One of the reasons why Christianity triumphed was because it did have a fairly consistent set of doctrines. But by the fourth century, the tools of Greek philosophy were being used to make these doctrines more and more precise. And as Christian bishops struggled with each other over power, they began to accuse one another of heresy, namely unorthodox doctrine. Some of them claimed that Jesus was of the *same* substance with the father, *homoöusios*. Others maintained, quite to the contrary, that he was only of a *similar* substance, *homoiousious*. A lot of cynical people, at the time, said this is only the difference of an iota. But it was a great difference. It was the difference between being a finite being and being an infinite being, which is, of course, an infinite difference. So Constantine decided that Christianity wasn't bringing peace to the empire at all; it was bringing conflict and hostility. And so he felt it necessary to settle the difficulties: he called a great council which decided that Christ was really *homoöusios* with his Father. In other words, Christ was divine.

The emperor succeeding Constantine had to do the same thing, because once the bishops got the taste of calling each other heretics, they couldn't resist. There was a lot of competition for the control of wealthy churches, and there was a lot of power-lusting. And heresy-hunting became one of the essential means of this pursuit of power. Meanwhile, the emperors were doing their best to quiet down the whole ruckus, and so they began to call these councils and they would send out commands to come to the council, commands that were worded something like this (when there was both a man and a woman emperor at one time): "Constantine and Irene, by the grace of God Roman Caesars," command all you bishops to come to such and such a city, transportation paid. And indeed they did pay the transportation of the bishops to the councils and they granted them safe passage, and guarded them and protected them. (The Constantine mentioned immediately above was not the one who established Christianity but a successor of over 400 years later.)

At these councils, the old doctrines of Christianity became what we call dogmas. Now, a dogma is a precise statement which one is forced "sincerely" to agree with. The bishops at the council passed dogmas, that is they took a vote—under the inspiration of the Holy Spirit, of course. And frequently during the debate they were actually striking each other and pulling each others' beards. (There is a famous joke which claims that the Pope gained supremacy in the Western church by ordering that all clergy be clean-shaven.) At these councils they would debate and then pass dogmas. The dogmas were stated in very precise philosophical terms, and then at the very end of the dogmatic statement would come the words, "and if anyone believes to the contrary, let him be anathema, anathema, anathema." And the dissenting bishops would then be thrown out of the church and their sees taken over by more orthodox candidates waiting in the wings.

By the year 500, four important general councils had been held: the first council of Nicea, which met in 325; the first council of Constantinople, which met in 381; the council of Ephesus, which met in 431; and the council of Chalcedon, which met in 451. The first council declared Jesus divine. The second council declared the Holy Spirit divine. So now you had the Trinity by 381. The council of Ephesus proclaimed that Jesus was one person, not just a human person dwelled in by the son of God, another person. The council of Chalcedon proclaimed that Jesus had two natures, divine and human.

The results of these four councils I call *classical Christianity*. Classical Christianity is the essential position out of which came the two main churches of Christendom; Catholic and Orthodox, who make up three-quarters of all Christians today. Classical Christianity is characterized by belief in the Trinity, in the radical fall of man, in salvation by being incorporated into Christ by baptism and communion. It accepts the radical ethics of Jesus as the ideal, but this is for monks and nuns primarily; the rest are allowed to follow a minimum standard. The ideal life is one of chastity, poverty, and obedience. For centuries, classical Christianity existed in alliance with the state, which imposed its doctrines and its values by force upon the people. You know the story of the Inquisition; it is moot whether the church has yet fully renounced this position.[20]

I want to consider for a moment the free-will controversy in the church. About the year 400, there arose a great Christian teacher whose doctrines were to have an enormous effect on the whole future of Western civilization. This time it was a good effect. His name was Pelagius. Pelagius was a defender of free will, the main defender of free will in the history of Christianity. He was shocked by the common teaching that sin was unavoidable. He said that this was a gross insult to both God and man.

Pelagius preached unconditional free will and unconditional moral responsibility for our acts. Man alone among creatures, he said, is free and responsible. Evil is always possible as a choice, but the possibility of choosing good implies the possibility of choosing evil. Free will itself is a gift of God, but its exercise is up to us. According as we act, we merit praise and blame. There is no overwhelming bias toward wrongdoing, no original sin, as Christians are accustomed to teach, not even an evil inclination as the Jews teach. The doctrine of original sin, he said, is a moral nightmare. It claims that we are to blame for things we have never done. It is also a *metaphysical* nightmare. It implies that souls as well as bodies are inherited from our parents. In effect, it says our souls are just pieces of Adam's soul, and that they have been handed down the generations with the "acquired characteristic" of sin, to put it in the language of modern biology.

Pelagius was asked by his opponents, "If there's no original sin, why do *you* baptize infants?" Pelagius, who was a very clever man, turned this question around against his adversaries and said, Why do *you* baptize infants? According to your theory, the infant should have inherited the forgiveness bestowed upon his parents in *their* baptism. No, he said, baptism is merely a rite allowing membership into the church. As for man, he is neither good nor bad by nature, but free. If there is no evil impulse, there is no good impulse. What then is grace? Grace is the power of choosing, he said. Secondly, it is reason, which reveals to us proper values and virtues. Thirdly, it is the revelation of God's Law. Men were so surrounded by bad customs and bad examples that the light of reason grew dim, he said. And the will became clogged, and God had to intervene, and that's why revelation was given. This is a very mild doctrine of grace. It is possible, however, for everyone to be virtuous, no matter how strenuous the acts of will required. God will reward the good and punish the evil man.

What about predestination? Well, that is merely God's foreknowledge of who the good people are going to be and who the bad people are. He looks ahead and he foresees the bad committing evil acts and the good performing good acts, and he predestines the evil to condemnation and the good to heaven. God is no favorer of persons. "By merit alone, men advance in holiness," he said. "It is possible to observe all the commandments without sinning." Pelagius's ablest disciple, a bishop named Julian of Eclanum, went on to proclaim that man's free will put him in a position of complete independence with respect to God. "*A Deo emancipatus homo est.*" "*Man is emancipated from God,*" said Bishop Julian. Now this was a very radical position to take in the church. Then, along came the man who answered Pelagius, Augustine.

Augustine's theory started with Adam. Adam was created as a perfect man with a stunning IQ, the king of the Bell Curve, in perfect health and perfect innocence. His emotions and his physical urges, according to Augustine, were under the control of his reason. Thus his being was in a state of inner order, because reason is of higher intrinsic value than the lower parts of man. Hence, the lower parts ought to be subject to reason. This, of course, was a premise derived from Plato. But in addition to the hierarchy of intrinsic values within man, namely reason, the emotions, the physical appetites, there was another hierarchy of supreme importance. There was the hierarchy of, at the very top, God, the supreme good, then the angels, then man, then the lower animals. Man would be in God's favor, in the beginning, in Paradise, as long as he observed this hierarchy, and did not try to make himself equal to God. This would be a sin. (Now, included here we have a Platonic premise in Augustine's thought, that there is a great chain of being, with the divine being being of intrinsically the highest value at the top.) Adam was in perfect health and would enjoy perfect youth once he was allowed access to the tree of life.

But there was another tree to which he was *denied* access. That was the tree of knowledge of good and evil, the eating of whose fruit would make him equal to God. Now, Adam had free will which Augustine defines as the freedom to sin or not to sin. But, Adam did sin, preferring the lower intrinsic value, himself, to God, who was the higher intrinsic value. This was an act of rebellion against the cosmic order of intrinsic values, putting oneself above God.

As soon as Adam had committed this sin, a punishment struck at his inner order. Adam's lower faculties, his emotions and his appetites, revolted against his reason. Thus, a microcosmic disorder was the price paid for a violation of the macrocosmic order. Since Adam's reason was now powerless against his emotions and appetites, it was *impossible for him not to sin.* In Augustine's words, "Man cannot not sin." *"Non posse non peccare."*

At this point, God blocked Adam off from the tree of life, and man became subject to disease and death. God expelled Adam from Paradise, which supplied automatic economic abundance. From now on, Adam had to toil for his bread by the sweat of his brow. These curses Adam passed down to his descendants. But he passed on the *guilt* of his actions as well. All of Adam's descendants share his guilt and share it from the moment of conception. Why do we all share his guilt? Because in Augustine's words, "All were already *identical* with him in that *nature* of his." You see the Platonic concept involved there. We all participate in universal human nature, and universal human nature was totally and exhaustively present in that nature of his. In other words, our identity *consists* literally of broken off pieces of Adam's identity. As the old New England primer put it, "In Adam's fall we sinned all."

I want to conclude with a few words on the Christian view of God, man, and values. I present this in greater detail in the next chapter. The Christian view of God, man, and values shares some essential points with the Jewish, and adds some of its own. Like the Jewish, the Christian view postulates a transcendent, all knowing, all powerful God who created the universe out of nothing, saw how good it was, and who rules over it by his providence. Like the Jewish, the Christian view of man postulates a sharp distinction between the good way of life and the bad way of life. And also like the Jewish, locates the standard of value beyond the reach of human reason, in the incomprehensible, divine mind. Like the Jewish, it believes in a first sin, and a primal fall of man. But it adds to this the doctrine that man's fall was the catastrophe such that there is no way in which he can save himself to get back into God's good graces, and that therefore he needs a divine savior. And that since this Savior must come down, must descend to rescue man, he must become incarnate in human flesh, must become man. This Savior, now half human and half divine, must then incorporate the men he saves into himself, by sharing his body with them through the sacraments of Baptism and the Eucharist and taking them back to heaven with him.

So that in Western Christianity, which formally adopted Augustinianism at the Council of Orange in 529, we have an emphasis on the depressed state of man, on his passivity in being saved, and on his mystical incorporation into the Godhead. What does this mean? It means a sense of tremendous tension between the possibility of total eternal depravity on the one hand, and the possibility of an ecstatic, mystical union with God. *This is the essence* of the classical Christian metaphysics of the Catholic and Orthodox churches. This is the essence of the classical Christian ethic, this tremendous difference between the possibilities of horrible depravity and ecstatic joy forever with God.

Notes

1. I am here adopting the recent chronology of John P. Meier. Of his *A Marginal Jew Rethinking the Historical Jesus*, vol. 1, New York, Doubleday, 1991, p. 402. Meier opines that the date of the crucifixion was Friday, the 14th of Nisan (April 7), A.D. 30.
2. Kurt Rudolph, *Gnosis, the Nature and History of Gnosticsim*, San Francisco, Harper and Row, 1984, pp. 343-66.
3. Matthew 23:2–3 RSV
4. Luke 17:9–10 RSV
5. Matthew 5:27–28, 21–22 RSV
6. Matthew 23:24 KJV
7. Leviticus 19:18 RSV
8. Matthew 5:43–44 RSV
9. Matthew 5:39–40 RSV
10. Matthew 5:29 RSV
11. Matthew 18:18, 19:12 KJV
12. See his *The Mythmaker: Paul and the Invention of Christianity*, New York: Harper and Row, 1987, pp. 39–40. This book may be described as a "sympathetic polemic" against Christianity.
13. Mark 10:25; Matthew 19:24; Luke 18:25 RSV
14. Most commentators treat this as a cry of despair or as simply inexplicable, but it is actually the first verse of Psalm 22, which ends on a note of triumph. The original tradition attributing the words to Jesus may have been motivated by the desire to make the crucifixion of an innocent holy man the prelude to that very man's vindication as the "suffering servant" who turns out to be the Messiah.
15. I am adopting Meier's dating. See John P. Meier, *A Marginal Jew: Rethinking the Historical Jesus*, New York, Doubleday, 1991, vol. 1, p. 402.
16. Acts 2:13 KJV
17. Acts 24:16 KJV
18. It was apparently in Syria that the followers of the Jesus sect were first called "Christians."
19. Philippians 3:6 RSV
20. See *Catechism of the Catholic Church*, Libreria Editrice Vaticana, Liguori, MO, Liguori Publications, 1994, main entries 2106–09.

7

The Ethical, Political, and Economic
Teaching of the Judeo-Christian Tradition

This chapter will deal with the ethical, political, and economic doctrines of the Judeo-Christian tradition. We will first focus on the basic
ethical position of the tradition, and then consider the application of
that position to politics and economics. That basic ethical position I
will refer to as *ethical dualism*. Ethical dualism is the doctrine that the
values which should govern our daily living are given to us from a
transcendent source outside the universe and that these values are, on
many crucial points, opposed to the values that we might follow were
we to depend merely on reason. The values revealed from the transcendent source are regarded as higher and purer then worldly values,
and they are supposed to be definitive of true morality. They are the
values that characterize what some of the professors of our academic
establishment call "the moral point of view" or simply "moral values,"
or "morality."

Historically, the observant Jews identified the true and pure values
with those of their Law, the Torah, and they identified the false values
with those of the Caananites and other non-Jewish people living around
them; the "high rollers" of the time, who lived a life of luxury and
corruption. This transcendent source had to be a *god*, and the god had
to be *formless*, for if the god had a form he would represent a *limited*
area of human concern, and would be opposed by other gods repre-
senting other human interests. Think of Venus versus Diana, in Roman mythology. Venus was the goddess of eroticism and Diana was
the goddess of chastity, and they worked against each other all the
time.

All pagan religions were of this nature. They manifest a pluralism of values. For instance, Kali, the goddess of destruction, is the patroness of thugs in India. This is to deify contradictory human values. But the God of the Jews was above and beyond all human values. He did not have to struggle with any other God. He was the supreme master of the universe, the creator. His values and his laws were above any merely worldly values. That is why I have called this position ethically dualistic.

Now, you must not confuse this with the sharp distinction between black and white that characterizes Objectivism. Objectivism believes in the ethical *duality* of good values on the one side and bad values on the other, and adds that they are in sharp conflict. In contrast, ethical dualism believes that true values come from beyond, from outside the world, which is quite a different thing. In other words, ethical dualism is based on metaphysical dualism. The position took centuries of conflict before it finally crystallized and was proclaimed, once and for all, in the most uncompromising way, by the scribe Ezra in 400 B.C.

Judaism asserts the existence of two opposing sets of values, good values, those revealed in the Law; and evil values, those deviating from the Law. What now of man? Does he have the ability to choose between the good values and the bad values? In other words, does man have free will? Well, the Jews assert that in every human being there are two urges, one which is called the evil inclination, and the other which is called the good inclination. Now the Jews were not *radical* metaphysical dualists like the Zoroastrians. I quote the Talmud now to give you the Jewish point of view. "The holy one, blessed be he, created both inclinations, the good inclination and the bad inclination. The evil inclination exists from birth and continues for the whole of one's life. The good inclination is thirteen years younger."[1] It comes into existence at one's Bar Mitzvah, and continues for the rest of one's life.

What is the nature of the evil inclination? The evil inclination consists of self-assertion, ambition, and sexual desire. It is man's natural impulse as an inhabitant of this world. "How do you know when a person is under the influence of the evil inclination?" the Talmud asks. "Just watch him. It is when he ogles with his eyes, straightens his hair and walks with a swaggering gait." Now, we have already said that God created the evil inclination, and it is written in the Bible that God looked upon all his creation and saw that it was very good. "Therefore," argued the Rabbis, "the evil inclination is good, in fact very good." "Why is the evil inclination good?" asks the Talmud. This is the answer: "Were it not for that impulse, a man would not build a house, marry a wife, beget children, or conduct a business." In other words, he would not survive. The distinction is between worthiness to live and ability to live.[2]

Now, what is the good inclination? It emanates from the Law. It is the influence of revelation upon man. It checks, shapes, and also contradicts the evil impulse. There is an ethical ambivalence inherent in the Judaic tradition. The evil impulse is necessary to survival. It is necessary in order to thrive in the world. The world is good. Therefore, the evil impulse is naturally good. Why is it evil then? Because it is liable to tempt man to get too big for his breeches. It is liable to be misused because it leads man to be over-assertive so that he threatens God, and the Bible tells us that Yahweh is a jealous God. The evil impulse led man to build the skyscraper of Babel. Against this pride of the evil impulse is set the good impulse or inclination which comes from studying the Law. To quote again from the Talmud, "The holy one, blessed be He, said to Israel, 'My children, I have created the evil impulse and I have created the Torah as an antidote to it. If you occupy yourself with the Torah, you will not be delivered into the power of the evil impulse.'" So there is an ethical ambivalence in Judaism. The natural impulses of man are called the evil inclination, even thought they are necessary to survival, which is good. True morality consists in following the Law which is set over and against the evil impulse.

In between the evil and the good impulses stands free will. The Judaic tradition more than any other gave us the concept of free will. Although all other events may have been decreed by God, the choice between good and evil has not. Man can decide whether to act virtuously or viciously. "Behold . . . " says God in the book of Deuteronomy, "I have set before you life and death, blessing and cursing: therefore choose life, that both thou and thy seed may live."[3] Free will thus stands in between the good inclination, which urges the individual to do good, and the evil impulse which urges him to do evil. Man must choose by throwing the weight of his will with one or the other impulse. Some men choose good. They are the good people, the righteous. Some men choose evil. They are the wicked people, the unrighteous. Since both groups are descended from Adam, you cannot blame

Adam. The individual is responsible. This is the rabbinical view, the view of the Pharisees, whose intellectual descendants are, today, the Orthodox sect.

Free will has always been the majority view among Jewish religious authorities, and they passed it on to some Christians whom we will deal with later. The good impulse is embodied in studying the Law. If you want to be really good, you study the Law. To quote the Talmud again, "If this despicable thing, the evil inclination, meets you on the way, drag it along to the house of study."

But there is some hint in the Talmud of a tendency toward determinism. The evil impulse may take possession of a man even though he has struggled earnestly against it. What is such a person to do? Well, the determinism is mixed with pragmatism. "If a man sees that his evil impulse is gaining the mastery over him, let him go to a place where he is unknown, put on black clothes and do as his heart desires, but let him not profane the name of God publicly." Now, obviously, this does not mean do a black cape like Batman, and commit murder: it cannot mean commit murder. It cannot mean commit idolatry. Readers of the Talmud obviously equate it here with illicit sex, as in Christianity. The text seems to assume that, although in theory (nevertheless in practice) it is possible to avoid sin, to expect everyone to avoid it is hopeless. The Talmud and rabbinical authorities are divided on the question of whether any man has ever been sinless. One school maintains that no man has ever been sinless. The other school maintains that four men have been sinless. This doctrine might be called statistical determinism, as in subatomic physics. Although the Jews are responsible, more than anyone else, for introducing into Western history the doctrine of the freedom of the will, nevertheless their interest was totally practical and confined to the choice, to sin or not to sin. They developed no metaphysical view of the nature of free will, or of how it could coexist with the evil and good inclinations. Indeed, as the great Jewish historian Josephus remarks, "They left all other events to the will of God." That is, to the predestination of God, except the choice between good and evil. It remained for Christianity and Islam to extend the idea of predestination to man's other choices as well. Nevertheless two of the ablest theorists of universal determinism were secularized Jews, Baruch Spinoza and Sigmund Freud.

We now come to the transcendent God, as the source of moral values. To simplify greatly, let us take the Ten Commandments. They were supposedly written on two tablets by Moses. The laws on the *second* tablet direct one to honor one's parents, they forbid murder, adultery, stealing, bearing false witness, coveting what is one's neighbor's. One might think they might be derived from reason, but the Judaic position is that once reason enters, doubt enters. All sorts of qualifications and exceptions may be introduced. Perhaps one's parents are not deserving of honor. In other words, the tradition wants to foreclose the possibility of exceptions. They want to make these rules unconditional, and the only way to do this apart from rational demonstration is to make them the commandments of an authority who by definition cannot be questioned. A set of authoritarian premises is required. These premises are required by the commandments on the *first* tablet—I am Yahweh your God, you shall worship no other Gods, nor make an image, nor bow down to it, for I am a jealous God, you shall not misuse my name, you shall keep holy the Sabbath. These commandments on the first tablet literally put the fear of God into the sinner. They establish all the other commandments with the force of taboos. And in Jewish history, the Law, once given, kept expanding as the rabbis built what they call "fences" around the Law, additional precautionary measures to prevent even unintentional encroachment. The official number of commandments of the law is 613.

We now come to the subjects of faith and reason, or the epistemology of Judaism. The interest in metaphysics, which so characterized the thinkers of Greece, was lacking in the Jews. The Jews started with ethics, and they moved on to metaphysical questions only when answering the metaphysical questions was absolutely necessary to buttress their ethical position. Beyond this, they believed it was dangerous to go. The Talmud says, "Whoever reflects on four things, it were better that he had never been born. What is above, what is beneath, what is before and what is after. Why does the story of creation begin with the letter Beth? Because the letter Beth is closed on all sides and only open in the front. Similarly you are not permitted to inquire into what is before and what is behind, but only what has existed from the actual time of creation." Action, not inquiry is the chief thing. This fundamental attitude characteristic of Orthodox Judaism was passed from them to the Christians and to the Muslims all the way down to the Ayatollah.

I want to add some remarks on Jewish economic ethics, and later to compare these with Catholic and Protestant views on proper economic behavior. Some people are confused by the fact that Jews have been so prominent in capitalistic activity and the defense of capitalism on the one hand, and on the other hand they have been among the foremost enemies of capitalism. I think I can answer this question. The Jewish attitude is this-worldly. But within the this-worldly attitude, there are two poles, the egoistic and the altruistic, the individualistic, the collectivistic, the ethics of the settled Jew versus the ethics of the nomadic Jew wandering in the desert. And so we always have with us the Jewish primitivist wanting to return to a communal state.

Nevertheless, the question may be fairly asked: is there *any* Jewish other-worldliness? The answer is yes, but it is different. It is found in the idea of a messianic age, projected to sometime in the future. And in that messianic age or kingdom of God all the goodies to enjoy will be material, physical, all the goodies will be here. But the *means* by which these goodies will be produced will be supernatural. The whole point of view is that of the consumer. Meanwhile, according to Jewish doctrine, Orthodox doctrine, the dead will be supernaturally raised, the whole family will be reunited. The millennial point of view, or messianic point of view as we call it, is still taught by ultra-Orthodox rabbis. Among secular Jews of altruistic orientation, we often see adherence to socialism and even to pure communism, as a millennial dream. All the goods will be here and they will be material goods, but how will they be produced, and how will process be determined? "That," replied the early Marxists, "is an unscientific question. We're not yet at that stage of the dialectic. We will know when we get there," which is just a secular way of saying the goods will be produced and distributed supernaturally.

We have already seen that an essentially tribal ethic, when applied to an urban or even an agricultural environment, will not work. Indeed, it does not even work in a nomadic environment. And that is why we have civilization, because a few superior nomads understood the message. The attempt to make the unselfishness ethics work in the world leads to worldly failure. Those who realize this became egoists, at least on one side of the brain, and they tried to combine that touch of health with a verbal allegiance to altruism on the other side of the brain. Those, on the other hand, who continued to take the tribal ethic seriously, generated the idea of a world wherein life is unconditional, and fruit falls off the trees into one's hands automatically, a world wherein all effort, mental and physical, is superfluous.

Why? The proof is simple, and it goes like this. Mental and physical effort require planning ahead, and evaluation with reference to the needs and wants of the self. But this is egoistic, and we cannot have that. We must have a world in which such activities are unnecessary. So we must somehow abolish the very conditional character of life. *Now, this is an argument which is implicit in the thinking of all Utopians.* The conditionality of life requires egoism, egoism is bad; therefore, we must abolish the conditionality of life. When we reach the fourth movement of this logical symphony, we come to a mad finale, *allegro molto vivace.* We must abolish reality. This abolishing of reality can be done in two basic ways: to spiritualize man completely by extricating his spirit from his body, and sending his spirit to heaven, which is the Platonic answer, the Greek answer; or, another way, the Jewish way, leaving man in his body on earth, and then to extricate that body, together with the whole earthly environment from the curse of egoism and therefore of conditionality. This is the millennial way. Now, the Jews by the very nature of their value system, were committed to life on earth, and they were committed in the latter part of their development to the doctrine of the resurrection of the body. So they were committed to the second view, that an ideal life lay in a golden age in the future, wherein the Garden of Eden would be restored, all work abolished, the conditionality of life for all animal species abolished, food simply drops from the trees into one's hand, the lion lies down with the lamb, the slaughter of animals is abolished, and everyone lives contentedly albeit on a vegetarian diet. Remember, the Garden of Eden was on earth.

How could such an order be established? Only supernaturally, said the really consistent Jews and Christians. By God's literally taking power and establishing his kingdom over the whole earth; this is what is meant by the kingdom of God, or the millennium. Now, there have been Jews and Christians, really ex-Jews and ex-Christians, who have tried to retain the value system of the millennium without the supernatural apparatus necessary to maintain it. And of course, they are the socialists and Marxists that I referred to a few minutes ago. They proclaim that what they want to establish on earth are the values of the prophets, the ethics of the Sermon on the Mount, without the dogmatic religious beliefs that lie behind them.

I mentioned before the existence of two sects. I want to remind you of them once again, the Rechabites and the Essenes. In the Judeo-

Christian tradition, some people have attempted to revive the pure life, the pure ethics of the tribe. We have seen this in Judaism among the Rechabites and the Essenes. The Rechabites refused to dwell in towns or to build houses. They were sworn to remain tent dwellers. They refused to plant vineyards. They refused to drink wine. At one time, also, there was a kind of religious order among the ancient Jews known as the Nazirites, who also abstained from wine, and who were forbidden to cut or trim their hair in any way. Then there were the Essenes, probably identical with the Dead Sea sect, who lived in a great commune, administered daily baptisms, and laid out military plans for the coming war of the sons of light against the sons of darkness. In Christianity, of course, we have monasticism, but we also have messianism and millennialism. In Islam we have all sorts of strange sects like this, especially among the Shiites. And we can see it in the present Iranian revolution, with its veiling of women and its lust for blood. All these phenomena represent tribalist movements within a settled civilization, which by its nature calls for individualism.

Now we come to Jesus' teaching concerning the politics of the kingdom. Remember it was a kingdom. He did not preach a republic of God with a bill of rights, but a Kingdom of God with a bill of duties. The Messiah was to rule absolutely over the whole earth. Needless to say, there would be no separation of church and state. The incident in which Jesus said, "Render therefore unto Caesar the things which are Caesar's and unto God the things that are God's,"[4] means that he is giving that advice as long as the Romans are in power, although he expected God to abolish the Roman power. As for those who were to be the subjects of the kingdom, Jesus expected they would be a select group chosen from the beginning of the world. The evidence of the Gospels is that he believed in predestination, for in one place he says that he is speaking in parables lest certain people understand and be forgiven.[5] Again, the use of force is not ruled out by Jesus. Everyone is invited to a great messianic banquet, but then people give all sorts of excuses, whereupon Jesus directs his disciples to scatter and kidnap people, bring them in to replace the people who have refused the invitation.

Let us look at his teaching concerning the economics of the Kingdom of God. If Jesus had written a book called *Superhuman Action: A Treatise on Economics*, his views on production would have been summed up in the following formula: Consider the lilies of the field and the birds of the air, they toil not, neither do they spin, but their heavenly father supplies all their needs. Let it be the same with you, take no thought for the morrow, what you shall eat or what you shall wear, your father in heaven knoweth all your needs. Which of you by taking thought (that is by planning) can add to his stature?[6] So just as one's height is a brute fact of nature, so is the appearance of products on the scene. As for consumption, Jesus' ethics is one of self-sacrifice in sharing, combined with suspicion of wealth. "It is easier for a camel to go through the eye of a needle,"[7] he says, "than for a rich man to enter the kingdom of God." "If thou wilt be perfect [if you want to do more than follow the law]," he said to the rich young man, "go and sell that thou hast, and give to the poor."[8]

Now we come to Christianity's introduction of a true dualism between the spiritual and the secular. By the year 100, Jesus had not yet returned, and the church began to de-emphasize its belief in the nearness of the end of the world. Instead, the church began to claim that *it* was the Kingdom of God on earth, a spiritual enclave opposed to what was called "the world." The work of the church was now conceived as the salvation of individual souls by rescuing them from "the world." This meant freeing them from bodily values, and transporting them to a higher realm of spiritual values. Where did the church get that idea? Plato. This is the Platonic influence coming into the church. Life in the church was conceived as a strenuous preparation for entrance into heaven. Just as Plato had conceived philosophy as preparation for death (those are his exact words), so now the church conceived the Christian life. The old Jewish messianic doctrines were replaced by a Platonic scheme. The resurrection of the body in the millennium was replaced by the immortality of the soul and its life in heaven contemplating the divine essence (Roman Catholicism) or being vitally united with the divine energies (Eastern Orthodoxy).

The church now made a sharp distinction between the spiritual realm and the secular. The spiritual was good, the secular bad. We are moving slowly into the Catholic-Orthodox scheme of things. In the years 100 to 300 when the church was being persecuted to take any political or military office, or to enter the fields of drama, art, or rhetoric was frowned upon for all these were inextricably mingled with idol worship or emperor worship. The church excommunicated any member who became a school teacher, because every school teacher had to lead the class in divine reverence to the emperor in the morning. Prayer in the schools! It excommunicated carpenters, stucco workers, cabinet makers, gold-leaf beaters, painters, workers in bronze, engravers, florists, and anyone else who indirectly contributed to pagan temple worship. No participation in war, gladiatorial fighting, or capital punishment was allowed. The pagan naturally felt that, if Christianity prevailed, society would go to pieces. This did not happen immediately, for there were many Christians during this period who managed to find a way of compromise. Some of them even became pagan priests or flamines. They would preside at ceremonies in which the emperor's statue was worshipped even though they carefully avoided worshipping the emperor's statue themselves. These Christian/pagan flamines would have long sticks around which were wound flowers, and they would come to the fore in the Roman city and they would say, "would the emperor worshipping party please proceed," and the non-Christians then had to come out and worship the emperor, and the Christian posing as a pagan priest would lead them until suddenly he would disappear around the corner. So that gives you the idea of how some Christians managed to survive. It is an amazing fact that centuries later Immanuel Kant would perform the same disappearing trick at the door of his university chapel after he as Provost had led the faculty to prayer.

Society did not immediately go to pieces, and the overall reason was what we call the Constantinian establishment. By the Constantinian establishment, is meant, literally, the establishment of Christianity as the official religion of the Roman Empire. This took place in the fourth century by a series of official acts. But the term, "Constantinian establishment," has acquired, at the hands of historians, a far deeper meaning. In this deeper sense, it refers to the alliance between the church and the secular order that lasted from the fourth century to the nineteenth century. The dominant notes were compromise, mutual support, a sharing of the spoils, the blessings of the church on the established political and economic order, persecution of heretics, Jews, and pagans, by the State. Most of the professions were now reopened to the Christians. In many towns, the Bishop was the most important man in town. Augustine, for instance, complains that as Bishop of Hippo he spent more time mediating lawsuits and presenting petitions than he did on church matters.

In this situation, the church continued to preach its ideal, which was that of primitive communism. St. John Chrysostom, Bishop of

Constantinople, proclaimed from the pulpit his desire to turn the capital city into a communistic fellowship of *agape* or selfless love, but in the same sermon he calms the fears of his wealthy listeners by telling them that, in the present sinful world, such ideas are impossible to put into practice. Now, since most Christians in the fourth century lived in cities, they engaged in trade, but from the church's standpoint, trade was regarded as ethically lower than agriculture or manual labor. It was, in theory, permissible only when the selling price equaled the cost of production plus a moderate profit, the sum necessary to gain a living.

Only retail trade was regarded as respectable. The church forbade any wholesale business which involved credit and interest, which it called usury, of course. To justify this, it appealed to the Jewish law that interest must not be accepted from one's fellow religionist. The idea behind this prohibition was based on a complete ignoring of the role of interest in production. The idea, instead, was the concrete image of a man who is already ruined in business, who needs a loan to tide him over and of the money lender lying in wait for such men. He gives them their loans and then when they are unable to repay the loan, in interest, he seizes their property at law. That is the concrete image which the opponents of usury had in mind. Christians had no concept of increasing productivity, and a rising standard of living. The doctrine insisted that one could satisfy one's minimum needs at a moderate level of comfort by engaging in trade within the limits allowed by the church. These limits were meant to restrain "the sin of greed." The church got the state to prohibit the taking of interest on the earning of profit it deemed excessive. With the goal of restraining lust, the church got the state to regulate the arts and the theater and to censor books.

It is important to notice that all these prohibitions were based on the Jewish tribalist element in Christianity. It was not until the high middle ages that the authority of Aristotle was appealed to, to prove that the taking of interest was against natural law because money, by nature, was barren. So by and large, the life of a scrupulously observant Catholic Christian fluctuated between a moderate self-indulgence and ascetic severity. It was the deep conviction of many that moderate self-indulgence was conceding too much to the world. This conviction, added to the conviction that the church itself was becoming too worldly, resulted in the institution of monasticism. Thousands drew away from the worldly church in order to live in the *desert*. These monasteries became drains on the rest of society, and hot beds of fanaticism. Many monks unwilling to live in *monasteries* which they found too corrupt, withdrew to the *far* desert to become *solitaries*, where they practiced extremes of fanaticism. Some lived in swamps until they were covered with mosquito bites, others lived on the tops of pillars and were known as *stylites*. For instance, St. Simeon Stylites lived on a fifty-foot-high pillar with a fence around the top so he would not roll off when he was sleeping. He lived there for thirty-nine years. His food was sent up to him in a basket, and there was also a basket that came down . . . The Roman emperor himself used to go and stand at the bottom of the pillar and call up to Simeon for advice on how to settle theological controversies.

We have covered, at least in part, the Catholic point of view. Let us turn our attention to the Protestant ethic—that is, the economic ethics. The economics of the Judeo-Christian tradition must be understood not only in terms of Judaism and Catholicism, but also of Protestantism. We cannot pause to discuss the theology of the Protestant Reformation, except to note that it included a breakdown of the distinction between the sacred and the secular, repeal of the doctrine of the superiority of the monastic life, proclaimed the everyday workaday life of the ordinary man as the road to salvation, proclaimed business and the secular family home as workshops of salvation. All this was based in turn on the doctrines of absolute predestination, justification by faith alone, and individual responsibility to God without the mediation of the priest.

It is important to realize that there were two version of the Protestant ethic, the Lutheran and the Calvinistic. The Lutheran prevailed in north and east Germany, in Scandinavia, Finland, and Estonia. The Calvinist prevailed overwhelmingly in Protestant Switzerland, the Netherlands, Scotland, among the French Huguenots, and to a sufficient degree in England and the United States for us to identify it as the "White Anglo-Saxon Protestant (WASP)" ethic.

Now, let us look for a moment at the Lutheran economic ethics. Lutheranism is closer to Catholicism than is Calvinism, and Lutheranism retains much of the medieval agricultural class-stratified outlook. The raw materials of nature are gifts of God, and the fact that man has to appropriate them by toil is his punishment for sin. Hard work is a remedy for sin, and its significance is ascetical, and manifests itself in precision and technical exactitude in work.

Stability in one's work is a matter of self-discipline. There you have the basis for the German devotion to good work, the production of technically precise products. There is no recognition of the role of increasing productivity or capital formation in Lutheranism. *Work is just a penance.* Private property is ordained by God as a second thought, to preserve the social order. The ideal state would be primitive communism, reversion to which is permissible in times of famine, state need, or economic need. This is known as the doctrine of the compulsory bargain. *Men should be allowed to accumulate as much private property as they need to maintain their class rank.* The economic order consists of living within one's class standards. It is the duty of the government to protect this order and to guarantee its permanence. Those classes in direct contact with nature, the feudal land owners and the peasants, are to be regarded as naturally superior orders, together with the soldiers and bureaucrats who protect them. *Middle men and merchants are necessary evils.* Here we have the doctrine behind Bismarckian conservatism, German blood-and-soil socialism, and ultimately nazism. It has also influenced Scandinavian welfare statism.

Now let us look at Calvinism, which is the real WASP economic ethics. Calvinism shared with Lutheranism a high evaluation of work, regarding work as a form of worship to which all men were equally called, and also as a means of self-discipline and sublimation of aggressive and lustful desires. Work was a universal duty. Monks were banished and beggars were arrested as vagrants. The economic ethic of Calvinism also shared with Lutheranism its anti-Mammon spirit, and its emphasis on modesty and moderation. It instituted laws against luxury, which it prosecuted with unusual severity. Calvin also believed that poverty encouraged Christian virtues. He violently denounced the great Catholic trading centers of Venice and Antwerp. However, special circumstances reversed the anti-capitalistic trends in Calvinism. Calvin's own city, Geneva, was a town of 20,000 people based on a mercantile rather than agricultural economy. It could maintain its independence, and therefore Calvin's rule, only by successful competition and trade with nearby cities like Lyons. When Geneva lost its cloth and velvet trade to Lyons, Calvin acted vigorously and introduced the manufacture of the watches which are on everybody's wrists today.

Calvin was a practical man who emphasized those aspects of behavior which were possible for men to achieve. He therefore quickly integrated his work ethic with the rising capitalistic spirit. He repealed the Catholic laws against usury and supported a doctrine of credit that was at least a little nearer the modern idea. However, lending at interest was regulated. Only that interest was allowed which was to be plowed back into production. People were not allowed to live on interest. No interest was to be taken from the poor. Loans were not to be refused for lack of securities.[9] The maximum rate of interest was to be set by the state. The Calvinist ethic had more appeal to the businessman than the Catholic or Lutheran ethic. The reasons were that success in business was regarded in Calvinism as a sign that one was one of the elect, predestined by God to eternal salvation. This was because success in business was the result of planning ahead, and putting order into one's life.

In Calvinism, order was a sign of the divine rule. Disorder or chaos was a sign of the rule of the devil. He who rules his own life is probably himself under the rule of God. Since the doctrine of predestination creates a certain anxiety in people as to whether oneself is one of the elect, the presence of signs of order in one's life is a reassuring external mark that a person is one of the elect. Those who wasted their time and threw away money on gambling and women were called the reprobates, or the unchosen. No pity was to be wasted on them. However, Calvin taught there is no one-to-one correlation between wealth and salvation; there were the idle rich and there were the deserving poor. The idle rich flaunted their wealth. These were to be condemned. The deserving poor, worked hard, but circumstances deprived them of success. To the deserving poor, charity was proper; to the bums, none. What ought a businessman to do with his wealth? He ought not to spend it, in luxury or vulgar display, but save it and plow it back into the business. Thus arose the Calvinist social ethic, which has two elements; the productive and the altruistic. The altruistic element is evident in the emphasis *on charity for the deserving poor as a major virtue*, scholarships and foundations of every kind, and on dedication to a life of "public service." Calvinist man must show his worth, not merely by hard work and the amassing of wealth, but by public service. This is the WASP ethic.

Now, we come to the contemporary reversion to primitive messianism. Finally, the uncomfortable alliance between Christianity and capitalism began to dissolve in the nineteenth century, when churches were more and more disestablished, and became more voluntary organizations. One of the results was that the major Christian denominations ceased to be so interested in saving individual souls and began to turn their attention once more to changing the social order. This meant the breakdown of the Constantinian establishment in the broad sense, and the reversion to primitive Judaic messianism, the belief that the Kingdom of God could be established on earth. This took three forms: (1) the expectation that Jesus would soon return to establish the millennium; (2), the social gospel; and (3) liberation theology. The first we have already discussed.

Let us look at the second form, social gospel. In the first half of the twentieth century, the leaders of many of the Protestant churches in America had basically lost their faith in supernatural Christianity. This loss of faith was intellectual. It was due to their knowledge of science and of the critical study of the Bible. They asked themselves what was left of Christianity. They answered, the values it teaches. The values of altruism and self-sacrifice. The importance of Christ's death on the cross was not that it had saved the world, but that it was the supreme example of self-sacrifice. A ministry, therefore, could regain a sense of social relevance by preaching and working for the ethics of Jesus, rather than for the doctrine that he was the savior of mankind. In this way, they could help "bring in the kingdom" as they put it. Pulpits subsidized by businessmen resounded with denunciations of the selfishness of capitalism. The Protestant clergy, in this way, implanted in the minds of American businessman the thought that they were doing something unworthy and immoral in making money. And that they could only put meaning back into their lives by large donations to charity, by working in public service, or by participating in various kinds of prison reform, or other social reform, or by promoting government regulation of business. Once the depression had hit, businessmen influenced by the preaching of such clergy were foremost in supporting the New Deal. The most articulate clergyman of the social gospel movement was a man named Walter Rauschenbusch. Another was the Reverend Norman Thomas, the perennial Socialist candidate for president. It should be noticed that the movement spread to Reform Judaism as well, and many Reform rabbis were led to declare that as long as the teachings of Jesus, rather than his divinity, were preached in Christian churches, there was little to distinguish Christianity from Judaism. It was at this time that the term "Judeo-Christian tradition" became current. But the social gospel was an upper- class movement, largely dissociated from anything revolutionary. We cannot say the same of the third movement which will be the final topic of this chapter. This movement is *liberation theology.*

In the 1960s, a new school of thought came to the fore in the Catholic Church. This school of thought had first called itself *the theology of hope,* but later adopted the name of liberation theology. It was led by the left-wings of the Jesuit and Dominican orders, two of the most learned orders in the Catholic Church. They were assisted by priests and nuns of all orders in the church, especially Franciscans, who have always worked with the poor, as well as by thousands of parish priests and hundreds of bishops, in transforming what was essentially a school of thought into an active social movement.

The liberation theology people made the Protestant social gospelers look like parlor pinks. The Protestant social gospelers had been essentially reformers, whereas the liberation theology people were revolutionaries of the most radical kind. A consideration of their theological position and of their activities will throw much light on everything we have been saying so far. The liberation theologians reject entirely the Constantinian establishment: its vertical concept of salvation (extricating the individual soul from the body) and its compromise with the world, its telling their parishioners, "don't worry, we're not going to put the kingdom of God into effect in this world." The liberation theologians advocate that the church go back to the original Jewish concept of redemption, in the sense of redemption from slavery in Egypt. It is the duty of the church, they say, to redeem people, not to "save" them, to redeem them from all sorts of oppression, economic oppression by capitalism, political oppression by dictators (they mean right-wing dictators), racial oppression, and war.

All these kinds of repression are only expressions of selfishness, say the liberation theologians. Man must be liberated from selfishness, in order that the kingdom of God may come in. The liberation theologians point out that wherever there is a movement to liberate oppressed people, some Christian within the movement is at the forefront, Martin Luther King for example, who conceived himself as another Moses. The starting point of Christian theology, they say, is Christian commitment to the poor, and their struggle for liberation. This commitment grows out of Christian faith working through love.

Borrowing the Marxist concept of *praxis,* or intellectually guided action in the world, the liberation theologians call for orthopraxy, or correct practice, as prior to orthodoxy or correct belief. In the experience of orthopraxy, or solidarity with the oppressed, comes the insight that the church as an institution must give up the notion of an otherworldly salvation that tolerates or condones what they call the social injustices of the world. If individual Christians wish to be redeemed, they must get involved in the historical process of liberation here and now. In other words, they must go into politics, left-wing politics, now, especially in the Third World, they must join with the Marxists in their war against capitalism and colonialism.

Most liberation theologians are explicitly committed to a socialist economy, and most are committed to active cooperation with Marxists in achieving it. In some mysterious way, human political action is the incarnation of God's redemptive plan for mankind. Union with Christ is relating to this redemptive process, it is struggling to build the Kingdom of God. "This struggle to build the Kingdom of God involves," writes one Jesuit, "a priority of Utopian perspectives over factual ones, to those who work in hope." In other words, we need not devote ourselves to a factual study of economics in order to discover whether a socialist economy is workable. Whereas Marx had declared that any such factual study is unscientific, the liberation theologians proclaimed that it is irreligious. It goes against hope, they say, and the dimension of hope *negates* that of fact.

You see the Hegelian influence here. This is merely a Christian version of Marxism. Or you can put it another way : Marxism is the secular version of Christianity. Consider the three main virtues of Christianity: faith, hope, and charity. The Marxist equivalent of faith is raised class consciousness, the feeling that one is being oppressed, plus commitment to the proletariat as the agent of liberation. The Marxist equivalent of hope is the blind trust that somehow a socialist economy is possible. And the Marxist equivalent of charity, is identification with all the oppressed. "Arise ye wretched of the earth" is therefore, just another way of saying "blessed are the poor for theirs is the kingdom of heaven." All this may throw some light on why some Latin American right-wing military men converted to a pro-capitalist Protestantism and regarded anti-capitalist Jesuits who advocated "land reform" as looters and therefore fair game.

Notes

1. Abraham Cohen, *Everyman's Talmud*, New York, E.P. Dutton, 1975. All further passages from the Talmud are from this volume.
2. Nathaniel Branden, *The Psychology of Self-Esteem*, Los Angeles, CA, Nash Publishing, 1969, p. 110.
3. Deteronomy 30:19 KJV
4. Matthew 22:21 KJV
5. Mark 4:12 KJV
6. paraphrase of Matthew 6:25–28; Luke 12:27–31 KJV
7. Matthew 19:23–24. There was a narrow gate in Jerusalem called "The Needle."
8. Matthew 19:21 KJV
9. Notice the Calvinistic basis for opposing "red-lining" mortgage policies in certain urban areas today.

8

The Sexual Ethics of the
Judeo-Christian Tradition

This final chapter has three parts. The first section deals with the sexual and family ethics of the Judeo-Christian tradition. The second deals with the principal theses or major assertions of the Judeo-Christian ethic, not all of which are unique to that ethic. In the third section, I come to some general conclusions.

First we begin with the sex laws of ancient civilization. Here I am thinking primarily of the Greek and Roman civilization. The sex lives of ancient civilizations were not primarily concerned with what the sex act meant to individuals but with their relation to the social order in general—to the family, to property, and to the class structure. They were also concerned to reinforce both authority and class lines. Roman law punished the crossing of class lines in one's choice of sexual partners either in or outside of marriage. Now, the laws governing sexual behavior in ancient Greece and Rome in no way derived from the gods or from religious values. While the wrath of the gods might be called down on the heads of those who strayed from the social norms, or who broke the laws, the attitude of the gods was pictured as, "Do what your society tells you," not "do as I do." Indeed it has been well observed that if the Olympian Gods had to pull some of their sexual escapades on the streets of downtown Athens or Rome, they would have been immediately arrested. It was the establishment of Christianity as the official religion of the Roman Empire, at the end of the fourth century, that changed all this. From this time on, sexual transgressions aroused enormous condemnation and enormous guilt because they were conceived as personal affronts to an innocent God.

In other words, sexual transgressions were conceived as *sins* from the time that Christianity was established.

Sexual transgressions are conceived as sins in Judaism also, in other words, as affronts to God. But the difference between the Jewish and Christian traditions is that the Christian tradition itself comes very close to regarding sexual pleasure as something that is intrinsically evil, whereas the Jewish certainly does not.

The Jewish tradition, in its earliest form, sought to regulate sexual behavior in the real or supposed interest of society as a whole. The primary interest was to safeguard reproduction and to encourage it. At the same time, it viewed marital sex and its pleasures as a divinely ordained component of human life. God had commanded human beings to increase and multiply, and had attached supreme pleasure to such activity. Since the main interest was reproduction, even divorce was allowed and sometimes even urged on people if they did not have children; that is, it was urged for a man to take a wife who would give him children so that the focus was on reproduction. Nevertheless, any violation of the approved limits of sexual activity was regarded as a sin, again, in the sense of an offense against an innocent God who was an idealized father figure.

Although the range of permitted activities in Judaism was at first very broad, including polygamy, and the keeping of concubines was permitted, things began to narrow, at least after Ezra's time in 400 B.C. You see I marked Ezra as a villain throughout these studies. It was not always easy to find happiness within a structure of arranged marriages and complicated regulations regarding ritual purity. Therefore, the Jewish sexual code appeared as a heavy burden to pagans.

The sexual teaching of Jesus, as it is portrayed in the Gospels, introduced some new elements into the Jewish environment, elements that came to be rejected by the Jews. First of all, Jesus announced that in the coming Kingdom of God there would be no marriage, which has generally been attributed to mean no sex, although that is not the only possible interpretation; it could also mean that there is to be promiscuity on the premise that the angels have sex but no marriage. "For in the resurrection they neither marry, nor are given in marriage, but are as the angels of God in heaven," said Jesus.[1] Now again some commentators have justified that in the light of an Old Testament text, in the book of Genesis, that said that the angels looked down and "saw the daughters of men and they were fair," and they came swooping down to earth, and from the resulting union there came the race of giants. "There were giants in those days."[2] But I don't think Jesus meant to refer to that passage as a justification of promiscuity. I think he had a more spiritualized conception of angels. If he did, he had a clear *asexual* ideal.

Since Jesus also talked of how the bodies of the dead would be literally raised, you can see that he was predicting that the faithful would have their bodies but that they would be spayed or castrated. "Indeed . . . " he said, "there are some . . . which have made themselves eunuchs for the kingdom of heaven's sake."[3] And we know in the history of the church that one of the great fathers of the church (Origen) was accused of having castrated himself. So that what Jesus is predicting is not escape *from* the body as in Plato, but escape *in* the body, from sex. At the same time, Jesus preached a stricter attitude towards divorce. There should be no divorce allowed for *any* reason, he taught."[4]

What is the actual meaning of adultery? What does the word *adulterate* mean? To water down, to introduce something new into a stream. To commit adultery is to create a situation in which a father does not know if his children are his own. That was the basic reason for forbidding it. Jesus, of course, tightened the teaching on adultery. "But I say unto you," he said, "That whosoever looketh on a woman to lust after her hath committed adultery with her already in his heart."[5] He was thus proposing that the Jewish code be interpreted as referring to even fleeting desires as well as actions—certainly an inadequate basis for a law code. You could get arrested for your free associations. By the same logic, he was more ready to forgive the breaking of external prohibitions. He is pictured as having saved a woman from being stoned to death for adultery by challenging the man without sin to come forward and cast the first stone.[6] And he was known for his association with prostitutes as well as others ostracized for their way of life by ordinary Jewish society. We have, thus, in the teaching of Jesus, some elements of the later Christian ethic, the teaching that moral ideals should be very strict and suited for another world. The teaching also that morality is primarily a matter of intention. With these two elements in place, we can see the natural conclusion. All men are equally sinners needing forgiveness and deserving forgiveness. Anyone who takes a different attitude is condemned as self-righteous and it is sometimes suggested by Jesus' statements and actions that self-righteousness is practically the worst of all sins. The path from here to the doctrine of original sin is now clear.

Let us look at the contributions of St. Paul. His teaching on sex is governed by a number of factors, one of which is his seeming personal aversion to sex, sexual anorexia, so to speak . A hatred for the licentiousness of the Greco-Roman world of his time is a second factor; a third is the belief that the world is about to go through a period of tribulations followed by the second coming of Christ. And fourth, the belief that only the traditional family structure will preserve the Christian church from sexual chaos, a chaos that might be caused by a misinterpretation of the doctrine that salvation cannot be obtained by adherence to moral law, which doctrine is what Paul actually taught.

Here are Paul's words in a letter to the church in Corinth:

> Now concerning the matters about which you wrote. It is well for a man not to touch a woman. But because of the temptation to immorality, each man should have his own wife and each women her own husband. The husband should give to his wife her conjugal rights, and likewise the wife to her husband. For the wife does not rule over her own body, but the husband does; likewise the husband does not rule over his own body, but the wife does. Do not refuse one another except perhaps by agreement for a season, that you may devote yourselves to prayer; but then come together again, lest Satan tempt you through lack of self-control. I say this by way of concession, not of command. I wish that all were as I myself am. But each has his own special gift from God, one of a kind and one of another. To the unmarried and the widows I say that it is well for them to remain single as I do. But if they cannot exercise self-control, they should marry. For it is better to marry than to be aflame with passion. To the married I give charge, not I but the Lord, that the wife should not separate from her husband (but if she does, let her remain single or else be reconciled to her husband)—and that the husband should not divorce his wife . . . Now concerning the unmarried, I have no command of the Lord, but I give my opinion as one who by the Lord's mercy is trustworthy. I think that in view of the present distress it is well for a person to remain as he is. Are you bound to a wife? Do not seek to be free. Are you free from a wife? Do not seek marriage. But if you marry, you do not sin, and if a girl marries she does not sin. Yet those who marry will have worldly troubles, and I would spare you that. [He could have said that on a completely worldly basis.]
> I mean, brethren, the appointed time has grown very short; from now on, let those who have wives live as though they had none, and those who mourn as though they were not mourning, and those who rejoice as though they were not rejoicing, and those who buy as though they had no goods, and those who deal with the world as though they had no dealings with it. For the form of this world is passing away.[7]

You see, he really expected the end to come. These last words about withdrawing from society seem to be influenced by Stoicism. As for the place of women, Paul, or perhaps disciples writing in his name, are quite explicit. The man is the head of the woman as Christ is the head of the man. Let women not speak in churches, but ask their husbands later the meaning of what was going on.

Christianity's attitude toward sex is in part derived from Platonism. As we have seen, Platonism entered the Judeo-Christian tradition via Judaism. The leading Hellenistic Jewish intellectuals were Platonists, and the greatest of them was Philo Judeus, whose views we've already discussed in chapter 5. The chief influence of Platonism on Christianity was the doctrine of the two-layer structure of reality and the mind/body dichotomy.

Two aspects of Plato's doctrines on sex found particular acceptance among the monks and clerics of the Christian church. One was his doctrine of love as celebrated in the Symposium. That dialogue set forth that love or eros is the desire of the imperfect for the perfect, ultimately culminating in love for the divine beauty. One starts with love of mere persons. In Plato, quite evidently it is persons of the same sex, and this was especially appealing to monks. One starts with love of individual persons and gradually ascends to love of higher things, the whole process being fueled by a kind of sublimated desire for the less and the less concrete. The fathers of the church and other writers elaborated on this basis a doctrine on the "ladder of perfection" which the Christian gradually climbs until he finally attains the ecstasy of the vision of God. This is celebrated in Dante's *Divine Comedy*.

Plato was, of course, a puritan. This comes out in his late work, *The Laws*, where he rages against all sex which is not procreative, especially homosexual sex. I think this is probably a reaction-formation on Plato's part to his own homosexuality. Now, these two apparently contradictory but really complementary aspects of Plato's views on sex were incorporated into Christianity through the early fathers of the church. Now, there was also some influence from Stoicism. The Stoics saw as their goal perfect tranquillity or peace of mind—you know you cannot have this with a lot of sex, so they claimed In order to attain this tranquillity, they taught, it is necessary to achieve a state of total indifference—you *know* you cannot have a lot of sex and a total indifference to everything that goes on in the world.

This includes pain. The story is told of the Stoic philosopher, Epictetus, who was a slave, that when his master was torturing him by tightening an iron boot around his leg, he said to his master, "If you make it any tighter you'll break it, sir." Crack! "I told you sir." We still call stoical the kind of person who can meditate on the mind/body dichotomy while having a root canal. It is a psychological law that, when you repress pain, you have to render yourself indifferent to pleasure as well. The Stoics thought to improve on this law. They urged the direct repression of pleasure before it could even get off the ground. Thus they could avoid all commitment and all disappointment. Now you can imagine what was the attitude of even the moderate Stoics toward sex. It was an especially intense form of pleasure they said, which is objectionable because it is so distracting. It causes a loss of control of over both the mind and the body, and is therefore not conducive to sobriety or dignity.

The second-century Stoics, Sextus Empiricus, taught that it is wrong to lust even after one's own wife. The statement was taken over and elaborated by St. Jerome, whose revised version was referred to admiringly by Pope John Paul II whom I will quote in a few minutes. The Stoics, you see, were afraid of a loss of control, which is the picture of the modern obsessional neurotic. Since sex, then, is so low on the scale of values, chastity must be equivalently high on the scale of virtues. And Sextus Empiricus advised self-castration for those who found it difficult to practice celibacy. So much for the application of Stoic principles to private life. Many Stoics were men who participated in politics out of a sense of public responsibility, including even the Roman emperor Marcus Aurelius. You can imagine what their attitude would be, since marriage and the family are essential to the state as its instrument of appropriating and rearing children. All sex, they said, has basic implications for the public order. None of it is simply one's private business. The state therefore has a legitimate interest in regulating it. Now the early fathers of the church were ardent students of the Stoics, as ardent as they were of Plato. They incorporated the idea of the Stoic sage or wise man into that of the Catholic ascetic. Layer after layer of material, some of it of pagan origin, was being added to the Judeo-Christian tradition.

Now we come to Augustine. Think of this as about 400. The thought of Augustine marks a major step in the development of the Christian doctrine of sexuality. What disturbed Augustine about sex was that it was involuntary, intense pleasure, in which various parts of the body began all on their own to expand, contract, throb, undulate, spasm, and generally go wild without so much as a word of permission from the conscious reason or will. In other words, Augustine got right to the center of the matter and objected to the orgasm as such because it was not under the complete control of the conscious mind. If you cannot believe this, I will quote some excerpts. Realize, Augustine is speaking from a pious Christian point of view, although the point of view of a man who has had much experience before he became a Christian: on the way to conversion he prayed, "Oh Lord give me chastity but not yet."[8] The following is from *The City of God*:

> And [sexual] lust not only takes possession of the whole body and outward members, but also makes itself felt within and moves the whole man with a passion in which mental emotion is mingled with bodily appetite so that the pleasure which results is the greatest of all bodily pleasures. So possessing indeed is this pleasure that at the moment of time in which it is consummated, all mental activity is suspended. What friend of wisdom and holy joys who being married but knowing as the apostle says, "how to posses his vessel in sanctification and honour; not in the lust of concupiscence, even as the Gentiles which know not God"[9] would not prefer if this were possible to beget children without this lust, so that in this function of begetting offspring the members created for this purpose should not be stimulated by the heat of lust but should be actuated by his volition in the same way as his other members serve him for their respective ends? But even those who delight in this pleasure are not moved to it at their own will whether they confine themselves to lawful or transgress to unlawful pleasures; but sometimes this lust importunes them in spite of themselves and sometimes fails them when they desire to feel it, so that though lust rages in the mind it stirs not in the body. Thus strangely enough this emotion not only fails to obey the legitimate desire to beget offspring, but also refuses to serve lascivious lust; and though it often opposes its whole combined energy, to the soul, that resists it, sometimes also it is divided against itself, and while it moves the soul, leaves the body unmoved.[10]

Augustine believed that the original sin of Adam and Eve was not lust, it was not sexual sin, it was ambition and self-assertion: the desire to be equal to God. It was not, then, a sin of the flesh that was the original sin. It was not lust. Had they not committed the sin of pride and self-assertion, our first parents would have been given the marvelous pleasure of producing children without lust. This again from *The City of God*. "The man then would have sown the seed and the woman received it as need required. The generative organs being moved by the will not excited by lust"[11]—at the appropriate time and in the necessary degree, and had not been excited by lust. Bring it under the control, the full control, of the central nervous system, you see, is what, in modern terms, he means. "Thus the instrument created for the task would have sown the seed on the field of generation. As the hand now sown seed on the earth should have been sown by the organ created for this purpose as the earth is sown by the hand."[12] These words became definitive for Catholic theology.

The Catholic Church objects to sex without children. Some years ago, a leading British analytic philosopher named Elizabeth Anscombe wrote an article called, "Sex Without Children?" She is a very strict Catholic and does not believe in birth control(this article was actually printed in the philosophical journal *Mind*). The Catholic Church objects to sex without children. In the twentieth century, it has generally presented a milder version of the doctrine by merely prohibiting artificial impediments to conception. In other words, it no longer objects to the so-called rhythm method, which has been called "Vatican roulette," nor does it any longer object to sex after menopause. It used to. The real meaning of this general attitude is however to be found in the words of Augustine. *What the Catholic authorities wished they could have is not merely no sex without children, it is children without sex.* That this ideal has not been abandoned, even today, by those in the highest positions in the church can be proved by these words of the present Pope John Paul II, in his audience of 8 October 1980, in which he reiterated as his own belief a statement of St. Jerome to the effect that married men who felt desire for their own wives were guilty of adultery.

By the end of the tenth century A.D., the church had incorporated in its official manuals for hearing confession, which are called the "penitentials"—these are manuals that medieval priests used in order to determine whether a thing is a sin or not, or the degree of the sin— the church had incorporated in these penitentials the Augustinian doctrines that only married persons should have sex, and they should do so primarily to conceive children. Pleasure was rejected as a legitimate purpose of sex. Conjugal love was not even mentioned. Love was not even mentioned. The sex act itself was prohibited on a very large number of days in the church year, indeed only about five days were left open per month. It was also prohibited during menstruation, pregnancy, and nursing. It has been calculated that the overall results of following these rules would have reduced sexual activity to one-third the frequency of modern industrial nations without having any appreciable effect on the frequency of conception. It is important to note that the penitentials were written by celibate monks who were simply applying certain philosophical doctrines. These doctrine were: Plato's mind/body dichotomy; the Stoic doctrine of rigid self-control by suppressing sexual urges and suppressing such emotions as love; and finally the old Pythagorean doctrines of ritual impurity on certain days. So far as the influence of the monastic environment itself is concerned, it is not surprising that homosexuality was classified as the most serious sin. Thus we have the amazing phenomenon of a society in which the only specialists in sex were those committed to never practicing it, and many of whom had intense psychological disgust for it. Furthermore, these specialists were all males. Male sexual anorectics imposed for centuries upon the men and women of Europe a code that was the result of their own special philosophical premises, their own special living conditions, and their own peculiarities of psychology.

Figure 8.1 shows a flowchart of the times and occasions on which it were permissible to have sex. Every time it says yes, it means advance. If at anytime it says no, you get a "Stop! Sin!" on your theological computer.

A wrong answer, contrary to those above would result in prohibition of the act. I have taken this flow chart from a large book called *Law, Sex and Christian Society in Medieval Europe* (James A. Brundage, University of Chicago Press 1987, p. 161).

The penitentials could not be enforced except in the privacy of the confessional. The only penalty available was the refusal of absolution to those who would not promise to give up the sin. But the majority of the clergy were relatively broad-minded and lax compared to the monks, hence many of the rules of the penitentials remained unenforced this just illustrates the ideal. Even as unenforced they laid a heavy burden of guilt on those who read them. But in the twelfth century, the enforcement of Christian sexual morality went much more public. This was due to the occurrence, at this same time, of an intellectual revival and a great reform of the church in the direction of stricter observance. Canon law, that is, the public law of the church, was systematized in the twelfth century and made into a juristic structure of great effectiveness. One major effect was on divorce. This came to be permitted only when the husband proved to be impotent, or it was shown that the marriage had violated one of the church's laws on blood relationships. These incest laws were extremely complex and the tradition was passed on not only in the Catholic Church, but in the Anglican church. I remember once in far northern Canada entering an Anglican church and when I opened the door I saw in front of me a sign saying, "Church of England in Canada. Table of Forbidden Degrees: It is forbidden to marry one's mother, one's grandmother, one's wife's grandmother, one's daughter," and so forth and so on. I wondered about these Canadian Anglicans and their urges.

FIGURE 8.1

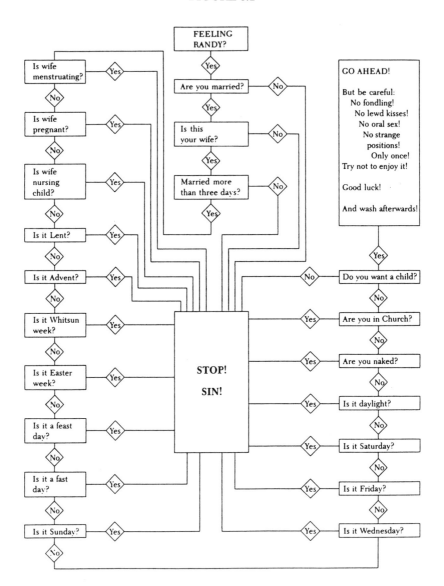

A second change was the increasing enforcement of clerical celibacy which resulted in the parish priests developing narrow mentalities similar to that of the monks, because the priests often went on retreats to monasteries. In the middle of the twelfth century a textbook of Canon law appeared. It is called *Gratian's Decretals*. This book declared that all extramarital sex was not only sinful but criminal and should be subject to public punishment by ecclesiastical courts, which at this time constituted a separate system of courts with their own police. *Gratian* also formulated the principle that men, as well as women, should be punished for adultery. Gradually things were tightening. By the end of the century, intercourse and the so-called missionary position became a matter of law, deviations being condemned on the ground that they were motivated by the desire for *"extraordinaria voluptas."* The concept of the "marital debt" became formalized. The marital debt was the right to intercourse and could be demanded by either party, even when payment of the debt was forbidden at a certain time, like Pentecost week. Refusal was sinful and consent was sinful, so their principles were at odds with each other.

During the thirteenth century, St. Thomas Aquinas made a significant change in the accepted doctrine of St. Augustine concerning the acceptable motive for sex. Augustine had held, you will remember, that within marriage, sex for pleasure alone is a mortal sin resulting in condemnation to hell forever. Aquinas made what, on the surface, was an apparently timid and slight modification, never admitting he was contradicting Augustine. "It is only a venial sin," he said, "to enjoy legitimate sex." But in effect that meant that the punishment in the next world was only a quick and short scorch in purgatory, not eternally roasting in hell. That was all poor Aquinas could do in his delicate Dominican situation. The Dominican order to which he belonged was under the suspicion of preferring Aristotle to Augustine.

Now we go to the Protestant sexual ethic at the time of the Reformation. The Protestant Reformation of the sixteenth century was characterized by considerable change in the attitude toward sex. The most conspicuous changes were: (1) a more positive attitude toward marriage, an emphasis on personal affection in marriage, and on sex as a proper expression of that affection, and on that proper expression as an end more important than procreation of children; but (2) now that sex had become respectable, everyone was expected to confine his or her activities within the sphere of marriage—anyone who does not will lose social respectability and become liable to severe civil penalties. In other words, the Protestant ethic (we discussed this in connection with economics, see chapter 7) in the sexual sphere, expected everyone to conform literally to its somewhat easier requirements—whereas the Catholic ideal was set on so strict a level that nobody could possibly follow it.

The Italians expected all good Italians to violate it and then seek forgiveness in the confessional. Whereas in the Catholic world the confessional was an institution of such one-to-one secrecy, that not even the Pope could demand to know what had been told inside it—in the Protestant world, everyone's sins were everyone's business, and if anyone was even suspected of sin, the immediate action was to call the police. Whereas in the Catholic world the moral hero was the saint whom the ordinary person was hardly expected to emulate—in the Protestant world, the moral hero was the respectable man, and everyone was supposed to emulate him under the minimum penalty of malicious gossip or ostracism or maximum penalties that could be, well, quite maximum. Thus the Protestant reformer John Calvin, as I mentioned before, is said to have approved of the beheading of a child for striking its father. Calvin's whole attitude was so censorious toward people that when he was a student in the early grades of school, his classmates called him "the accusative case." Catholic sexual morality could be exceedingly lax in Judeo-Christian terms, as in Italy, or at its most extreme in Brazil, where there is said to be a saint who specializes in finding lovers for old ladies. In one case however, in Ireland, it was applied in the Protestant spirit and the result was a form of Catholic puritanism that is today truly horrendous, that seeks to impose some form of the Christian sexual ethic on the whole community. This has in America been fueled by an alliance between Anglo-Saxon Protestants and Irish-American Catholics with their own brand of puritanism.

Now the concept of sexuality, which has dominated the Christian tradition, consists of two parts. The first is the reproductive model of the function of sexuality: the purpose of sex is the procreation and rearing of children. This view it shares with Judaism—no surprise because they are both based on Old Testament revelation. The Bible undeniably declares that God said to Adam and Eve, "Be fruitful and multiply." So this model is shared by the two religions and may be regarded as pervasive of the whole Judeo-Christian tradition. But there's a second model which Christianity has superimposed on the Jewish model; this is the doctrine of sexual pleasure as something evil, impure, or degrading. This is the opposite of the Jewish view according to which the pleasure is bestowed upon mankind for the procreation of children and the strengthening of the bond between husband and wife. The doctrine of sexual pleasure as something evil surely is based on the mind/body dichotomy of Plato and the Stoic doctrine of self-control.

The radical dualism of the Manicheans likewise comes into it. The Manicheans were a type of Persian dualists and St. Augustine was a Manichean for a time before he became a Christian. So it was partly the influence of the Manicheans. Christianity was able to combine the reproductive model with the sex-as-evil model in the developed doctrine of original sin of which Augustine was the chief proponent. Sex before the Fall would have been fine, he said, but sex afterwards has been shameful in its nature. We must try to combine the two models, carry out God's demand to be fruitful and multiply, and yet not enjoy it. Therefore the tremendous ambivalence in Christianity resulting in the conclusion that sex is a necessary evil. And any sexual activity not incorporated into the reproductive model is either utterly condemned or is highly suspect; therefore the opposition to birth control, therefore the dim view of marriage after the age appropriate to procreation, therefore opposition of course to any sex outside of marriage. This last prohibition—no sex outside of marriage—is shared by the Jewish tradition which sees the proper place of sex as being within marriage. But the premises are somewhat different. Judaism seeks to confine sex within marriage in order to avoid wasted energy and divided loyalties, and also as a sign of reverence for God's gift. Christianity seeks to confine it within marriage because it regards reproduction as the only excuse for a bad thing.

We now come to some basic ethical features of the Judeo-Christian tradition, namely sin and guilt. I want to say a few words about this. Sin is conceived in the Judeo-Christian tradition as a special kind of wrongdoing. It is not merely wrongdoing, it is a special kind of wrongdoing. It is a wrongdoing against parental figures such as God the Father, or in the case of Catholicism, the Virgin Mary. And it involves the defiance of the one, God the Father, or the soiling of the honor of the other, the Blessed Virgin. This leads to a deep sense of the loss of love of these figures, for the sinner, which when combined with fear amounts to religious guilt.

Let us now look at the doctrine of hell. The Jews at the time of Jesus had a very undeveloped idea of rewards and punishments after death. Sometimes they spoke of all the spirits of the dead as wandering in a place called Sheol, a place like the Greek Hades. Sometimes they spoke of a place of punishment called Gehenna, which was a dump for burning refuse on the outskirts of Jerusalem. Sometimes they spoke of the souls of the righteous as resting in Abraham's bosom waiting for resurrection. Jesus, in his preaching, pictured the righteous as in Abraham's bosom and he threatened Gehenna or eternal burning for the unrighteous. In the early church, a doctrine of hell, of eternal torments, quickly developed. This was partly the result of Roman traditions. The Romans may have gotten the concept of hell, an infernal place, from the Etruscans. As a matter of fact, the Etruscans were a very grim people. The fear of hell became a central aspect of Christian teaching. As time went on, Catholicism developed a detailed theology of hell. All those who died in mortal sin went to hell. Now, mortal sin means, to a Catholic, three things. First it has to be a grave matter, a serious matter such as murder, adultery, major theft, or an internal act of the mind in which you cursed God. It must also be committed, secondly, after serious reflection and, thirdly, with the full consent of the will. This doctrine was taught to little children. I will quote from a Catholic childrens' book published in the late nineteenth century. It is a book called *A Sight of Hell*. A childrens' book, believe it or not. This was Sunday school stuff.

According to this book, hell, in the late nineteenth century, is an actual enclosure in the center of the earth. It is flooded with streams of burning pitch and sulfur, and showered by sparks in a veritable fog of fire. Tormented souls are shrieking, roaring like lions and hissing like serpents. There are six dungeons, each with its own mode of torture. There is a burning press, a deep pit, a boiling kettle, a red-hot floor, a red-hot oven, and a red-hot coffin. The author reminds us that according to Catholic doctrine a child is capable of committing mortal sin and therefore meriting hell from age seven on, the age of reason and moral responsibility, at which age children must start going to confession. Now the author asks his child readers to picture a little eight-year-old child who has committed a mortal sin and who has died before getting to confession. I quote: "The little child is in the red-hot oven, hear how it screams to come out, see how it turns and twists itself about in the fire, it beats its head against the roof of the oven, it stamps its little feet on the floor. God was very good to this little child. Very likely God saw that it would become a worse sinner and never repent, and so it would have to be punished more severely in hell. So God in his mercy called it out of the world in early childhood." The name of the author of this book is, believe it or not, the Reverend Joseph Furniss, a Priest of the Congregation of the Most Holy Redeemer, a Redemptorist Father.

With regard to hell, the Christian often thinks in terms of Pascal's wager. Blaise Pascal was a great mathematician of the seventeenth century, the author of the modern theory of games, an anticipator of the computer and generally one of the great minds of his age and of all ages. He was also a fervent Catholic attached to the Jansenists, an extremely reactionary party in the church. The Jesuits he regarded as mealy-mouthed soft-liners in the church—liberals.

Pascal's approach to religion was one of the weirdest applications of rationalism to religion ever known. It is called Pascal's wager, and it goes like this: The basic option before me is to believe what the Catholic Church teaches or not to believe. If I believe what the church teaches and live like a good Catholic, then if the church is right, I will gain an *infinite* reward, eternal reward, but I will also have to renounce a *finite* amount of earthly goodies of the kind forbidden by the church. If the church is wrong, then I will never know the difference and will merely have missed a finite amount of pleasure on earth. If I disbelieve what the church teaches, and then if the church is right, I will have lost the infinite reward and earned Father Furniss's furnace, and I will merely have gained a finite amount of pleasure on earth. And if the church is wrong, I will again have made only a finite gain. Now I don't know whether the church is right or wrong, so I must wager. In wagering Pascal used what later became to be known as the "minimax principle" in games. He thought of playing a game with God here. The minimax principle tells you to minimize the maximum damage your opponent can do to you. He pictured himself playing against a possible God. The maximum damage this possible God could inflict on him was infinite. To minimize this, he made the "leap of faith." The loss he might suffer could not be more than finite. Many Catholics, and indeed many of all faiths who believe in hell, make this kind of bargain. As a matter of fact this kind of bargain is no solution because there are several different religions which threaten hell if you do not believe they are the one true religion, so the thing to do is to be completely prepared so that if you are awakened by a Muslim angel remember to say this, "There is but one God and Muhammad is his prophet." If you doubt what I am saying about people's motivations, about people's accepting religion on Pascal's wager, and many do try this: on Sunday morning, note the number of cars parked in front of the churches that preach hell and damnation as opposed to those who are more liberal on the subject.

* * *

I would like to summarize the basic theses of the Judeo-Christian ethic. The first thesis is *that morality as such needs no justification, no derivation from the facts of reality*. The basic principles of morality serve as quasi-axioms within the system. There is no demonstrable source from which they can be derived. Of course they are not axioms in Aristotle's sense of first principles or in the sense that one must affirm them in the act of denying them. But some traditional moralists even claim this; for instance they say that unless one first accepts the moral axiom that one should reason honestly, one will never arrive at A is A. Although Kant would not go as far as this, the Kantian view does imply that the categorical imperative is an independent first principle within the field of morality. The second basic thesis of the Judeo-Christian morality is the concept of duty; what one owes to God or to one's neighbor. Sometimes the duties are regarded as axiomatic, as in Kantianism. A twentieth-century example is the moral philosopher, W. D. Ross, who wrote a famous book called *The Right and the Good*, which he modified later in the book *The Principles of Ethics*. Ross claimed that certain actions are right or at least *prima facie* right regardless of whether they have good consequences. Other Judeo-Christian thinkers base duty on some mystical I-thou encounter, as does the Jewish philosopher Martin Buber, or on an existential encounter with God, as does Kierkegaard. At any rate, duty is an uncontracted debt and is generally regarded as preceding all rights.

Now we come to unselfishness. *Judeo-Christian thinkers include unselfishness* among the axiomatic principles of morality. Generally they will say that the very concept of an egoistic morality is a contradiction in terms. Morality as such, they tell you, implies unselfishness, *therefore the genuine egoist, they say, is amoral*. In his theory he is self-contradictory; in his feelings, if his feelings follow his theory, he's a psychopath, for he has no conscience, conscience being the awareness of one's duty to others. So Objectivists would be psychopaths to many of these thinkers. Generally these thinkers will affirm that man is, by nature, selfish although he is obliged not to be. This results in a divided theory along the lines of St. Paul's famous statement, "For the good that I would I do not: but the evil which I would not, that I do."[13]

Then there is *sacrifice*. The original concept of sacrifice is found among primitive tribes. It was that a man takes a certain small portion of what he owns and he offers it to the god. In return, he keeps the larger portion and the god protects him in possession of this larger portion. For instance, the man sacrifices one lamb from his flock of sheep and thus protects his stake in the rest of the sheep from the god's anger. This is more like a baseball sacrifice, the giving up of a lesser good for a greater. However, when human sacrifice is involved or when a father offers his child, then at least from the child's point of view this is no baseball sacrifice. He's losing the greater good —his own life. This, perhaps, is the most radical example of Ayn Rand's definition of sacrifice and, if voluntary, it involves complete altruism. In the Judeo-Christian tradition we have an exultation of this latter kind of sacrifice as the prototype of all sacrifice. In order to do God's will, that which is most precious in value is to be given up; as when Abraham prepared to sacrifice Isaac; or when the whole nation of Israel is compared to the lamb which is led to the slaughter, as in Second Isaiah; or when Jesus is conceived of offering his life for the sins of the world. Christianity is primarily a sacrificial religion with its supreme symbol of the cross. But Judaism was ritually sacrificial in character as long as the temple remained, and there was a daily slaughtering in the temple (See Paul Johnson's *History of the Jews*, if you want a good description of that.)

The basic content of the offering, in the Christian doctrine of sacrifice and to some extent in the Jewish concept of sacrifice, is an offering of reason, independence, and happiness. So in principle, the Judeo-Christian tradition demands that we make an offering. To make an offering means to renounce one's claims to something. In the religious tradition, the offer is primarily made to God. In the secular version of the Judeo-Christian tradition, of course, the offering is made to society, to the tribe. Whatever the superficial content of the offering, its evidence is the giving up of oneself as an absolute end. This involves the renunciation of one's reason. I believe it because it is absurd, or because it is impossible said Tertullian, one of the most extreme advocates of this position. Another equally extreme advocate, St. Ignatius Loyola, the founder of the Jesuits, said in his spiritual exercises, "if the hierarchical church tells me that black is white I must believe it." A less extreme position is that of St. Anselm, the Augustinian position, "I believe in order that I may understand." The least extreme position is that of St. Thomas Aquinas, "I first prove the existence of God by reason, then I take on faith what God has revealed." Now in my mind one has to be crazy to accept the Tertullian position. The most dangerous of the three positions is the Augustinian-Anselmian one—I believe in order that I may understand—for here one accepts a formula on faith, and then warmed by the security afforded by faith, examines the arguments with an attempt at rationality. However sincere the attempt, the fear of losing one's faith is likely to persuade one to think one grasps the proof when in fact one has not done so. The result is a faith convinced that it is rational instead of a perfectly straightforward confession of subjectivity, as you have in Tertullian. The Thomist position is obviously the least harmful, but even it is full of holes, since the Thomists insist that the grace of God is necessary to help one see the truth of the proofs for the existence of God.

The Judeo-Christian tradition, like all tribal traditions, insists on the surrender of personal independence in every area of life. Full adherence to the synagogue or church requires one to be ready to accept not only old rules but a new interpretation that is fully supported by consensus of rabbis, general councils, or popes. Such rules govern all aspects of life such as friendships, relationships with one's parents, marriage, sex, the books one reads, the arts, commercial relations; I need only mention, abortion, birth control, circumcision. A Jewish women is regarded as unclean at certain times, twice as long after the birth of a female child as after the birth of a male child. A Greek Orthodox mother may not attend her child's baptism because she is regarded as ritually unclean. A Greek Orthodox priest may not celebrate mass on the morning after he has had intercourse with his wife. I merely mention behavioral rules that spring to my mind. I am sure there are worse examples yet. As for happiness, it is obvious that happiness as an end must be sacrificed. Now this does not mean that long- term contentment and peace is not possible in certain religious institutions where a heavy dose of Aristotelian sanity is introduced by venerable abbots wise in the ways of the world. As for short-term ecstasies and enthusiasms and joys, one has only to watch a procession of Hari Krishnas—they are having fun (up until age thirty—sex stops after thirty for the Hari Krishnas).

Happiness as a goal, however, is something quite different and *that* really has to be renounced and sacrificed in the Judeo-Christian tradition. A man who is often called the father of modern poetry, Gerard Manley Hopkins, a Jesuit, destroyed many of his works as an act of sacrifice. The Augustinian monk, Gregor Mendel, the father of genetics, had to see his pea gardens put into extreme jeopardy by an ignorant abbot. These are examples of the sacrifice of reason, independence, and happiness all at the same time.

Now I come to the payoff or communion. Every sacrifice has a payoff. Sacrifices are not made for nothing. In the Judeo-Christian tradition the sacrifice of reason, independence, and happiness is answered with a warm welcome to a life of security in the bosom of the tribe. This payoff is promised. It is a basic belief that it is there to be found. It is a basic thesis. Since security depends on unity, the tribe must retain identity. This is relatively easy to do in Judaism where the unity is supplied by the ethnic factor, and subscription to nothing but the survival of Jews qua Jews is absolutely required. Proselytism or conversion is an additional factor keeping the door slightly ajar to admit new blood.

In Christianity the situation is totally different. In a strict sense, there is no such thing as a born Christian. All Christians in some sense must be born again—go through rebirth rituals of baptism, confirmation, finding Christ in a conversion experience subscribing to a creed or a set of dogmas. Both of these methods of keeping identity are collectivistic however. Both the Jewish and the Christian communities are collectivistic by nature.

Now I come to the last two points. The Danish philosopher Kierkegaard, in his book *Either/Or* and in his many other writings, spoke of the necessity of making critical life choices founded on no good reason at all. In saying this, he founded the philosophical movement known as existentialism. Existentialism is the culminating burst of the Judeo-Christian tradition. It declares that one achieves meaning and life only by a leap of faith even if that leap is into atheism. This very fact, this surprise in the history of ideas, shows that what is of first importance in the Judeo-Christian tradition is not God, but faith.

How many of us, when arguing with an adherent of the Judeo-Christian tradition, has not encountered the objection, "even atheism is a faith, even science is based on faith." The either/or of existentialism offers either the faith which welcomes to the warmth of the tribe or the faith in the worship of one's personal arbitrariness and subjectivity. To this the rational person must answer, "neither/nor."

Notes

1. Matthew 22:30 KJV
2. Genesis 6:4 RSV
3. Matthew 19:12 KJV
4. Mark 10:11, Luke 16:18; the exception clause in Matthew 5:32 and 19:9 is not genuine.
5. Matthew 5:28, KJV
6. John 8:7 KJV
7. 1 Corinthians 7:1–11, 7:25–31, RSV
8. *Confessions*, translated F.J. Sheed, bk. 8i, ch.7. New York, Sheed and Ward, 1942, p. 139.
9. 1 Thessalonians 4:4–5, KJV
10. *The City of God*, translated by Marcus Dods, bk.14 , ch. 16. New York, Modern Library Random House, 1950, pp. 464–465.
11. Ibid., bk. 14, ch. 23, p. 472.
12. Ibid., p. 476.
13. Romans 7:19 KJV

Selective Bibliography

Augustine (St.). *The City of God.* New York: Random House, 1950.

Holy Bible, The. (Old and New Testaments). Revised Standard Version. Cleveland, OH and New York: The World Publishing Company, Meridian Books, 1962. The Old and New Testament sections are derived from the Revised Standard Version of the Bible, [1946] 1952, Division of Christian Education, National Council of Churches of Christ.

Brundage, James A. *Law, Sex and Christian Society in Medieval Europe.* Chicago, IL: University of Chicago Press, 1987.

DeBary, Wm. Theodore, ed. *Sources of Indian Tradition.* New York: Columbia University Press, 1967.

Fox, Robin Lane. *Pagans and Christians.* New York: Alfred A. Knopf Inc., 1987.

Frithjof, Schuon. *Understanding Islam.* Baltimore, MD: Penguin Books, 1963.

Jonas, Hans. *The Gnostic Religion* 2d rev. ed. Boston, MA: Beacon Press, 1958.

Koran Interpreted, The, tr. A.J. Arberry. London: George Allen and Unwin Ltd., 1955.

Leibowitz, Yeshayahu. *Judaism, Human Values and the Jewish State.* Cambridge, MA: Harvard University Press, 1992.

Maccoby, Hyam. *The Mythmaker, Paul and the Invention of Christianity.* San Francisco, CA: Harper and Row, 1987.

Meek, Theophile James. *Hebrew Origins.* New York: Harper and Row, 1960.

Meeks, Wayne A. *The Social World of the Apostle Paul.* New Haven, CT: Yale University Press, 1983.

Meier, John P. *A Marginal Jew, Rethinking the Historical Jesus.* New York: Harper and Row, 1991 (vol. 1); 1994 (vol. 2).

Neill, Stephen. *The Interpretation of the New Testament, 1861–1961.* London: Oxford University Press, 1978.

Organ, Troy Wilson. *Hinduism: Its Historical Development.* New York: Barron's Educational Series, 1974.

Reik, Theodor. *Mystery on the Mountain: The Drama of the Sinai Revelation.* New York: Harper and Bros., 1959.

Rudolph, Kurt. *Gnosis: The Nature and History of Gnosticism.* San Francisco, CA: Harper and Row, 1987.

Segal, Alan F. *Paul the Convert.* New Haven, CT: Yale University Press, 1990.

Smart, Ninian. *Doctrine and Argument in Indian Philosophy.* London: Allen and Unwin, 1964.

Stevenson, J. Creeds. *Councils and Controversies.* London: S.P.C.K., 1966.

Wells, G.A. *The Historical Evidence for Jesus.* Buffalo, NY: Prometheus Books, 1988.

Zimmer, Heinrich. *Philosophies of India.* Princeton, NJ: Princeton University Press, 1969.

Index

this-worldly attitude, 154, 155
view of world and man as good, 67
Judeo-Christian ethics. *See also under*
        Christianity; Jesus; Judaism
    duty, 182
    morality as needing no justification,
        182
    payoff/communion, 185
    sacrifice/self-sacrifice, 136, 183–85
    surrender of personal independence,
        184
    unselfishness, 182–83
Judeo-Christianity, 140, 149. *See also*
        Old Testament
    ability *vs.* worthiness to live, 70
    message of prophets, 115
    origin, 113
    puritanism and neo-primitivism, 115
    social justice, 114
    wealth sharing, 114
Julian, Bishop, 146

Kaaba, 84
Kant, Immanuel, 182
Kantianism
    ancestry, 133
    Jesus compared with, 132–33
    pharisaism as foreshadowing, 132
karma, 33–35
Kelley, David, vii, 33
Kharijites (seceders), 94–95
Khomeini, Ayatollah, 95
    as representative of Imam, 95
Kierkegaard, 185
Kingdom of God, 55, 130, 131, 156,
        157, 165, 168
knowledge. *See also* divine revelation;
        Gnosis; Old Testament,
        Adam and Eve
    salvation by, 32
Koran. *See* Qur'an

liberation movements, 164
liberation theology, 164–65
life after death. *See also* dead;
        reincarnation
    heaven theory, 10
    rebirth theory, 10–11
    wandering shade theory, 11
Logos, as mediator between God and
        man, 123

love
    groundless, 60
    unconditional, 134–35
Loyola, St. Ignatius, 184
Lutheran economic ethics, 160–61

Maccoby, Hyam, 135–36
magic, 3–4, 11–13
    assumes primacy of consciousness,
        12
    banning of/taboo on, 46, 49
    as based on association of ideas,
        11–12
    contagious, based on law of contact,
        12
    fetishism compared with, 13
    imitative, based on law of similar-
        ity, 12, 13
    sympathetic, based on law of
        sympathy, 12
malevolent universe, in Gnosticism, 71,
        141
Malinowski, Bronislaw, 16
Mandeans, 130–31
Manichean, dualism of, 179
mantras, 28
Marxism. *See also* communism; wealth
    in Christianity, 158–59, 165
mäyä (veil of illusion), 32
meaning, achieved by leap of faith, 185
Mecca, business *vs.* tribal ethic in, 87
mercy
    in Gnosticism, 72, 77
    Jesus and, 75, 134, 169
Messiah, 123
messianism, 156
millennialism, 156
mind-body dualism, 33, 171
mind-body unity, 91
mitzvah/mitzvoth, 70, 71
moksha (release), 29, 32, 38
monasticism, 156
money. *See* wealth
monism, 32. *See also* Brahmanism
moral prohibition, 7. *See also* ethics;
        *specific religions and
        prohibitions*
Moses. *See under* Judaism
Muhammad, 87
    doctrine of God, 90
    life history, 82–87